Students, Markets and Social Justice:
higher education fee and student support policies in Western Europe and beyond

Students, Markets and Social Justice:
higher education fee and student support policies in Western Europe and beyond

Edited by
Hubert Ertl & Claire Dupuy

Oxford Studies in Comparative Education
Series Editor: David Phillips

SYMPOSIUM
BOOKS

Symposium Books
PO Box 204, Didcot, Oxford OX11 9ZQ, United Kingdom
www.symposium-books.co.uk

Published in the United Kingdom, 2014

ISBN 978-1-873927-57-1

This publication is also available on a subscription basis
as Volume 24 Number 2 of *Oxford Studies in Comparative Education*
(ISSN 0961-2149)

Printed and bound in the United Kingdom by Hobbs the Printers, Southampton
www.hobbs.uk.com

Contents

INTRODUCTION

Comparative Perspectives of the Contexts and Rationales of Fee Policies in Higher Education

CLAIRE DUPUY & HUBERT ERTL

This edited volume examines recent changes in tuition fee policies in a number of Western European countries, Canada, the USA and China, and investigates the impacts of these changes on access to higher education. The contributions of the volume are twofold: first, it provides an overview of recent reforms in a comparative perspective, including a diverse range of national context; second, it elaborates a systematic analysis of tuition fee policies' rationales, instruments and outcomes in terms of access to higher education. The volume thereby argues that tuition fee policies provide fruitful grounds to explore the variety of neoliberal trends in higher education, that is, how marketisation trends and concerns about social justice are intertwined in contemporary higher education systems.

Variety of Neoliberal Trends

This volume [1], as many others, takes stock of a major change in the understanding of the role of the state and the purposes of its intervention that is commonly depicted as the neoliberal turn. From the early 1980s onwards, this turn, which started with Margaret Thatcher and Ronald Reagan coming to power in their respective nations, has come to characterise a growing number of policy areas in an ever-increasing number of Western countries. Even countries whose political traditions and elites were distant from neoliberalism converted to varying degrees at some point. France is a case in point, as the neoliberal turn was initiated in 1983 by the first socialist government of the Fifth Republic (Jobert & Théret, 1994), and despite their not admitting it, subsequent socialist and right-leaning governments introduced neoliberal policies (Gualmini & Schmidt, 2013).

Neoliberalism is unquestionably a much debated notion and reality. The issues in defining 'neoliberalism' are inherent to its multifaceted nature: originally a concept in economic and political theory (Hayek, 1944; Friedman, 1962), it has been used by political actors either intentionally as a label for their own ideology and policies (e.g. Margaret Thatcher in England) or as a criticism and a blame placed on their opponents (e.g. policy debates in France where being 'neoliberal' is certainly not an advantage in the political competition, even for right-wing politicians). Social scientists have used the term 'neoliberal' as well, but in conflicting ways: some of them use it to denote a normative assessment of contemporary politics, while others, conforming to Weber's axiological neutrality (Weber, 1971), refer to neoliberal trends to describe ideas and policies without including any normative connotation. When discussing neoliberalism, the present volume follows this latter path. Despite the diversity of intellectual traditions and the general polysemy of the word in the political scene, a minimal consensus is that neoliberalism refers to a set of ideas and practices revolving around markets being as 'free' as possible 'meaning governed by competition and open across borders, while the state should have a limited political economic role in creating and preserving the institutional framework that secures property rights, guarantees competition, and promotes free trade' (Schmidt & Thatcher, 2013, p. 4).

In Western countries, the neoliberal turn is multidimensional and goes far beyond the economic domain. In this field, it pertains to the move away from Keynesian policies (Hall, 1993) to a growing role of markets and market-like resource and service allocation. The neoliberal turn also relates to redistribution and the growing emphasis put on incentivising individuals to participate in the labour market and to limiting redistribution (Le Galès & Faucher-King, 2010), and, lastly, to a variously broad transformation of the scope and objectives of public sector through the import from the private sector of targeting, performance assessment and management devices, that is new public management (Pollitt & Bouckaert, 2000). Overall, the last decades have witnessed a profound process of change, affecting the role of the state and its activities, as we knew them until the 1970s.

The neoliberal turn is also heterogeneous. Exploring this heterogeneity provides leverage not only to accurately describe recent evolutions of higher education systems, but also to compare their features and outcomes. This is the main task of this volume. Over the past 40 years, neoliberalism in Western countries has in fact taken various shapes in different countries, different policy sectors and across time because of the distinct political dynamics generating ideational and policy changes. One reason for this is probably 'the generability, the flexibility and mutability of neoliberal ideas themselves' (Schmidt & Thatcher, 2013, p. 1).

One main characteristic of neoliberal turns in different countries and sectors is a trend toward marketisation. But marketisation per se says little on how markets actually work in different national and sectorial settings and how political actors may shape markets. Jane Gingrich (2011) provides a thorough and sophisticated analysis of 'market-making' in the welfare state. She contends that markets differ along two dimensions. The allocation dimension concerns 'whether price and selection mechanisms are used to allocate services, or whether services preserve a strong collective guarantee of access and funding'. In other words, the allocation dimension distinguishes markets where the responsibility for access to the service or the public good is collective or individual. The second dimension, the production dimension, describes whether 'the structure of competition gives the state (or third-party payers), users of new producers control over the incentive structure in the delivery of services' (Gingrich, 2011, p. 10). The combination of both dimensions distinguishes different types of markets.[2] For instance, the market for care for the elderly in England since the mid-1990s is a case of a 'private power market' where public authorities contract providers without tightly regulating them. This type of market is therefore producer-driven (the production dimension), where producers shift costs onto individuals and reduce service quality to pursue profit (the allocation dimension). By contrast, the recent English contracting in education is a case of a 'managed market' where the state controls the market as competition is created to respond to the state's preferences, while there is a collective responsibility for access to education. Another example is provided by the Swedish health care market in the early 1990s which can be characterised as a 'consumer-controlled market'. In this case, users were able to choose among health care providers given that the market regulation incentivised clinics and hospitals to be responsive to patients' demands, as opposed to national or local governments (the latter play an important role in the Swedish health care system). In addition, the allocation of benefits was still collective and not market-driven. Overall, as these brief examples show, there is a wide variation in markets regarding the costs they place on citizens, the incentives they offer producers and, therefore, the relative power of users, the state and producers. Gingrich explains it by focusing on political parties under institutional constraints. She argues that right- and left-leaning political parties introduce different types of markets in the welfare state for diverging reasons. Beyond this particular explanatory line, what is worth emphasising is that exploring recent changes in higher education systems would gain from thoroughly looking at the policy devices at stake, their variation, and how they combine, sometimes unexpectedly, various components.

There is also wide variation in time of neoliberal trends. In other words, just like there is variation in space and across policy sectors, neoliberalism and its specific features have taken different forms over time. This can be illustrated with the evolution of neoliberal ideas in the social realm. Maurizio Ferrera contends that 'the influence of neoliberalism on the welfare state has followed a broad parabola, which reached its peak in the early 1990s but started to decline thereafter in the wake of ideological changes and discursive reorientations' (2013, p. 77). More specifically, the Keynesian welfare states in most European states were first challenged in the 1970s after the first oil crisis. They were accused, among others, to be partly inefficient, to be unfavourable to entrepreneurship and to discourage risk-taking and individual responsibility. Opponents also criticised the excessive bureaucratisation of the welfare states and the undue constrains they put on individual freedom. In the 1980s and the early 1990s, an 'anti-welfare ideology' succeeded in the United Kingdom (UK) and the USA, but less so in continental Europe. During this ascending phase, neoliberalism had a tangible impact on European welfare states, even though not as strong as its proponents wished for (in the English and US case, see Pierson, 1994).

However, from the early 1990s, there has been an anti-neoliberal fight-back where neoliberal arguments against the welfare state faced counter-arguments built on strands of European intellectual traditions, like social democracy and Christian solidarism, and also egalitarian liberalism.

> In part because of necessity, in part because of (conditional but genuine) conviction, the new discourse came to internalize some of the cognitive and normative elements and institutional constraints of the neoliberal stream: for example, financial stability, the need to regain competitiveness, organizational efficiency, individual responsibility, and work incentives.
> (Ferrera, 2013, p. 84)

In the social domain there has therefore been a shift from neoliberalism to what Ferrera suggests to refer to as 'liberal neo-welfarism', that is a 'genuine ideological innovation, which recombines, redefines, and updates concepts drawn by those traditions that had most suffered by the neoliberal conservative attacks during the 1980s and early 1990s' (2013, p. 100). With this analysis of how neoliberal ideas in the social realm have varied over time in Western European countries, it is important to stress that studying recent policy changes requires that we pay attention to possible reconfigurations over time of ideational elements and policy devices, for instance the re-combination of marketisation and social justice rationales in tuition fee policy.

Based on the insights of this strand of scholarship, our volume comparatively examines the variation in time and space of tuition fee policy. The volume thereby contributes to the analysis and understanding of actual variations of neoliberalism in higher education.

A Comparative Analysis of Tuition Fee Policy

Among higher education policies, tuition fee policy is prominent as it most visibly embodies recent neoliberal trends in higher education, and illustrates the contemporary tensions between marketisation and social justice. Among the major transformations higher education systems have undergone in the last two decades, the emergence of marketisation, and in particular the introduction of tuition fees, have received a lot of attention indeed (Leuze et al, 2007; Brown, 2011). In Europe, these trends seemingly break with a long dominant representation of higher education as a public good, which stood at the centre of the process of massification of higher education access since the 1960s in most European countries (Trow, 2006). However, despite strong arguments made in favour of turning higher education into an industry (European Commission, 2005), the reasons and rationales underlying the trend towards (increased) tuition fees are complex. The many debates and the social mobilisations ensuing reform proposals to introduce or increase tuition fees in various European and North American countries illustrate very clearly the weight of alternative understandings of the nature of higher education systems. Opposing the idea that tuition fees are a necessary efficiency-oriented answer to reduced public funding, student groups and left-leaning political groups, most notably, have pointed at the issue of social justice in access to higher education. Recent reforms and resulting counter-mobilisations highlight the intrinsic political nature of tuition fees, and call for a fine-grained and systematic analysis of the variety of tuition fee policies in order to understand their impact on actual access to higher education. This is the present volume's main task. More specifically, the volume will explore three related issues: first, the various rationales for increasing (or not increasing) or introducing tuition fees; second, the policy instruments applied, i.e. the question of how tuition fee policies are set; and, third, the implications of (increased) fees for access and enrolment behaviour.

The issue of tuition fees came to the top of education ministers' political agendas when public funding for higher education started to decrease. This decline in public spending for higher education affected European and non-European countries unevenly (Estermann & Pruvot, 2011), but in most countries the 2008 economic and financial crisis gave a new impulse to funding diversification. In this context, the question arises what are the implicit and explicit political rationales for introducing or increasing tuition fees? How do political actors justify policy reform along the lines of increasing fees in their national setting? Research points at a variety of rationales that governments may use to advocate their tuition fee policy (Jongbloed, 2004; Marcucci & Johnstone, 2007; Musselin, 2010). Clearly, not all rationales are economic in nature (for instance, related to the compensation of the decrease in public funding), and some rationales articulate the increase in fees with a concern for social equity. The first objective of the volume is to investigate the rationales for tuition fee policies, and the drivers of such rationales: how does the political, social and economic context lead governments to choose certain tuition fee policies over others?

The connection between policy rationales and policy instruments is sometimes very weak (Palier, 2005). An analysis of the ways in which tuition fee policies are set and work is therefore indispensable. Previous investigations suggest several funding models that are available to policy-makers (Ward & Douglass, 2006; Brown & Carasso, 2013), and some research has developed an inventory of the various mechanisms through which fees are paid in different national settings (Jongbloed, 2004; Marcucci & Johnstone, 2007). Upfront payment, deferred tuition fees, loans or income contingent policies are the main instruments. The literature also pays attention to the levels of tuition fees. The second objective of the volume is to deal with the question of tuition fee policy instruments and fee levels by looking at some of the most recent reforms in different national contexts, and by including in the analysis some countries that are usually not part of comparative studies as their tuition fee policy reforms have been less dramatic than, for instance, in England. One ambition of this volume is therefore to provide a systematic analysis of national cases along the continuum between marketisation and social justice, avoiding merely focusing on the marketisation end.

The issue of the impact of tuition fee policies on access to higher education is crucial. A further aim of this volume is to bring together existing qualitative and quantitative data on the connection between fees policies and patterns of participation and to critically assess the potential and the limitations of research in this area. To what extent do increased tuition fees change patterns of student enrolment? How do financial assistance policies compensate certain groups of potential higher education students for fee increases and sustain access to higher education of students from less privileged social backgrounds? How do the various tuition fee policy instruments impact on student enrolment? How price and debt-averse are students from different social backgrounds? For this area of investigation a careful consideration of the question of causality is crucial: what is the evidence that changes in fee and student support patterns drive changes in higher education participation? The third objective of this edited volume is to go beyond econometric models built to test the elasticity of student demand to higher tuition fees, and to answer these questions in a comparative perspective.

The comparative design is key to this edited volume. The volume draws on eight case studies of different national and regional contexts. Given the recent reforms of tuition fee policies, England stands on the marketisation end of the continuum. Germany can be regarded as moving towards the other extreme as the last German federal states have abolished fees for undergraduates altogether. France is another extreme case, as, while higher education policy has been massively reformed in the last ten years, tuition fees have never been part of the reform packages. Three diverse intermediary cases will also be included. Québec is a case where the government framed the issue of increased student fees as cost-sharing, but failed in the end to adopt the reform because of massive student and broader social mobilisations making a 'social justice' argument. Portugal is an example of a country where external pressures, i.e. the conditions of the international bail-out agreement, are instrumental in the discussion surrounding increased fees in higher education. The fees policy in China demonstrates how tight government control on the one hand and increased market forces on the other can lead to a complex higher education system comprising of a number of distinct institutional types, each of which follow a different rationale for fees, resulting in starkly different levels of fees. These cases are supplemented by chapters on tuition fees in the USA, and more specifically their role in the Californian higher education set-up, and on recent changes to fee and support regimes in the Netherlands.

Fee Policies in National Contexts

Helen Carasso's chapter on tuition fees in England sets out the evolving contexts of the introduction of fees from the late 1990s onwards, discussing the rationales of the main policy documents, from the 1998 Dearing Report, to the 2004 Higher Education Act, to the 2010 Browne Review, and White Paper of 2011. In addition to outlining the changing fee policy, the chapter provides an overview of the student support mechanisms that have accompanied each increase in fees.

While the introduction and increase in fees over the period covered has dramatically changed the funding regime for higher education, this seems to have had only limited impact on longer term trends in participation in English higher education; the chapter provides a summary of the relevant participation data. However, it also needs to be recognised that interventions in the shape of bursaries and scholarships for students from non-traditional backgrounds seem not to have encouraged equity in participation or achieved 'fair access' to higher education; this is the case despite fees being re-payable only retrospectively, i.e. when graduates start to earn over a prescribed income threshold. The development of the fee landscape also shows the emergence of a quasi-market that has been a political aim of reforms in English higher education. However, the chapter argues that the quasi-market does not match the expectations of policy-makers, with the majority of institutions and courses charging at or very near the maximum fee level allowed by the state. The chapter concludes that, considering the far-reaching changes in a relative short period of time, the higher education sector and applicants now would benefit from a period of stability and consistency. However, the analysis of the current model of higher education funding and student support demonstrates increasingly clearly that the model is not sustainable financially and that further changes will be required (Thompson & Bekhradnia, 2013).

The chapter on Portugal reminds the reader of the particular characteristics of higher education as a labour intensive activity and the associated challenges of reducing cost and increasing productivity that higher education institutions are facing. In order to fulfil their main tasks of conducting high level teaching and research, there is a limited labour market pool higher education institutions can recruit from, resulting in cost pressures. If this situation is compounded by restrictions on public spending, such as currently in place in Portugal and a number of other European countries, this leads to an increasing emphasis on cost-sharing and the imperative to look for new funding sources in higher education. The chapter identifies a number of factors that potentially influence the ability of higher education institutions to generate income from tuition fees and provides insights into the risks that different types of institutions face in the current funding context in Portugal.

The 2008 reform of student support in France seems to have initiated significant changes affecting a number of aspects of higher education. The reform abolished interest-free loans provided by private banks for students who fulfil certain needs-based criteria. These loans were replaced by interest-paying loans, available to all students. The chapter on France highlights that the low fee, low aid model for student finances creates significant challenges for students. While the financial support available for students from lower socio-economic backgrounds is redistributive in nature, its scale and scope is too limited to substantially change traditional participation patterns. Since support is dependent on parents' income, particular problems arise for mature students. The chapter also demonstrates the variety of rationales for setting fee levels, some based on the cost of providing education, some on the pressures of a marketplace in which price is often seen as a marker of quality. The fee regimes emerging in France aim to combine notions of cost-sharing and principles of open access to higher education, seemingly squaring a circle that other countries are struggling with. This is achieved in parts by a system of means-tested, variable up-front fees, dependent on the income of students' parents. This emerging fee regime is based on the same principles as the much older system of determining the eligibility for student grants. The chapter also provides evidence for fee schemes being developed and tested at the 'margins' of the higher education systems and then introduced in mainstream provision; a strategy that can be observed also in other national contexts.

In comparison with other countries, the discussion on the introduction of tuition fees has been relatively insignificant in the German context. The contribution by Hüther and Krücken provides an overview of the introduction of fees in some of the 16 German federal states from the mid-2000s, as well as political and societal rationales for their abolition in all of these federal states in recent years (see also Alecke & Mitze, 2012). The introduction of fees in several federal states happened in the context of the growing importance of new public management approaches in the late 1990s and early 2000s and at a much lower level than in many other national contexts. The importance of new public management strategies, in turn, can be considered as a consequence of politicians of all main political parties acknowledging the potential role of market forces in rationalising and improving efficiencies in a number of societal areas, including higher education. It can also be argued that the early 2000s saw a reform agenda taking hold of higher education that can be linked to Germany signing up to the Sorbonne and Bologna Declarations. While this agenda was primarily concerned with the structure and duration of degree programmes, the analysis of legislation and regulation of the time also demonstrates that the Bologna agenda was used to introduce higher education reform in a number of areas in which change had been regarded as desirable in the 1980s and 1990s already, but due to political reasons never succeeded (Ertl, 2013).

Hüther and Krücken demonstrate that the issue of higher education fees has been highly politicised in the German context, proving to be a 'vote-loser' for parties in favour of fees in a number of regional elections. Maybe more importantly, there never was a strong consensus on the introduction of fees in the first place and public opinion on the issue has proven rather volatile. The contribution also highlights that the 'rise and fall of student fees' demonstrates the persuasive influence of the notion of higher education as a public good in the German context. The German case certainly disproves the notion that once university fees are introduced there is 'no way back' and that fees will inevitably have to rise in order to secure the funding of higher education.

The chapter on fee increases in the Netherlands demonstrates that policy-makers rely heavily on predictions of future student numbers when they design fee regimes and accompanying student support mechanisms. Wrong predictions can lead to significant problems in funding for higher education institutions and students. In the Dutch case, the underestimation of student numbers in the 1980s meant that the generous student support scheme designed by the government at the time proved to be unsustainable.

The Dutch student support system includes a performance-related aspect according to which support initially given as a loan is converted into a grant if students successfully complete their degrees in a given period of time. It can be seen from the Dutch case that the introduction of performance-related criteria for student support can affect the choices that students make regarding the subject and the type of institutions they choose. Performance-related support can be regarded as a merit criterion that is not applied before students start their higher education careers (as in conventional merit-based arrangements) but during their studies.

The Dutch system also includes a means-tested grant that takes into account whether students live with their parents or not. Another feature worth considering is the ability of the Dutch system to recoup loans, evidenced by a repayment rate that is significantly higher than in other national contexts.

The chapter by Rebekah Nahai outlines the diverse and complex tuition fee regimes and student funding mechanisms in US higher education at federal and state level. This requires at least some level of understanding of the historical formation of the higher education system in the USA and the development of fee policies over time which is provided by the contribution. The decentralised nature of higher education policy in the USA means that regulation at federal level is minimal and that fee levels for individual students vary greatly between different states and depend on whether students enrol at an institution located in their own federal state or not. The complexity is compounded by the differentiated institutional set-up of the system, with large differences in fee levels according to institutional types.

On the basis of a map of this complicated terrain, the chapter discusses the connection of student funding and social justice. The analysis highlights the positive but limited effect of federal mechanisms for student support on higher education participation of under-represented groups. However, the existing research in this area does not provide a conclusive understanding of the effects of different types of student support on participation rates and success of different groups of students in a system that is highly marketised and increasingly dependent on students making efficient economic choices regarding their higher education studies.

In order to develop a deeper understanding of the effect of state regulation and fee regimes on questions of social justice, the chapter narrows the focus on the University of California system. This focus demonstrates the evolution of tuition fee policies in a particular political context, including the rationales for differentiated fees and substantial fee increases over time. The connection between the over-arching economic situation, dwindling public funding for higher education and the impact of increasing fees on participation patterns is outlined. The Californian context illustrates how financial constraints can severely limit the effectiveness of a system explicitly historically geared towards high participation in higher education and how federal support mechanisms cannot prevent steep increases in student loan debts and the detrimental effects thereof.

In the Chinese context, the introduction of fees can be regarded as a by-product of the wholesale transformation of the economy from a state-planned to a market-regulated system, with the opening up of the economy from the late 1970s onwards paving the way to the introduction of market forces in higher education. As a result of this path of economic policy, higher education was no longer part of the socialist development process, but became essentially a process that benefits primarily the individual student. From this assumption the step to asking students to contribute to the cost of their education is only a short one. As the economy started to grow strongly, and as a result of increasing family incomes, it became possible for families to fund the studies of their children.

China is also an example of a country in which tuition fees were used to enable the rapid expansion of higher education, accounting for around a third of the income of higher education institutions (HEIs). The introduction of fees also signified a change from a situation in which HEIs were only responsible to the state to a position in which higher education plays a much broader role in society. However, sharp rises in tuition fees in the 1990s have put higher education practically out of reach for large parts of the Chinese society, particularly the population in the rural, economically less developed areas of the country. The research in this area shows that efforts of the Chinese government to counteract this trend with student support programmes have so far had only limited effects. Yu and Jin's chapter demonstrates how fees in general and substantial differences in fee levels according to types of institutions and subjects perpetuate inequality in Chinese society as a whole; a phenomenon mediated by the institutional hierarchies of the Chinese higher education system. This is compounded by the competition between various types of public and private institutions with vastly different fee regimes.

The chapter on Québec and Canada demonstrates how tuition fee levels can vary within federal systems according to policy priorities in different federal jurisdictions. With federal funding being cut, different Canadian provinces have found different ways of funding universities, and therefore the contributions that students are asked to make vary significantly.

Discussion of three opposing narratives on the role of higher education in society at large, and of higher education funding in particular, exposes very different views on the nature of benefits higher education can generate and the recipients of these benefits. This leads to an insightful debate on different perceptions of students, ranging from students as citizens, as investors in their own human capital or as users and buyers of a service. These different notions have consequences for how higher education should be paid for and guide theories of action.

Notes

[1] The editors are grateful to David Phillips for offering to include this volume in this series. They are also grateful for the support of Jane Caplan, Kalypso Nikolaïdis from the European Studies Centre, St Antony's College, Oxford, and Sophie Duchesne from CNRS – University of Paris-Nanterre.

[2] Gingrich (2011) identifies six types of markets. Besides the three types presented here, there are austerity markets, two-tiered markets, and pork-barrel markets.

References

Alecke, B. & Mitze, T. (2012) Studiengebühren und das Wanderungsverhalten von Studienanfängern: eine panel-ökonometrische Wirkungsanalyse, *Perspektiven der Wirtschaftspolitik*, 13(4), 357-386.

Brown, R. (Ed.) (2011) *Higher Education and the Market*. Abingdon: Routledge.

Brown, R. & Carasso, H. (2013) *Everything for Sale? The Marketisation of UK Higher Education*. Abingdon: Routledge & Society for Research into Higher Education (SRHE).

Ertl, H. (2013) German Higher Education and the State: a critical appraisal in the light of post-Bologna reforms, *Oxford Studies in Comparative Education*, 22(1), 131-152.

Estermann, T. & Pruvot, E. (2011) *Financially Sustainable Universities II. European Universities Diversifying Income Streams*. Brussels: European University Association (EUA).

European Commission (2005) *Mobilising the Brainpower of Europe: enabling universities to make their full contribution to the Lisbon Strategy*. Brussels: European Commission.

Ferrera, M. (2013) Welfare-State Transformations: from neo-liberalism to liberal neo-welfarism?, in Vivien A. Schmidt & Mark Thatcher (Eds) *Resilient Liberalism in Europe's Political Economy*, pp. 77-111. Cambridge: Cambridge University Press.

Friedman, M. (1962) *Capitalism and Freedom*. Chicago: University of Chicago Press.

Gingrich, J. (2011) *Making Markets in the Welfare State. The Politics of Varying Market Reforms*. Cambridge: Cambridge University Press.

Gualmini, E. & Schmidt, V.A. (2013) State Transformation in Italy and France: technocratic versus political leadership on the road from non-liberalism to neo-liberalism, in Mark Thatcher & Vivien A. Schmidt (Eds) *Resilient Liberalism in Europe's Political Economy*, pp. 346-373. Cambridge: Cambridge University Press.

Hall, P.A. (1993) Policy Paradigms, Social Learning and the State. The Case of Economic Policymaking in Britain, *Comparative Politics*, 25(3), 275-296.

Hayek, F. von (1944) *The Road to Serfdom*. Chicago: University of Chicago Press.

Jobert, B. & Théret, B. (1994) France : la consécration républicaine du néo-libéralisme, in B. Jobert (Ed.) *Le tournant néo-libéral en Europe, Idées et recettes dans les pratiques gouvernementales*, pp. 21-80. Paris: L'Harmattan.

Jongbloed, B. (2004) Tuition Fees in Europe and Australasia: theory, trends and policies, in J.C. Smart (Ed.) *Higher Education: handbook of theory and research*, pp. 241-310. Amsterdam: Kluwer.

Le Galès, P. & Faucher-King, F. (2010) *The New Labour Experiment. Change and Reform under Blair and Brown*. Stanford: Stanford University Press.

Leuze, K., Martens, K. & Rusconi, A. (2007) *New Arenas of Education Governance. The Impacts of International Organizations and Markets on Education Policy Making*. Basingstoke: Palgrave Macmillan.

Marcucci, P.N. & Johnstone, D.B. (2007) Tuition Fee Policies in a Comparative Perspective: theoretical and political rationales, *Journal of Higher Education Policy and Management*, 29(1), 25-40.

Musselin, C. (2010) Universities and Pricing on Higher Education Markets, in Dimitris Mattheou (Ed.) *Changing Educational Landscapes. Educational Policies, Schooling Systems and Higher Education – a comparative perspective*, pp. 75-90. Amsterdam: Springer.

Palier, B. (2005) Ambiguous Agreement, Cumulative Change: French social policy in the 1990s, in Wolfgang Streeck & Kathleen Thelen (Eds) *Beyond Continuity. Institutional Change in Advanced Political Economies*, pp. 127-144. Oxford: Oxford University Press.

Pierson, P. (1994) *Dismantling the Welfare State? Reagan, Thatcher, and the Politics of Retrenchment*. Cambridge: Cambridge University Press.

Pollitt, C. & Bouckaert, G. (2000) *Public Management Reform: a comparative analysis.* Oxford: Oxford University Press.

Schmidt, V.A. & Thatcher, M. (2013) Theorizing Ideational Continuity: the resilience of neo-liberal ideas in Europe, in Vivien A. Schmidt & Mark Thatcher (Eds) *Resilient Liberalism in Europe's Political Economy,* pp. 1-50. Cambridge: Cambridge University Press.

Thompson, J. & Bekhradnia, B. (2013) *The Cost of the Government's Reforms of the Financing of Higher Education – an update. HEPI Report Summary No. 64.* Oxford: Higher Education Policy Institute (HEPI).

Trow, M. (2006) Reflections on the Transition from Elite to Mass to Universal Access: forms and phases of higher education in modern societies since WWII, in James Forest & Philip Altbach (Eds) *International Handbook of Higher Education,* pp. 243-280. Dordrecht: Springer.

Ward, D. & Douglass, J.A. (2006) Higher Education and the Spectre of Variable Fees: public policy and institutional responses in the United States and the United Kingdom, *Higher Education Management and Policy,* 18(1), 1-28.

Weber, M. (1971) *Economie et société.* Paris: Plon.

CHAPTER 1

Reassuringly Expensive?
The Impact of Market Forces on
England's Undergraduate Provision

HELEN CARASSO

ABSTRACT Since 1998, home and EU undergraduates at English universities have found themselves at the receiving end of an evolving policy experiment in marketisation. They have seen their annual fees increase from zero to a maximum of £9000 in three steps and, in parallel, mechanisms for student support have changed at each stage. These moves were the result of the need to address underfunding of the sector during a period of increasing participation. However, at each stage the political case made for modifications to fees and funding concentrated on: equitable cost-sharing; the potential for market mechanisms to increase the options open to applicants (who would then make informed choices); and the expectation that universities would experience pressure from students for improved quality of provision. Opponents of each change expressed concerns about the potential for higher costs to discourage participation – especially among people from groups that are the focus of widening participation activities – resulting in several highly contested parliamentary debates on 'top-up fees'. While the most negative predictions about the impacts of increased fees have not proved entirely accurate, neither has a more market-based approach to the funding of undergraduate degrees obviously brought about the changes that politicians predicted. With questions about the sustainability of the current funding model, however, there is the potential for another politically controversial review of undergraduate fees and loans in the near future.

Over a period of just 15 years, Home and European Union (EU) undergraduates in England [1] have seen their annual contribution to fees rise from zero (until 1997) to a maximum of £9000 (from 2012). This change took place in three stages, with each initially presented by politicians as a long-term solution to the funding of universities and their students, not a step along a path of exponential growth in the tuition costs borne by students and graduates.

Contrary to the concerns expressed by critics when each increase in maximum fee was being considered, participation in higher education has grown significantly over this period – from around 33% in 1997 to approaching 50% in 2012.[2] However, beneath this headline figure, the picture is more complex and there is little evidence that means-tested non-repayable financial support (whether provided by universities themselves, or under national schemes) has helped to address the underlying imbalance in participation between different socio-economic groups of the population that is inherent in the English system. Answering questions in front of the House of Commons Business, Innovation and Skills Select Committee, Les Ebdon (in a pre-appointment session, prior to becoming Director of Fair Access) indicated that imbalance was, in fact, increasing in some areas: 'we have actually slid back in some universities in widening participation, and we must make up that lost ground immediately before we move forward' (Ebdon, 2012).

This question of the widening of participation – and the linked issues of equity of access [3] and of the role of higher education in social mobility – therefore remain at the core of the national debate in England about the funding of undergraduate degrees and students. At the same time, politicians argue that graduates benefit financially from their qualifications, in the form of a 'graduate premium' over their working lifetime, and thus that students should see the debts that they are now expected to take on (in the form of government-subsidised student loans) as an investment.

The value of this premium for today's undergraduates is highly contestable though as participation rates grow and the global economy shows only limited signs of growth (Thompson, 2012). Nevertheless recent modelling (Walker & Zhu, 2013) finds that the net lifetime benefits of a degree (compared to having two or more A levels, or equivalent, as the highest qualification) averages £168,000 for men and £252,000 for women. At the same time though, it estimates that the 'social benefit' of an individual having a degree is £264,000 for men and £318,000 for women which it notes is 'far in excess of likely exchequer costs' (p. 5).

The Application of Market Forces?

As each major change in undergraduate fees and funding was introduced in England (in 1998, 2006 and 2012), it was increasingly apparent that ministers viewed these reforms as introducing market measures to the provision of higher education. Politicians expected to observe consumer-like behaviours by students, such as demanding choice and quality of provision, as the amount that they contributed towards the cost of their degree (whether directly through the payment of fees, or indirectly through taking out loans to cover living costs) increased. This, in turn, ministers envisaged would encourage universities to seek to satisfy the wishes of applicants and students, while also aiming to operate more efficiently.

But this potential change in the relationship between an institution and undergraduates concerns many academics who see the introduction of market mechanisms as a path to the abandonment of the valuing of education for its own sake (Grove, 2011). In practice, however, no politician in England has suggested that a market should be allowed to operate unfettered among providers of undergraduate education. They have instead moved towards the introduction of what could most accurately be described as a quasi-market (Le Grand & Bartlett, 1993). This is a system in which not all suppliers have profit-maximisation as a primary objective and purchasing is not expressed strictly in terms of money (with vouchers or state purchasing agents involved). As we shall see though, even this form of a market does not operate entirely as the theorists might expect between English universities and their undergraduates, particularly as the ultimate costs of obtaining a degree (in terms of loans taken out for fees and living costs, offset by grants, scholarships and bursaries) are at best opaque to applicants.

Taken together, however, the introduction of up-front means-tested fees of up to £1000 in 1997, 'top-up fees' of up to £3000 in 2006, and a 'student contribution' of up to £9000 in 2012 for Home and EU undergraduates at English universities are arguably the most fundamental set of changes that any established higher education system has undergone to its funding over this period. In parallel with each of these there were also significant changes to the principles behind the availability of funding for student support, creating additional complexity for applicants and their advisers. These changes to the funding of tuition and of students is summarised in Table I.

	Fees	State student funding
Late 1970s-90	No student fee contribution	Means-tested grants
1990-98	No student fee contribution	Loans and means-tested grants
1998-2006	Means-tested student contribution – max £1000 (index-linked)	Loans for living costs only
2006-12	Deferred partial fee liability –max £3000 (index-linked)	Loans (for tuition and living costs) and means-tested grants (grant eligibility adjusted for 2008 and 2009)
2012- present	Deferred (partial) fee liability – max £9000 (not index-linked)	Means-tested grants, NSP[4] and loans (revised loan repayment terms)

Table I. A summary of undergraduate fees and student funding for home and EU students at English universities.

While some may therefore judge that the sector and its undergraduates now need a period of stability as far as funding goes, it is already probable that the current model of student support will quickly prove unsustainable (Institute for Public Policy Research [IPPR], 2013, pp. 120-127), with Universities Minister David Willetts confirming (Morgan, 2013) that his department estimates that some 35% of student loan debts will ultimately be written off, a figure which he also acknowledges may rise. So what will recent history tell policy-makers, should they start to consider a fourth remodelling of the funding of undergraduate fees and funding at English universities?

The Dearing Report and the 1998 Act

From 1979 to 1997, the UK had a Conservative government (with Margaret Thatcher as prime minister until 1990). During this period, undergraduate numbers more than doubled, while the unit of public funding per student reduced to 76% of its 1979 value (Watson & Bowden, 1997). This under-resourced expansion meant that 'by the mid-1990s the higher education system was facing a financial crisis' (Blackstone, 2007, p. xiii), a situation which was recognised by politicians from all the national parties.

The problem was so acute that, by 1996, vice-chancellors (through their representative group the Committee of Vice-Chancellors and Principals) were sending strong signals to ministers that, if this growing funding gap were not addressed nationally, they would recommend that a 'special levy' of £300 be charged to undergraduates entering university in 1997-98 (Brown with Carasso, 2012, p. 82; Shattock, 2012, pp. 132-133; Hillman, 2013, p. 11). At the same time, it was widely seen as almost inevitable that the long period of Conservative rule would come to an end at the following year's general election. It was in this context that the Dearing Committee [5] (formally the National Committee of Inquiry into Higher Education [NCIHE]) was established by the Conservative Secretary of State (supported by her prime minister) with the endorsement of Labour's Shadow Secretary and the leader of the opposition. Its terms of reference were:

> to make recommendations on how the purposes, shape, structure, size and funding of higher education, including support for students, should develop to meet the needs of the United Kingdom over the next 20 years. (NCIHE, 1997)

The bipartisan approach meant that, when the Committee reported in July 1997, two months after the general election had led to the widely predicted transition to a Labour government, it was still politically acceptable for ministers to welcome its recommendations. Speaking in the House of Commons on 23 July 1997, the day of the publication of the report, Prime Minister Tony Blair said:

> there will be proper protection for low-income families. We will not tolerate people being put off going to university as a result of

the means of their parents. That is point number one. Point number two is that we want a loans system that is fair and geared to people's ability to pay. That will also be part of the settlement. Point number three is that we do not want additional parental contributions. Point number four is that we must get more money into our university system.

We face a clear choice. If we want to increase student numbers and raise the amount of investment in universities, and we were to do it with taxpayers' money, it would cost a very substantial amount – something that people simply would not tolerate – so we must look for a better way to do it. Dearing was set up as an all-party initiative by the previous Government.

I believe that decisions on the funding of post-16 education must be taken in the interests of the long-term future of Britain and we will not shrink from taking them. (Hansard, 23 July 1997, col 1945)

The full report of the Dearing Committee filled some 2000 pages, included 5 appendices of commissioned research and made 93 recommendations; however, on the day of its publication, the government announced measures to fund undergraduate teaching and students which disregarded the proposals made by the Committee. The recommendations of the Committee and the ultimate legislative outcome are summarised in Table II.

Dearing Committee recommendation	Provisions of the 1998 Act
Flat fee of £1000 p.a. for all higher education institutions and courses – covered by income-contingent loans	Tuition fee to be paid upfront (with no loans available)
Replace 'mortgage' loans with income-contingent loans	Tuition fee to be means-tested
Retain means-tested maintenance grants for low-income students	Grant abolished and replaced by loan

Table II. Dearing Committee recommendations and the provisions of the 1998 Act.

In launching his government's response, the Secretary of State, David Blunkett, presented the fee an undergraduate would pay as a rational long-term individual investment, within the context of a wider package of financial support for institutions:

I have given a clear indication this afternoon of the investment in universities and colleges, and the whole purpose of the exercise upon which we are embarking has been to achieve that goal. I want to make it clear that we are not charging students at the time they are students. We are relating what they have to pay to their ability to pay at a point in the future when they have become

better off because of the higher education that they have received.
(Hansard, 23 July 1997, col 1962)

The measures that were subsequently introduced – in the Teaching and Higher Education Act (1998) – set fees at an index-linked maximum of £1000, a figure which did not redress the long-term reduction in the unit of resource; thus this immediately became the standard fee for Home and EU undergraduates at English universities. Furthermore, at a macroeconomic level, according to Barr (1998, p. 185) it was difficult to see how the immediate problem of underfunding for the sector could be ameliorated to any extent by the 1998 package of changes to undergraduate fees and funding. This was because the government had made a commitment not to increase public spending on higher education and the additional loans that became available to students were accounted for as public spending (because of the way that they were underwritten), off-setting any saving made by the abolition of grants. There was also no declared political intention to increase the private contribution to the system (in the form of high net parental contributions to fees or living costs).

Such public and political opposition as there was during the passage and introduction of the 1998 Act focused on the ending of 'free degrees', and almost entirely ignored the abolition of any element of non-repayable means-tested support (in the form of grants) to students from lower income backgrounds (Carasso, 2010, p. 7). Watson and Bowden (2007) take the view though that the 1998 changes to student support were at least as significant, in terms of wider perceptions and social impacts, as the introduction of the £1000 fee:

> New Labour's first-term policy on higher education ... was structured around Dearing, with the serious modification of his recommendations on fees and student support, which has haunted them ever since. Essentially, the government was too greedy. Ministers took the Dearing recommendation of a student contribution to course costs and ignored what the report said about living costs, especially for poorer students. Simultaneously, they completed a Conservative policy of turning all student grants into loans ... This precipitate decision has become the Achilles heel of subsequent New Labour policy on higher education. Almost every major policy initiative has been drawn back into a kind of maelstrom of misunderstanding, of posturing and of bad faith about costs and charges to students, exacerbated by an aggrieved middle-class sense of entitlement. (p. 29)

From the economist's perspective, Barr (1998) also critiques the introduction of a *price* subsidy (through means-testing the fee contribution) rather than an *income* subsidy (effected through the design of the loan scheme):

The problem with this approach (which is rather Old Labour) is that it can frequently hurt the very people it is intended to help, for example excessive rent subsidies, which have led over the years to waiting lists and labour immobility. It is therefore not surprising that the proposed arrangements, not-withstanding the Government's strong commitment to improve access, are profoundly unhelpful.

Access is harmed in several ways. Student living standards are inadequate because the total of loan and parental contribution is 25 per cent too low to support an adequate standard of living. Second, strengthened reliance on parental contributions ... makes bad policy worse. Under the Government's proposals, third, the fee contribution is deemed to be paid through the parental contribution, in effect introducing up-front fees. No government committed to access should contemplate such a policy. Finally, all these problems are regressive with respect to gender. (p. 185)

So, from both the political and the economic point of view, the changes introduced to Home and EU undergraduate fees and funding in 1998 were poorly thought through. This was quickly recognised by influential figures within the Labour party as they considered the long-term viability of these measures. Explaining how, early in the 2000s, he viewed this legislation, Andrew (now Lord) Adonis [6] said:

My view then was that it was too little, the [1998] reform, and that it was flawed in one or two key respects, particularly the up-front nature of the fee that made it very inflexible and secondly the lack of any mechanism or flexibility for increasing it over time, when it was clear that universities were going to need a substantial additional fund of non-state income and, on any credible co-payment basis, this was probably going to involve more student contribution over time. (Adonis, quoted in Carasso, 2010, p. 236)

The combination of £1000 up-front fees, with all student support in the form of loans, might have been expected to discourage participation, especially from sections of society that were already under-represented in higher education. A study looking at the 2002 admissions round identified attitudes to debt as playing a significant role in the choices made by potential applicants to higher education:

Debt aversion, and aversion to debt arising from student loans in particular, may not appear to be economically rational, especially given the in-built safeguards on repayments for low earners. However, decisions and choices are not informed purely by economic calculations. Other important factors, such as cultural values, also play a role ... However, given the risks of failure, non-completion and financial hardship associated with HE participation, especially for those from low-income families, debt aversion and concerns about debt may be highly rational. Research clearly shows that the costs of participation and debt levels on graduation are inversely related to the risks involved. They are highest for those with the lowest rates of return on HE and who take the greatest risks – low-income students. (Callender, 2003, p. 155)

The study found that a tolerant attitude to debt made an individual 1.25 times as likely to go to university as someone who was debt-averse, but in all other ways similar. Groups identified as being particularly debt-averse were: those from the lowest social classes; lone parents; Muslims (especially Pakistanis); and members of black and ethnic minority groups (Callender, 2003, p. 10), tending to reinforce concerns about the effects of the 1998 fees and funding changes on patterns of participation among different socio-economic groups.

However, admissions statistics show that the proportion of first-year ethnic minority students from the UK rose from 0.133 to 0.141 between 1997 and 2001, while, in the same period, students known to have a disability rose from 0.038 to 0.047 of the annual intake (Watson & Bowden, 2007, pp. 43-45). Although these headline figures summarise more complex data sets (participation rates vary significantly between different ethnic minority groups and disability statistics depend on self-disclosure by students), they do suggest that any differential deterrent effect of the financial provisions of the 1998 Act was complex, as their implementation in fact was followed by a small increase in the overall participation of certain under-represented groups.

The Higher Education Act (2004) and the Operation of a Limited Quasi-market

Even before detailed analysis of the impacts on undergraduate admissions of the £1000 fee and abolition of grants was available (such as Callender, 2003), politicians were starting to become concerned about the possible consequences of this funding regime. Mirroring thoughts expressed by Adonis (quoted earlier), the then Secretary of State for Education, Estelle Morris (2001), said:

Four years ago we took the brave and right decision to expand higher education by changing the way we funded student support. However, it was clear during the General Election [held in June 2001] that student debt was a major issue. I recognise that for many lower-income families the fear of debt is a real worry and could act as a bar to higher education. I want to make sure that our future reform tackles this problem. Our aim is to get more children from less privileged backgrounds into higher education and we hope to better achieve this by changing the combination of family, student and state contributions.

So, within three years of the introduction of substantial reforms to undergraduate fees and funding, there was already recognition at senior levels of government that further work was needed if it was to achieve its policy of equity of access to higher education. At the same time, institutions continued to argue that undergraduate teaching was underfunded to the extent that quality could be put at risk (Brown, 2003, p. 4), an argument that was accepted at the very top of the government:

> It was the Prime Minister's view in 2001 that we couldn't continue to duck [the underfunding of university teaching] if we wanted world-class universities and to expand student numbers. It was that decision, in the knowledge of the fact that any reform would be politically controversial, that put the issue very firmly on the agenda. If it hadn't been for his personal support for it, there's no way of course that the Education Department alone would have been able to start formulating quite radical policies in a controversial area. (Adonis, quoted in Carasso, 2010, p. 240)

But, as Andrew Adonis suggests, policy-makers were fully aware that the issues of university fees and undergraduate funding were highly contentious, both politically and publicly. Charles Clarke MP, who was Secretary of State for Education during 2003-04, when reform was being debated, has since described the context as:

> a very hotly contested political process where the opposition parties abandoned any rational consideration of the issues in order to try and gain political advantage from the potential unpopularity of the proposals, particularly amongst the relatively wealthy individuals and families who would end up having to pay more for the advantages they gained from university qualifications and resented the reduction in government subsidy to them. (Clarke, 2010)

At this point, policy-makers may have thought to revisit the funding recommendations of the Dearing Committee which had largely been ignored in the design of the 1998 reforms. However, they were particularly interested in possible models from the evolving market in Australia (Adonis, quoted in Carasso, 2010, pp. 51-52), where undergraduate contributions to fees had first been introduced in 1989. The Australian regulatory framework had already been modified several times and universities there were adopting a number of competitive market behaviours, although not necessarily with the outcomes expected by national legislators (Meek & Wood, 1997, pp. 265-266).

Given the political climate in the UK, the Labour government had to make a number of compromises between the publication of the White Paper outlining its plans (Department for Education and Skills [DfES], 2003) and the crucial Commons vote on 27 January 2004 on what was to become the Higher Education (HE) Act (2004). Most notably, it had been widely expected that the new fee cap would be set at £5000, a level which would have been likely to have resulted in universities setting a wider range of fees than resulted from the £3000 cap.

Even with its parliamentary majority of 161, the government won the vote with a majority of just 5. In a subsequent debate, on 31 March 2004, one previously hostile Labour MP, Peter Bradley, explained why he had been prepared to accept the government's revised plans:

> A free market in higher education would indeed entrench privilege
> – that is why I originally opposed the concept ... Under a free
> market model, the elite universities would get richer at the
> expense of the poorer universities ... but what is now on offer is a
> firmly regulated market, if it is a market at all. We are no longer
> talking about top-up fees, but about top-down fees. We are no
> longer talking about variability, but about a fixed fee with a
> discount. (Hansard, 31 March 2004, col 1682)

Under the resulting legislation, Home and EU undergraduates entering English universities from 2006 would be charged variable fees (capped at £3000, but index-linked); however they would have access to low-cost loans to pay these fees, as well as towards living costs, and those from lower income families would receive non-repayable grants. In an attempt to allay concerns that higher fees would discourage some groups of potential applicants more than others, the Act also introduced the Office for Fair Access (OFFA – although nicknamed 'Off-toff' by the media at the time). Any university wanting to charge more than the 'basic fee' of £1200 could do so only with the authorisation of OFFA, something which would depend on its approval of that university's access agreement. This document would specify an institution's planned fees, outreach activities, bursaries and scholarships offered, retention measures in place, and the monitoring it would be conducting to determine the extent to which it was recruiting students from diverse backgrounds.

Universities were concerned that OFFA would threaten their independence, particularly in relation to the selection of their students. However, writing soon after his appointment as the first Director for Fair Access, Sir Martin Harris was clear that this was not his intention:

> OFFA's role is about supporting universities and colleges so that
> they can, where appropriate, broaden the pool of applications
> right across higher education. There will be no predetermined
> targets or benchmarks, no social engineering – merely a
> determination, which I know is widely shared across the sector, to
> seek applications from those most able to benefit. (Harris, 2004)

All English universities took advantage of the provisions of the HE Act (2004) to charge more than the basic fee from 2006. OFFA estimated that, once three cohorts of students were funded under the new arrangements, commitments in access agreements for 2006-07 would result in some £350m being spent annually on bursaries and scholarships and around £37m used to fund additional outreach activities (OFFA, 2007, p. 11).

With only four English universities charging less than the maximum £3000 fee in 2006-07, and all charging the maximum by 2010-11 (with index-linking this had by then risen to £3290), any market that was created by the HE Act (2004) was to be found in those bursaries and scholarships offered by institutions, rather than fees charged. The categories of financial support offered by institutions included: a flat-rate sum given to all students (in effect a fee-reduction); means-tested bursaries (with levels for eligibility varying from university to university); and scholarships (fixed sums offered competitively on the grounds of excellence in music, sport, etc., or to local residents).

However, while these bursaries and scholarships did reduce the net cost to certain students of their degrees, eligibility criteria for many were complex – particularly in the first few years of this new funding regime – and applicants could not be certain how much financial support they would receive from different institutions (Callender & National Institute for Social Research [NISR], 2009; Corver, 2010). This made it unrealistic to expect them to include cost as part of their decision-making process.

Universities – as 'suppliers' – were attempting to use market mechanisms to influence the choices of applicants – as 'consumers'. However the information deficit in relation to net cost that was created by the complexities and uncertainties of bursary and scholarship schemes restricted the effective operation of any quasi-market (Carasso, 2010).

Politicians had also hoped (DfES, 2003) that the funding regime that was ultimately introduced through the HE Act (2004) would encourage other recognised aspects of market behaviour, with institutions becoming more directly responsive to their students wishes and interests, quality improving, and increased diversification as fees grew (Brown, 2011, p. 1). In this context, the National Student Survey was introduced in 2005 to monitor what in commercial markets would be called 'customer satisfaction', however it recorded little immediate evidence of such a shift in the relationship between universities and their undergraduates.

The greatest questions in relation to the introduction of £3000 fees, however, were about their possible impact on participation in higher education – a concern that had led to much of the initial parliamentary opposition to the raising of the cap to this level. In this context, Universities UK commissioned a series of annual reports to track the impacts on students and institutions of the new variable fee regime from 2006, against a baseline of 2004 data. The fourth of these studies (Brown & Ramsden, 2009) found:

- an overall increase in the number and percentage of acceptances from minority ethnic groups between 2004 and 2008 (with some differences in trends between applicants from different ethnic groups);
- in 2008 (after a period of relative stability from 2004 to 2007) a drop in the proportion of students from the highest socio-economic group (higher managerial and professional occupations), offset by increases in proportions from backgrounds of semi-routine and routine occupations;
- no evidence that maximum levels of bursary offered had an influence on application rates to individual institutions.

Whatever the variations in application rates between different socio-economic groups and to different institutions, the overall trend for growth (as shown in Figure 1) in undergraduate numbers continued under the new model of fees and funding, once the immediate impacts of the introduction of the £3000 were past.

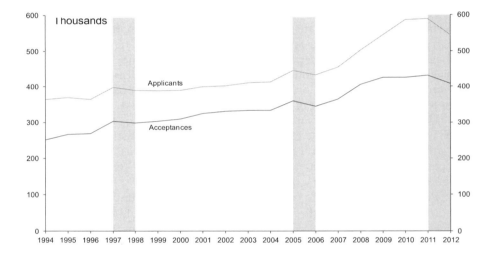

Figure 1. Home undergraduate applications and acceptances to UK universities by year of entry (data from UCAS annual end of cycle reports).
Source: Tuition fee statistics, House of Commons Library Standard Note SN00917, p. 8 (Bolton, 2013).

The sharp increases in applications and admissions in both 1997 and 2003 that are shown in Figure 1 are generally attributed to individuals who would otherwise have taken a 'gap year' entering university immediately after leaving school or college, to avoid higher fees the following year. In both cases, this is then followed by a drop in admissions – in the year in which higher fees were introduced – before numbers return to reflecting a broader trend of growing participation in higher education.

The Browne Review and the 2012 Fee Increase

When the HE Act (2004) was passed, the government guaranteed that there would be no substantive change in the undergraduate fees and funding for at least three years following its implementation. It also committed to commission a major review of the impacts of the 2006 changes, before proposing any new structures for fees or student funding. This came in the form of the Independent Review of Higher Education Funding and Student Finance, chaired by Lord (John) Browne of Madingley.[7]

Announcing the review in the House of Lords on 9 November 2009, the then Secretary of State, Lord (Peter) Mandelson said:

> Variable tuition fees have provided institutions with a secure income stream worth £1.3 billion per year, which has helped to sustain the long-term financial health and viability of this crucially important sector. Over this time, the number of students attending university has continued to rise, as has the number coming from lower-income backgrounds.
>
> To continue to thrive in the coming decade, institutions will need to respond to the changing needs of students, businesses and the wider community as well as adapt to demographic changes and growing international competition. The independent review will consider the balance of contributions from all those who benefit from the higher education system. (Hansard, 9 November 2009, col, lWS36)

Under its terms of reference, the review was tasked to:

> analyse the challenges and opportunities facing higher education and their implications for student financing and support. It will examine the balance of contributions to higher education funding by taxpayers, students, graduates and employers. Its primary task is to make recommendations to Government on the future of fees policy and financial support for full and part time undergraduate and postgraduate students. (Independent Review of Higher Education Funding and Student Finance, 2010, p. 57)

Thus the review was framed firmly in the context of 'cost sharing' (Johnstone, 2004) with the clear suggestion that the costs of a degree should be divided between three categories of beneficiary – the student or graduate, employers and the nation. However, the Secretary of State also placed some emphasis on the importance of widening participation.

The work of the Browne Review coincided with a period of national (and international) financial stringency and some judged that its assessment of likely public spending plans limited the options that it felt it could realistically consider (Baker, 2010; Morgan, 2010). The report, which was 61 pages in length, was published on 12 October 2010 (Independent Review of Higher Education Funding and Student Finance, 2010) and recommended abolishing any cap on undergraduate fees, but encouraging efficiencies within institutions by placing a levy on amounts charged above £6000 (so that, for example, an institution charging £7000 would receive £6600, with the additional £400 being returned to the public purse, and higher levels of fees would incur larger percentage levies). It also recommended retaining grants for students from low-income backgrounds, simplifying the subsidised student loan scheme and extending loans to part-time students; loan repayments would begin when the graduate was earning £21,000 as opposed to £15,000, but any outstanding debts would not be written off until 30 years after graduation as opposed to 25. In addition, the report suggested that universities should be free to recruit as many undergraduates as they wished.

To limit what could potentially have become an open-ended commitment of public funds, the Browne Review recommended that direct public funding (in the form of Higher Education Funding Council for England [HEFCE] grants for teaching) should be withdrawn from all but 'priority' subjects (i.e. sciences, technology and modern languages). Furthermore, student funding (in the form of subsidised loans and means-tested grants) would only be available to a pre-determined maximum number of students nationally, with the numerical threshold translated annually into an academic standard based on pre-entry qualifications obtained.

With funding 'following the student', the report argued that there would be clear incentives for institutions to ensure the quality of the education and other services they offered. In this context it suggested that formal responsibility for quality assurance and for student complaints should lie with a new public body that would combine the roles of HEFCE, the Quality Assurance Agency (QAA), the Office of the Independent Adjudicator (OIA) and OFFA.

This issue of the national regulatory framework for higher education was however not the immediate focus of political or media concern when the Report of the Browne Review was published.[8] Perhaps mindful of the response to the Dearing Review 12 years previously, when his Review Panel published its report, Lord Browne was quoted (Baker, 2010) as saying:

> This is a holistic system; all the key pieces fit together. This is a
> system that opens up choice and difference in university and I
> believe it is sustainable for the future.

However, the political situation in 2010 was more complicated with a coalition government of Conservatives and Liberal Democrats now in office. The Liberal Democratic Party had a long tradition of opposition to tuition fees, a policy on which it had continued to campaign during the general election of 2010 (Liberal Democrats, 2010), but one of its MPs, Vince Cable, held Cabinet responsibility for higher education as Secretary of State for Business, Innovation and Skills (BIS). Nevertheless, the wider economic climate – in which almost all areas of government spending were facing cuts and the Department for Business, Innovation and Skills itself was expected to make savings of 25% over four years – made a new funding model for universities unavoidable.

Given that economic context, it is perhaps not surprising that the government's initial response to the Report of the Browne Review was to focus on undergraduate fees and funding. It adopted a strategy that reduced the potential for highly contentious parliamentary debates (including between members of the coalition government) to a single vote on 9 December 2010 to alter the cap on fees. In the month before the vote there were a number of protests around the country, with students occupying university buildings and a national march in London resulting in violence and 35 arrests when some demonstrators tried to occupy the building housing the headquarters of the Conservative Party.

The coalition government had an overall majority of 83, but the increase to the cap on fees passed with a majority of only 21; of the 57 Liberal Democrat MPs, 28 voted for it and 21 against, with 8 abstentions. Thus, without the full scrutiny of new legislation, provisions for student finance and the funding of undergraduate teaching were altered from 2012 so that:

- there is no contribution towards the cost of undergraduate teaching (through a grant distributed by HEFCE) other than for priority subjects – principally sciences, mathematics and modern languages;
- the cap on Home and EU undergraduate fees at English universities was raised to £9000 (but not removed) – for 2013 at least, this figure has not been index-linked;
- any university wishing to charge fees above £6000 must not only have an access agreement with OFFA, but it must also participate in the National Scholarship Programme (NSP);
- students from low income families are eligible for non-repayable grants (£3250 when household income is less than £25,000, reducing to £0 at £42,875 [2012 figures]);
- student loans become repayable once a graduate's salary reaches £21,000, with a real rate of interest charged on the debt;
- part-time undergraduates have become eligible for student loans.

With these changes, politicians expected to establish a framework in which market principles would operate to enhance teaching and the experience of undergraduates, as the Universities Minister (Willetts, 2011) wrote:

Our changes to the financing system will [also] drive structural reforms in higher education. The force that is unleashed is consumerism. We would not have been willing to put in the extra funds and go through the political pain unless it was for the benefit of students and their educational experience. I recognise that the very term 'consumerism' causes deep anxiety for some. But it is not a threat to the classic relationship between academic teacher and student – it is an opportunity to rebalance academia so that teaching gets its rightful place alongside research.

But it was quickly evident that, even with a £9000 cap on fees, there was going to be only limited variation in the fees that universities set; the average national fee was calculated to be £8393 – or £8161 with fee waivers taken into account (OFFA, 2011a) – creating significant indirect costs to the government in the form of subsidies for student loans for tuition. At least partly as an incentive to institutions to review their initial decisions on fees for 2012 entry, the government introduced a 'core and margin' policy in which 20,000 student places were redistributed in response to bids from institutions charging net fees of under £7500 (Cable & Willetts, 2011).[9] In response to this initiative, 25 universities established revised access agreements with OFFA, so they could bid for some of these places. These resulted in a small reduction in the national average fee to £8354 – or £8071 after fee waivers (OFFA, 2011b).

The government was also alert to the potential to reduce its long-term financial commitment, in terms of subsidised loans, in the way that it designed the NSP. This scheme was launched by the Liberal Democrat Deputy Prime Minister Nick Clegg on 10 February 2011 following criticism of his party for reneging on its pre-election commitment to oppose fees. He said (BIS, 2011a):

> Social mobility in this country has stalled. It will only improve if we throw open the doors of universities, especially the most selective, to more bright students from disadvantaged backgrounds ... We must ensure that our great universities – often the gateway to the professions – make active and measurable progress to widen participation and advance social mobility.

The NSP is co-funded by the government and institutions, with those charging fees of over £6000 required to participate. In 2012-13, £50m of public money was distributed to eligible universities on the basis of their undergraduate numbers, with institutions required to match this money and establish scholarships of £3000 for first year students from the lowest income backgrounds; however no more than £1000 of each scholarship could be distributed as cash, with the rest 'in kind'. This led to many universities setting up fee-waiver schemes for NSP students, which were then extended to offer indirect financial support to other bursary students, thus reducing the call on fee loans, and hence the related public subsidy for this funding reflected in the national average figures reported above.

Given the terms of the NSP (Shepherd, 2011), and past behaviours in the design of their bursaries (Carasso, 2010), it was not surprising that the 129 resulting university schemes, which were approved institution-by-institution as part of their individual access agreements with OFFA, varied significantly, creating a complex picture for applicants and their advisers. An evaluation of the NSP commissioned by HEFCE (Bowes et al, 2013) found that: there was limited awareness among potential applicants of this as a national scheme; that direct financial assistance – in the form of cash awards – was more likely than fee waivers to have an impact on application decisions; and that communicating and operating the scheme (given its complexities) was resource-intensive for institutions. Potentially the most significant finding – in the political context – was that:

> There is scepticism [among institutions] about the likely impact of the NSP on social mobility, including access to HE, and choice of institution or course. Emerging evidence and international research suggests that financial aid will have a greater impact on retention and attainment, rather than access to HE. (p. 5)

After it has operated for three cohorts of freshers (with £100m of public money committed in 2013 and £150m in 2014), the government has decided that the NSP will close, diverting the funds instead towards support for postgraduate students. This is hoped to address concerns that those graduating from 2015 onwards, many of whom can be expected to have student loan debts of up to £40,000, will be loath to continue on to further study without any financial support.

While the consequences of the 2012 changes for subsequent postgraduate study can only be predicted, initial undergraduate admissions figures are available. The overall picture of applications and admissions for 2012 can be seen in Figure 1. This shows that the trend seen in 1997 and 2003 for a significant rise in application and admissions (generally attributed in large part to individuals who would otherwise have deferred entry to university for a year, deciding to study immediately to avoid a new fee regime) was not so pronounced in 2011. Furthermore as Bolton (2013, p. 3) notes, the 2012 drop in applications and acceptances of 6.5% and 5.5% respectively were the largest since the Universities and Colleges Admissions Service (UCAS) was formed in 1994.

In a detailed analysis of applications for 2012 (UCAS, 2012), UCAS found that applications from 18-year olds from England had fallen by about 1% (when adjusted for demographics), representing about 15,000 people who might otherwise have applied to university at 2011 rates. The drop was significantly larger for older applicants, at 15-20%, representing 30,000 people who might have applied at 2011 rates. Contrary to some expectations, application rates for young people from more advantaged backgrounds fell more than for those from less advantaged backgrounds.

The same report also found no evidence that price was having an effect on applications – with no substantial move to or from courses with higher fees. Similarly, there was no significant change in the proportion of young people from lower participation backgrounds applying to institutions with the highest entry requirements (a measure of equity of access).

Although these figures may seem initially to reinforce concerns that raising the cap on undergraduate fees to £9000 would have a detrimental impact on applications, putting them in the wider economic and demographic context, Thompson and Bekhradnia (2012) are less clear that they show any firm trends:

> We should not conclude from this assessment that the new arrangements have had no impact on demand for certain, only that that seems more likely. As more data becomes available the picture will become clearer. Nor should we assume that if, say, higher fees in themselves (rather than their introduction) have not been a deterrent to apply in 2012, this will continue to be the case in the future. And in part the decisions of young people in future may depend on the experiences of those who are starting university this year, and what story they have to tell to their friends and family.
>
> Nor should we forget that while increased demand may be a necessary condition for increased and widening participation and 'fair' access, it is not sufficient. Both the total number of funded places, and the way they are distributed may turn out to be more important than any changes in demand. (para. 61-2)

At the time of writing this chapter, final figures for undergraduate admissions in England for 2013 are not yet available. However, data on applicants suggest that, after the significant reduction in 2012, 2013 enrolments for students progressing directly from school or college may at least approach the 2010 level when demographic factors are taken into consideration (Independent Commission on Fees [ICoF], 2013, p. 10).

This trend may reflect financial realities as the macroeconomic perspective suggests that the position for students from low income backgrounds has actually improved under the package of funding reforms that accompanied the introduction of the £9000 cap on fees in 2012. Indeed, speaking before their introduction, one influential economist (Barr, 2011) argued that the planned revisions to the repayment system could be considered over-generous:

> you have to make sure that graduates with good careers repay their loan in full. Under the present system, the bottom 20% of graduate earners don't repay in full. Under the new system, Nick Clegg [Liberal Democrat Deputy Prime Minister] has said up to 60% of graduates don't repay in full. Now that starts to me to sound like a mixture between a loan and a grant. I can see no case for having a loan system as leaky as that. There is no need for that.

More detailed modelling of the impacts of the revised arrangements for student loans from 2012 calculated that 29% of graduates with the lowest incomes would be better off than under the system that was in place for undergraduates enrolling at university from 2006 to 2011. The same modelling found that, at the other end of the spectrum, high-earning graduates would pay back more than under the previous arrangements, with the top 15% paying back more than the value of their student loans. The researchers commented:

> What implications do these results, and the reforms in general, have for social mobility? Our analysis shows that the reforms involve an increase in up-front support for students whilst they are at university, especially for those from the poorest backgrounds. It also demonstrates that the reforms will strengthen the insurance built into the loan repayment system, and will increase its progressivity. (Chowdry et al 2012, p. 234)

Thus, in theory at least, higher education funding in England has, since 2012, been able to support increased participation [10] while the terms of student loan repayments have been adjusted to the benefit of graduates with lower earnings.

Conclusions

As successive governments have made significant changes to the ways in which undergraduate tuition costs are paid and students receive support through their studies, funding mechanisms have tended to move the higher education sector in England closer to a quasi-market model. However politicians have tried to off-set the perceived potential deterrent effect of increases in fees (especially for those from backgrounds with lower rates of participation in higher education) with complicated packages of financial support and other constraints on the extent to which that market can operate freely.

While there is no reason to believe that the desire to offer financial support to those for whom policy-makers believed increased fees would otherwise be a barrier to participation in higher education was anything but genuine, at each stage of the funding reforms considered here this was converted into policy with limited recourse to research evidence. Furthermore, the constraints that were placed on the sector (again with the intention of supporting access, but also designed to protect the more vulnerable institutions from potential sudden cuts in teaching income) encouraged universities to develop their own bursary and scholarship schemes based on complicated eligibility criteria.

In many cases, students do not know how much financial support will be available to them on a particular course until after they have had to make their decision about where and what to study (Bowes et al, 2013, p. 32). It is therefore not surprising that, while perception of, and the level of concern about, the cost of a degree plays a role in an individual's decision about whether or not to apply to higher education, possible net cost differences between different higher education choices are less influential in decisions about where and what to study. Applicants do not expect to have a clear idea of the net cost of their studies until after enrolment (as it is not until then that accurate information about bursaries and scholarships often becomes available), and instead consider factors such as employability and graduate salaries as proxy indications of 'value' when choosing between courses and institutions (Ertl et al, 2013).

Hence this pattern of decision-making is understandable at an individual level – because of the lack of personalised financial information – whatever the macroeconomic picture may suggest. It is therefore entirely possible that varying levels of debt aversion among different groups of the population (Callender, 2003; Ertl et al, 2013) will again affect the profile of applicants nationally.

This issue remains a political concern, both within the coalition government and more widely. However the Liberal Democrat Deputy Prime Minister Nick Clegg had already announced (in August 2010) the appointment of a former Labour government minster, Alan Milburn, as Independent Reviewer on Social Mobility and Child Poverty. Reporting just after the completion of the 2012 admissions round, the Independent Reviewer wrote (Milburn, 2012, p. 80):

> One thing is already certain: the increase in student fees is a major change. It means that families who are above the breadline but by no means wealthy now fear that they will incur considerable costs – and debts – if their children wish to go to university. Higher education is no longer a free good. That is especially salient for the fair access agenda. People from poorer backgrounds are more than twice as likely as those from wealthier backgrounds to say they will choose a university with lower fees, and are nearly twice as likely to say that they will choose a university where they can live at home. Of course, where people are making an informed choice based on their own aspirations that is welcome, but the evidence suggests that they are not always making a free choice. Instead, they are being constrained by debt aversion and the barrier of living costs. There is a very real danger that the Government has under-estimated the extent to which fear of debt is part of the DNA of Britain's least well-off families.

Monitoring this is however not straightforward and, through each reform of undergraduate fees and funding, legislators have retained an inherent inconsistency – are students to be perceived as dependent members of their families or independent adults? When considering the extent to which access to higher education has been widened, the measures used include those relating to family background, family history of participation in higher education and home address. Eligibility for substantial elements of non-repayable support (grants, funds from the NSP and institutional bursaries and scholarships) is determined on the basis of Residual Household Income – in effect a means-testing of a student's parents, carers or spouse. But loan repayments are based on the graduate's own income alone. So potential applicants are encouraged to think of any student debt they accumulate as an investment in their future, but how much they need to borrow in the first place will depend on their family circumstances, potentially adding further confusion to an already complex message about the costs of studying for a degree.

The recent history of reform to undergraduate fees and funding in England, which has led to this complex system, has been a divisive one, provoking student sit-ins, violent street demonstrations and highly charged parliamentary debates which have, at times, become symbolic of wider political divisions. However fraught arguments have been though while changes were under consideration, there is little evidence that implementing what were viewed, at the time, as significant and contentious reforms has damaged a government when it has next faced a general election (Hillman, 2013, p. 16).

The next election in the UK is due in 2015, the time when any impacts of the £9000 cap on undergraduate fees on postgraduate applications may first become visible. With this possible cause for concern emerging, it remains to be seen whether history will repeat itself when the Conservative and Liberal Democrat coalition partners stand independently in the election, unless there is clear evidence that undergraduate fees of £9000 have not acted to discourage some groups of the population more than others from applying to university.

Notes

[1] Until 1998 higher education funding for all parts of the United Kingdom (UK) (England, Wales, Scotland and Northern Ireland) was determined by the national Parliament in Westminster. The 1998 Act enabled the Scottish Parliament to set fees for its universities and equivalent power was given to the Welsh Assembly in the 2004 Act. All the legislation reviewed here applies to England, and is reported in that context.

[2] The basis on which Age Participation Rates are calculated changed in 2006, making figures for 1997 and 2012 not directly comparable.

[3] 'Equity of access' relates to the type of institution that students from different backgrounds attend and specifically concerns that the most selective universities recruit disproportionately from schools and families with longer traditions of entering higher education (see, for example, Harris, 2010).

[4] *NSP is the National Scholarship Programme, a scheme funded jointly by the government and individual institutions to provide non-repayable financial support to undergraduates from the lowest income backgrounds. Only up to one-third of support given to an individual student under this scheme can be in cash, with the remainder 'in kind', for example in the form of partial fee waivers or discounted accommodation. The NSP is being withdrawn from 2015.

[5] Sir Ron (later Lord) Dearing was Chancellor of the University of Nottingham at the time of his appointment, after spending much of his career in the civil service, he served as Chairman of the Post Office from 1980 to 1987. Following that post, he served as Chair of the Council for National Academic Awards (CNAA) and then of the Polytechnics and Colleges Funding Council (PCFC) before moving to head the School Curriculum and Assessment Authority. The 17-strong membership of the Dearing Committee represented schools, students, staff, the private sector and a range of higher education institutions.

[6] Andrew Adonis played a key role in the formation of education policy within 10 Downing Street from Labour's election victory in 1997 until he became a Peer in 2005. He is widely viewed as the 'author' of the Higher Education Act (2004).

[7] A physics graduate, Lord Browne spent his career in British Petroleum (later BP), joining in 1966 as an apprentice and standing down as Chief Executive in 2008. At the time of his appointment, he was President of the Royal Society of Engineering, and sitting as a Crossbench (independent) Peer. His seven-member committee was made up of a former advisor to Prime Minister Tony Blair, an economist Diane Coyle, two vice-chancellors (neither from post-92 universities), a businessman and the former chairman of the British Youth Council.

[8] The national regulatory framework for the sector was considered formally by the government in its White Paper, Students at the Heart of the System, published in June 2011 (BIS, 2011b). This was never followed by legislative proposals and no provision has been made in the parliamentary schedule for any resulting bill to be debated. However, on 11 July 2013 (*Hansard*, col 23-26WS), Universities Minister David Willetts outlined plans for revisions to the governance of the higher education sector in England, which he described as: 'The reformed regulatory system ensures accountability for public funding, protects the collective student interest, gives priority to quality improvement, safeguards institutional autonomy, and sustains the reputation of English higher education'. These will be implemented initially without the need for new legislation.

[9] At the same time, the government announced that there would be no cap on the numbers of students with the highest pre-entry qualifications (at least AAB at A level or equivalent) that an institution could recruit for 2012-13. This measure was intended to enable institutions to respond to demand from the most well-qualified students by increasing the number of places they could offer to them, without the risk of exceeding the maximum intake they had agreed with HEFCE. For 2013-14, this was modified so that there was no cap on students recruited with ABB or above.

[10] As demonstrated by the government's removal of any cap on the numbers of students admitted with academic qualifications equivalent to at least AAB at A level in 2012 and ABB from 2013.

References

Baker, S. (2010) Lord of the Market: let competition and choice drive quality, *Times Higher Education*, October 14.

Barr, N. (1998) Higher Education in Australia and Britain: what lessons?, *Australian Economic Review*, 31(2), 179-188.

Barr, N. (2011) Presentation given at The Financing of Higher Education, Higher Education Policy Institute (HEPI) House of Commons Seminar, 15 February, in London.

Blackstone, T. (2007) Foreword, in D. Watson & M. Amoah (Eds) *The Dearing Report – ten years on*. London: Bedford Way Papers (Institute of Education).

Bolton, P. (2013) *Entrants to Higher Education. House of Commons Standard Note SN/SG/1446*. London: House of Commons Library.

Bowes, L., Thomas, L. & Moreton, R. (2013) *Formative Evaluation of the National Scholarship Programme – summary of findings presented to HEFCE by CFE and Edge Hill University*. Leicester: CFE.

Brown, N. (2003) *What's it Worth? The Case for Variable Graduate Contributions*. London: Universities UK.

Brown, N. & Ramsden, B. (2009) *Variable Tuition Fees in England: assessing their impact on students and higher education institutions – a fourth report*. London: Universities UK.

Brown, R. (2011) Introduction, in R. Brown (Ed.) *Higher Education and the Market*, pp. 1-5. New York: Routledge.

Brown, R. with Carasso, H. (2013) *Everything for Sale? The Marketisation of UK Higher Education*. Abingdon: Routledge & Society for Research into Higher Education (SRHE).

Cable, V. & Willetts, D. (2011) Higher Education White Paper: students at the heart of the system. Letter to Tim Melville-Ross, Chairman of HEFCE, June 28.

Callender, C. (2003) *Attitudes to Debt*. London: Universities UK.

Callender, C. & National Institute for Social Research (NISR) (2009) *Awareness, Take-up and Impact of Institutional Bursaries and Scholarships in England*. Bristol: Office for Fair Access (OFFA).

Carasso, H. (2010) Implementing the Financial Provisions of the HE Act (2004) – English universities in a new quasi-market. DPhil thesis, University of Oxford. http://tinyurl.com/26a57a3 (accessed August 10, 2013).

Chowdry, H., Dearden, L., Goodman, A. & Jin W. (2012) The Distributional Impact of the 2012-13 Higher Education Funding Reforms in England, *Fiscal Studies*, 33(2), 211-236.

Clarke, C. (2010) Submission to Browne Inquiry into Higher Education Funding. http://webarchive.nationalarchives.gov.uk/+/hereview.independent.gov.uk/herevie w/2010/03/submissions-to-the-first-call-for-evidence/ (accessed August 10, 2013).

Corver, M. (2010) *Have Bursaries Influenced Choice between Universities?* Bristol: Office for Fair Access (OFFA).

Department for Business, Innovation and Skills (BIS) (2011a) Ensuring Higher Education is Open to All, February 10. https://www.gov.uk/government/news/ensuring-higher-education-is-open-to-all (accessed August 20, 2013).

Department for Business, Innovation and Skills (BIS) (2011b) *Higher Education: students at the heart of the system.* London: BIS.

Department for Education and Skills (DfES) (2003) *The Future of Higher Education.* London: DfES.

Ebdon, L. (2012) Oral Evidence to the Business, Innovation and Skills Committee, House of Commons, February 2, *Hansard*, 1811 – i.

Ertl, H., Carasso, H. & Holmes, C. (2013) *Are Degrees Worth Higher Fees? Perceptions of the Financial Benefits of Higher Education. Research Paper No. 117.* Oxford: Skills, Knowledge and Organisational Performance (SKOPE).

Grove, J. (2011) Sector Must Reject Neo-liberal Business-speak, Event Hears, *Times Higher Education*, December 1.

Hansard, 23 July 1997, col l945.

Hansard, 9 November 2009, col lWS36

Hansard, 11 July 2013, col 23-26WS.

Harris, M. (2004) Strings Attached, *Guardian*, November 9, Education section.

Harris, M. (2010) *What More Can be Done to Widen Access to Highly Selective Universities?* Bristol: Office for Fair Access (OFFA).

Hillman, N. (2013) From Grants to All to Loans for All: undergraduate finance from the implementation of the Anderson Report (1962) to the implementation of the Browne Report (2012), *Contemporary British History*, 27(3), 249-270.

Independent Commission on Fees (ICoF) (2013) Analysis of University Applications for 2013/14 Admissions. http://tinyurl.com/otl656t (accessed September 15, 2013).

Independent Review of Higher Education Funding and Student Finance (Browne Report) (2010) Securing a Sustainable Future for Higher Education. http://webarchive.nationalarchives.gov.uk/+/hereview.independent.gov.uk/herevie w/ (accessed August 18, 2013).

Institute for Public Policy Research (IPPR) Commission on the Future of Higher Education (2013) *A Critical Path – securing the future of higher education in England.* London: IPPR.

Johnstone, B. (2004) *The Economics and Politics of Cost-sharing in Higher Education: comparative perspective, Economics of Education Review*, 23, 403-410.

Le Grand, J. & Bartlett, W. (1993) Introduction, in J. Le Grand & W. Bartlett (Eds) *Quasi-Markets and Social Policy*, pp. 1-12. Basingstoke: Macmillan.

Liberal Democrats (2010) Liberal Democrat Manifesto 2010. http://www.libdems.org.uk/our_manifesto.aspx (accessed August 18, 2013).

Meek, V. & Wood, F. (1997) The Market as a New Steering Strategy for Australian Higher Education, *Higher Education Policy*, 10(3-4), 253-274.

Milburn, A. (2012) *University Challenge: how higher education can advance social mobility – a progress report by the Independent Reviewer on Social Mobility and Child Poverty*. London: Cabinet Office.

Morgan, J. (2010) Focus on Cuts Undermines Value of Browne's Report, Critics Contend, *Times Higher Education*, October 21.

Morgan, J. (2013) Willetts Reveals Rise in Student Loan Write-off Costs, *Times Higher Education*, May 15.

Morris, E. (2001) Key Challenges of the Next Decade. Speech given at London Guildhall University, 22 October, in London.

National Committee of Inquiry into Higher Education (NCIHE) (1997) *Higher Education in the Learning Society*. London: Her Majesty's Stationery Office. http://www.leeds.ac.uk/educol/ncihe/ (accessed August 6, 2013).

Office for Fair Access (OFFA) (2007) *Annual Report and Accounts 2006-07*. Norwich: Her Majesty's Stationery Office.

Office for Fair Access (OFFA) (2011a) OFFA Decisions on 2012-13 Access Agreements, news release, July 12. http://www.offa.org.uk/press-releases/universities-and-colleges-to-increase-their-spending-on-access-to-600-million-a-year/ (accessed August 20, 2013).

Office for Fair Access (OFFA) (2011b) OFFA Announces Decisions on Revised 2012-13 Access Agreements, news release, December 2. http://www.offa.org.uk/press-releases/offa-announces-decisions-on-revised-2012-13-access-agreements/ (accessed August 20, 2013).

Shattock, M. (2012) *Making Policy in British Higher Education 1945-2011*. Maidenhead: Open University Press.

Shepherd, J. (2011) Tuition Fee Waiver Scheme 'Too Complex' to Help Poorest Students, *Guardian*, January 31.

Thompson, J. (2012) *Returns on Investment in HE*. Oxford: Higher Education Policy Institute (HEPI).

Thompson, J. & Bekhradnia, B. (2012) *The Impact on Demand of the Government's Reforms of Higher Education*. Oxford: Higher Education Policy Institute (HEPI).

Universities and Colleges Admissions Service (UCAS) (2012) *How Have Applications to Full-time Undergraduate Higher Education in the UK Changed in 2012?* Cheltenham: UCAS.

Walker, I. & Zhu, Y. (2013) *The Impact of University Degrees on the Lifecycle of Earnings: some further analysis. BIS Research Paper No. 112*. London: Department for Business, Innovation and Skills.

Watson, D. & Bowden, R. (1997) *Ends without Means: the Conservative stewardship of UK higher education 1979-1997*. Brighton: University of Brighton.

Watson, D. & Bowden, R. (2007) The Fate of the Dearing Recommendations: policy and performance in UK higher education 1997-2007, in D. Watson & M. Amoah (Eds) *The Dearing Report – ten years on*, pp. 6-50. London: Bedford Way Papers (Institute of Education).

Willetts, D. (2011) We Cannot be Certain about Every Step. But the Journey will be Worthwhile, *Times Higher Education*, May 26.

CHAPTER 2

For Whosoever Hath, to Them Shall Be Given? Analysing the Matthew Effect for Tuition Fees' Revenues in Portuguese Higher Education

PEDRO TEIXEIRA, VERA ROCHA, RICARDO BISCAIA & MARGARIDA FONSECA CARDOSO

ABSTRACT The dominant issue in recent years in public higher education's funding has been that of financial stringency, with growing pressures towards revenue diversification. This has been followed by debates about possible differentiation in the way public institutions are funded and about the advantages and risks of concentrating resources in a few institutions. In this chapter we analyse the Portuguese experience with cost-sharing to analyse some major factors – besides the total number of enrolments – that may explain the ability of public higher education institutions to accumulate more revenues through tuition fees. The results do not seem to confirm the existence of a so-called Matthew effect in the distribution of those revenues. Our analysis instead highlights that revenues from tuition fees have been particularly important for those institutions with lower research-intensity and with a more specialised programmatic offer. Our results also point out possible tensions in the current pattern of funding in Portuguese public higher education, notably in the current environment of crisis and financial retrenchment.

Introduction

Public higher education institutions (HEIs) face a demanding and complex financial context in which the traditional modes of funding have been transformed and public sources have become more demanding and competitive (Herbst, 2006). These pressures have become very significant in view of the financial demands from other types of expenditure related to an aging society, such as health and social security programmes. The financial outlook has become even more problematic due to the increasing trends on the cost side. As has been documented in the USA (Clotfelter, 1996; Geiger, 2004), higher education seems to have a significant inherent trend for expanding costs. An important factor usually presented to explain this rise in costs has to do with the nature of higher education as a labour intensive activity (the so-called 'cost-disease') and the difficulties in benefiting in large scale of the kind of productivity enhancements typically associated with the goods-producing sectors of the industrialised economies (Archibald & Feldman, 2010).[1] Another part of the explanation to the increasing costs lies in the use of more costly resources and in an increasing emphasis of high-quality services to which has contributed the emphasis in Europe on research universities as the institutional role model.[2] Hence, the contemporary financial and policy context has placed the issue of sources of funding at the centre of higher education policy debates (Greenaway & Heynes, 2003).

The current economic and financial crisis has exacerbated even further these problems, with growing pressures upon the sustainability of funding regimes of public higher education and the pressure mounting to explore complementary sources of revenue. One of the major issues in this respect has been the introduction of cost-sharing in higher education (Johnstone & Marcucci, 2009), which is still a very controversial topic in many European countries (Teixeira et al, 2006). Thus far, there has been a lack of empirical studies analysing the actual relevance of tuition fees for the total revenues of European HEIs and of potential institutional differences in that respect. For many years it has been noted that there is a so-called Matthew effect in science (Merton, 1973), with the most prestigious institutions receiving a disproportionately high amount of financial and non-financial rewards, which in turn allowed them to keep their prestige over time. There are reasons to think that a similar situation may exist in teaching revenues, with more prestigious institutions being able to obtain bigger revenues through tuition fees.

The main purpose of this chapter is to reflect about the development of cost-sharing and some of its impacts. We pay particular attention to the ability of public HEIs to accumulate revenues from student fees by exploring which factors (besides the size of enrolments) may influence the absolute and relative amount of revenues from tuition fees gathered by institutions over the period 2003-09. Using panel data from Portugal, we explore to what extent certain institutional characteristics may help explain why certain public HEIs are more successful than others in generating those revenues. In the next section we briefly review the main issues surrounding the debate about the introduction of cost-sharing in Portugal by placing it within the wider European higher education context. In the subsequent sections we present the empirical analysis, including the data and the methodology used in the study, and finally the main results. The chapter concludes with some reflections upon the relevance of the results for European policy debates about public higher education, namely to what extent the growing relevance of tuition fees in institutional revenues is leading to greater institutional differentiation.

Changing Times for Funding in Portuguese Public Higher Education

Portugal has been part of the discussion about funding changes, not least due to the fast and belated expansion of its higher education system. Portuguese higher education remained rather small and elitist until the mid-1980s (Teixeira et al, 2006), but by then the social and political pressures for expansion became very strong and the system has expanded massively, both in terms of numbers of institutions and numbers of students enrolled. Thus, the expansion took place within an economic and political context far less favourable to an exclusive reliance on public funding. At present, the Portuguese public higher education system comprises 14 public universities (including a distance learning university), 15 public polytechnics and 32 vocational colleges. In the private sector there are 7 universities (including a Catholic university), 4 polytechnic institutes and 72 smaller colleges.[3] As Table I indicates, the evolution of enrolments highlights a profound transformation of the system during the last decades. Nowadays, Portugal has a rate of gross enrolment similar to its European counterparts and a very diverse system.

The Introduction of Cost-sharing

The evolution in the funding of higher education tended to follow European trends, namely the move from earmarked funding to lump-sum transfers and the adoption of sector-wide criteria. Since the late 1980s, the funding of public higher education has been organised through a funding formula that is proportional to enrolments and that incorporates other cost parameters such as the study area and type of institution (see, for instance, Rosa et al, 2009). In more recent years there has also been a growing political willingness to introduce output indicators regarding graduation rates and research performance of each HEI. Recent years have also signalled the political adoption of a more hybrid view regarding higher education funding sources. In the late 1990s, the notion of complementary funding was introduced as one of the guiding principles of the funding of public higher education, meaning that institutions should find additional sources of revenue besides public ones. In 2003, a new funding law was passed which included a more explicit emphasis on diversification of funding sources. Subsequent financial regulations will consolidate the incentives towards revenue diversification, namely through a preferential treatment of those institutions capable of generating more revenues.

	1971		1981		1991		2001		2011	
	No.	%	No.	%	No.	%	No	%	No.	%
Public universities	43,191	87.3	64,659	76.8	103,999	47.0	176,303	44.5	197,912	50.7
Public polytechnics	2,981	6.0	12,195	14.5	31,351	28.7	108,486	27.3	113,662	29.1
Private institutions	3,289	6.7	7,319	8.7	51,430	24.3	111,812	28.2	78,699	20.2
Total	49,461	100.0	84,173	100.0	186,780	100.0	396,601	100.0	390,273	100.0
Gross enrolment rates			12%		22%		50%		65%*	

*Value for 2010.

Table I. Growth of enrolments and gross enrolment rates in Portuguese higher education, total and by sub-sector.
Sources: Barreto, 1996; Simão et al, 2002; OCES – Observatory for Science and Higher Education (Portugal).

A major initial legal impulse towards revenue diversification came through a move towards greater cost-sharing in the 1990s. Until 1992, the level of tuition fees in public institutions was very low (c. €6 per year) because its value had been frozen since its introduction in 1944. Then, a new tuition fees system was established which was means-tested and with far more significant values (c. €300 annually), although still low for international standards. This change led to significant student protests and political turmoil, with various ministers of education having to resign under the pressure of the protests. By 1997, the situation was eventually settled. The Funding Law of 1997 defined a level of tuition fees equal for all students in public HEIs and linked its annual value to the national monthly minimum wage. The new funding law of August 2003 did not only increase the annual level of tuition fees, but also introduced a range within which institutions could define their own fee level, although most institutions would tend to charge the permissible maximum.

In order to overcome the resistance of students and the fears of institutions that the value of fees would be subtracted from government transfers, two strategies were adopted by the government. The first was to promise students that fees would be used for quality improvements (notably in teaching activities) and would not cover current expenditures, notably staff salaries. The second strategy was aimed at the institutions and the fact that tuition fees were treated as self-generated income, thus enjoying a far greater flexibility in the way these could be used. To a large extent, these two strategies were conflicting and subsequent periods of fiscal retrenchment saw the promises made to students increasingly untenable, solving the conflict in favour of the second one.

The controversy about tuition fees was very much focused on undergraduate programmes, which was hardly surprising since they represented the bulk of enrolments. Nonetheless, since the mid-1990s, the consolidation of the higher education system, the qualification of academic staff, and the stabilisation of the undergraduate market turned the attention of many institutions to the postgraduate market. This appeared as an interesting opportunity, not only to compensate for the saturation of the undergraduate market, but also due to its potential for generating additional revenues. The level of tuition fees charged for postgraduate courses could be defined by institutions themselves. The legal framework also stipulated that this revenue, like that from undergraduate fees, was considered to be an institution's own income.

Several institutions have seized this opportunity, especially in certain fields in which a master's degree could provide important professional and financial advantages. Consequently, master's programmes have developed in a rather unregulated manner. The issue became more visible from a political point of view due to the Bologna process. In this new context, many senior undergraduate students came to be considered as master's students. On the other hand, the shortening of undergraduate degrees in many fields has stimulated demand for master's programmes, namely as an instrument of differentiation in the labour market. The market for master's programmes promised significant growth, but also much stronger regulation, especially regarding the levels of fees. Institutions could still fix their fee level autonomously, though they faced several restrictions if they wanted to get public funding for those programmes.[4]

With the adoption of Law 37/2003 of 22 August 2003 (Law on Financing of Higher Education), the responsibility of higher education funding was expanded to cover several stakeholders, calling on them to contribute financially for higher education. More specifically, the contribution of students was strengthened, and both a minimum and a maximum amount of tuition fees were set. In relation to tuition fees, the Law introduced a minimum amount corresponding to 1.3 of the national minimum wage and the maximum amount, which was established in the previous legislation, started being revised each year according to the Consumer Price Index. Starting from the academic year 2004-05, most institutions went for the higher end of the proposed price range. However, polytechnic institutions and less prestigious public universities kept tuition fees closer to the lower limit.

As we can see from Table II, the level of individual tuition fees has increased, although at a slow pace. The major exception was, of course, the period subsequent to the funding Law of 2003, with impact from 2004 onwards, which represented a major jump in tuition fees, especially for their maximum level. This is even more significant since the indications are that most institutions tended to move rapidly to the maximum level. With the exception of the academic year 2003-04, increases in tuition fees have only slightly been above that of annual inflation, and the fact that the boundaries are closely linked to other social transfers prevents a stronger increase. The introduction of variable fees took place at the same time as there were increasing financial constraints, thus stimulating all institutions to find alternative revenues. As a result, tuition fees became a prime candidate in that regard.

Fees boundaries	Year					
	1999-2000	2000-01	2001-02	2002-03	2003-04	2004-05
Minimum value	306	318	334	348	464	475
Increase		4%	5%	4%	33%	2%
Maximum value	306	318	334	348	852	880
Increase		4%	5%	4%	145%	3%

Fees boundaries	Year				
	2005-06	2006-07	2007-08	2008-09	2009-10
Minimum value	487	502	524	553.8	585
Increase	3%	3%	4%	5.6%	5.6%
Maximum value	901	920	949	972.14	996.85
Increase	2%	2%	3%	2.4%	2.5%

Table II. Evolution of level of annual fees, undergraduate degrees – 1st cycle (values in current prices, in euros).
Sources: Cerdeira, 2009; our own calculations.

This second phase in the development of tuition fees as a source of revenue was far less controversial due to several reasons. Firstly, the idea of tuition fees had been already a feature of the higher education system and the introduction of incremental changes tends to raise less resistance than new features. Second, the country was already experiencing serious financial problems, with cuts in public expenditure being implemented in other areas, which also affected the financial allocations to public higher education. Thirdly, since higher education graduates were regarded as a privileged part of society, especially due to their better employment and income prospects, this additional effort was regarded as acceptable for larger sectors of Portuguese society. Moreover, the development of a private sector charging full-tuition (the private sector enrolled almost one-third of the students at the time) enhanced further the advantageous situation of students enrolled in the public sector (especially vis-à-vis their future job market prospects). Finally, the student movement was clearly weakened in its capacity to mobilise protests against those changes due to a steady decline in student activism and political participation in general.

The Development of the Student Support System

The development of cost-sharing has given additional political and social visibility to the development of student support mechanisms, especially in order to minimise the potential negative equity effects of those changes. The first steps for the implementation of a student social support system in Portuguese higher education were taken after the April 1974 revolution, aiming at the system's democratisation by giving grants to students from disadvantaged backgrounds. In 1980, a comprehensive student support system was established for the first time by creating an autonomous service in each university or university institute. These services were given more financial and administrative autonomy than universities, and a flexible human resources management system was established given that the staff working for students' residences and canteens was hired under private law.

The development of institutional autonomy also had an impact on the management of the student support system and the University Autonomy Act (1988) awarded to public universities a significant degree of autonomy in this respect. Although there were general guidelines and the funding was provided by a national budget, it was up to HEIs to manage those resources and, for instance, to manage the criteria and the selection of those students entitled to receive a scholarship, be awarded free or subsidised accommodation in university residences, or be entitled to be exempted (fully or partially) of paying fees. The latter would be possible since these were considered institutional revenues, although HEIs did not have a strong incentive to do it since it would reduce their direct revenues.

With the increase of cost-sharing, the two topics became increasingly entangled and student support mechanisms attained greater relevance. The student social support system includes direct and indirect support mechanisms, irrespective of the enrolling institution (public or private, university or polytechnic). The direct support consists of means-tested grants (scholarships) for needy students who demonstrate academic merit. The grants are awarded every year and are meant to contribute to students' expenses (housing, meals, transportation, tuition fees, etc.). The value of the grants depends on the per capita income of the student's family (or their own, in the case of independent students), and their value has a monthly maximum equivalent to the minimum wage and a minimum equal to one-twentieth of that value. Because fees are the revenue of higher education institutions, the law determines that the grants include the amount necessary to pay fees, instead of adopting a fees remission policy. The indirect support, in turn, consists of housing in halls of residence (with priority being given to displaced students), meals in canteens, and other services related to health, cultural and sporting activities.

One of the aspects debated for many years regarding student support mechanisms was the possible introduction of a loan system. Both Law 37/03 and Law 113/97 established that the state would give support to a loan system, but none of those efforts were implemented. On the one hand, this could be explained by a strong negative reaction from the students, afraid that this would open the way to progressively convert the traditional grant system into a loan system. On the other hand, the state did not have the financial resources for the initial investment in a loan system and the vulnerabilities of the Portuguese fiscal system did not guarantee either the equity of the system or its success in terms of loan repayment. The loan system was finally introduced in 2007 by the government as a student loans scheme with mutual guarantee.[5]

Academic year	Number of loans	Total amount of credit planned (euros)	Total amount of credit actually used (euros)	Defaults (euros)	Defaults over total credit contacted %
2007-08	3,302	36,513,696	32,746,862	1,539,932	4.22
2008-09	3,886	44,097,135	37,726,563	1,000,775	2.27
2009-10	4,074	47,147,583	35,209,577	283,226	0.60
2010-11	4,537	52,102,335	26,493,329	60,857	0.12
2011-12	1,951	22,561,214	5,565,983	–	0.00
Total	17,750	202,421,962	137,742,314	2,884,790	1.43

Table III. Basic data on the system of public loans to higher education students.
Source: SPGM – Society for Public Mutual Guarantee (Portugal).

Looking at Table III, we can see that the number of loans contracted has not been very significant. The number of contracts represents a very small percentage of the total number of students enrolled in the public higher education sector (see Table I) and the value on loans contracted was often clearly below that of the amount of credit planned for each year. This is the result of various factors, namely the limited awareness of many students of this possibility and a preference to rely on personal and family sources of funding. Moreover, its limited effects have been affected by the ensuing political and financial context. The economic crisis has affected the amount of funding available to grants and loans, with a significant decline in 2011-12. In that academic year the system was temporarily suspended and this was reflected in the number of loans contracted and in the drop of the amount of credit awarded. Furthermore, the award of grants has been made more selective (showing a further decline in the proportion of credit contracted vis-à-vis the amount planned), based on the argument of greater rigour in administering public loans, which has helped the government to make some savings at a time it badly needed it. (In fact, the default rates had been rather low and were diminishing in previous academic years, thus the argument does seem to be related to financial limitations.) Overall, the system is unlikely to have had a major effect in increasing funding opportunities for higher education students at a time of rising cost-sharing and increasing financial difficulties affecting most families. This meant that the institutional mechanisms of student support have continued to play a major role in this respect and that its role has not been significantly enlarged, let alone replaced by the recent development of the loan system.

Reflecting about Some Institutional Effects of Increasing Cost-sharing

There has been a lack of empirical studies analysing the actual relevance of tuition fees for European higher education. Thus far, most of the research has concentrated on issues of students' price sensitivity and its possible impact on access and equity.[6] In particular, there is very limited knowledge about the effectiveness of institutions in raising those revenues and of potential institutional differences in that respect.

In the case of science and scientific achievement, it has been long-established that the most prestigious institutions tend to enjoy a cumulative advantage, in what became known as the Matthew effect in science (Merton, 1973), reaping a disproportionate share of pecuniary and non-pecuniary rewards. More recently, Ali et al (2010) have found that there were significant advantages both at the individual and institutional level for more prestigious institutions when competing for research funds. There are good reasons to think that a similar situation may exist in teaching revenues, with more prestigious institutions being able to obtain more revenues through tuition. For instance, more prestigious institutions may be able to charge higher fees, especially in postgraduate and professional programmes. In addition, their reputation will also be significant in attracting a higher number of students for more expensive programmes.[7] Finally, more affluent institutions may also be able to support students in need and fund ancillary activities (e.g. canteens, accommodation, etc.) that may indirectly subsidise students in their direct costs of attending higher education. In the following sections, we try to infer about potential impacts of these changes in funding regulations in Portugal by analysing the effectiveness of institutions to diversify their funding structure over subsequent years.

Data and Methodology

In the empirical part of this chapter we aim to analyse the ability of HEIs to accumulate revenues from students' tuition fees (and other related fees), exploring potential determinants other than the number of enrolments in the institution. Although we may expect that the larger an institution the bigger the amount of fees accumulated (both in absolute and relative terms), other factors may influence that revenue besides size. Using data from Portugal, we explore to what extent certain institutional characteristics may help explain why certain HEIs are more successful than others in generating those revenues when controlling for enrolments on both the postgraduate and undergraduate levels.

Data and Variables

Our data comes from two main data sources. Data on the funding and revenues of HEIs were obtained from the Portuguese Ministry of Finance (DGO – *Direcção Geral do Orçamento*). Data on the characteristics of HEIs comes from the Ministry of Education and Science (DGEEC – *Direcção Geral de Estatísticas da Educação e Ciência*). From DGO, we gathered information on total revenues and revenues from tuition fees for each institution and each year. From DGEEC, we have mainly obtained data on the total number of enrolments and academic staff at HEIs. Detailed data at both levels allowed us to compute the relative quality of academic staff (through the share of PhDs in total academic staff), the relative importance of postgraduate programmes (through the share of postgraduate students in total enrolments), and the subject mix of each institution in each year. Subject mix was measured through the computation of programmatic diversification, an index that allows us to quantify how widespread or concentrated the enrolled students are across eight different disciplinary fields – education; humanities and arts; social sciences, business and law; science; engineering, manufacturing and construction; agriculture; health and welfare; and services (see Teixeira et al, 2012, 2013, for details on the computation of this index of programmatic diversification).

These three variables are expected to influence the competitive position of HEIs, the relative preferences of students entering higher education and making their institutional choices, and consequently the relative importance of tuition fees revenues in the total income of public institutions. Institutions with a more qualified academic staff may signal a stronger academic reputation, as well as more intense research activity, which may attract more students, and thus result in a large amount of revenue from tuition fees. The same effect may be expected among institutions presenting a higher share of postgraduate students in their total enrolments and a more diversified programmatic offer. However, how these characteristics influence the relative importance of tuition fees in the total income of HEIs is, still, an open question. If, on the one hand, a larger absolute amount of income gathered through tuition may be a sign of the reliance of HEIs on this source of funding, recent evidence has also showed that there is a positive association between the ability of HEIs to collect funds from tuition fees and the ability to generate other non-public revenues (Teixeira et al, 2014). Our subsequent analysis thus intends to improve our understanding about this issue.

Finally, we have also collected information – from Statistics Portugal (INE – *Instituto Nacional de Estatística*) – about the purchasing power of the region (regions disaggregated by NUTS 3) where each institution is located in order to control for the different regional dispersion of polytechnics and universities. Leading universities have historically been located in the main cities along the Portuguese coast (where the purchasing power tends to be higher), while polytechnic institutions have been placed around the country, being more geographically dispersed (and consequently, relatively more present in the peripheral regions where the regional purchasing power is, on average, lower). The expectation is that institutions located in relatively richer regions may have higher levels of enrolments and thus accumulate more revenues from tuition fees. However, those located in poorer regions may be more reliant on tuition fee revenues in relative terms due to their lower ability to collect funds from other sources. Given the potential role of the regional context that HEIs are exposed to, we also control for this in our analysis.

Empirical Methodology

Our dependent variable is the 'share of revenues obtained from tuition fees' for each HEI i in each year t. The other aforementioned variables – the size of HEIs in terms of enrolments, the share of postgraduate students, the subject mix, the proportion of PhDs in total academic staff, and the purchasing power of the region where the institution is located – are included in the vector of explanatory variables. Time effects are also controlled for in our estimations.

As there may also be unobserved characteristics influencing the HEIs' relative reliance on tuition fee revenues, we have used panel data models in our empirical analysis. According to the Hausman test, random fffects (generalised least squares) panel data models were found to be more appropriate than fixed effects, thus suggesting that individual specific effects are uncorrelated with the independent variables. Accordingly, we estimated the following equation:

$$y_{it} = \alpha + X_{it}\beta + \varepsilon_i + u_{it} \tag{1}$$

where y_{it} is the proportion of total revenues gathered through tuition fees of institution i at time t; α is the intercept term, common across the institutions included in the analysis; and X_{it} is the vector of explanatory variables previously discussed (including time dummies). The two remaining components correspond to a composite error term, where ε_i is the cross-section (or institution-specific) error component and u_{it} is the combined time series and cross-section error component.

Empirical Analysis

Descriptive Statistics

Figure 1 illustrates and compares the evolution of our dependent variable over time for the subsamples of public universities and public polytechnics. From these data, we confirm that tuition fees have been gaining increasing importance in the revenues of HEIs over the last decade, during which pressures for revenue diversification and HEIs' independence from public funding has become stronger. Besides, the experience of universities and polytechnics may have been different during these years – the data show that tuition fees have been accounting for an increasing share of revenues among polytechnics; in universities, this source of revenues has also become more important over the years, but at a slower pace. In 2009, 20% of revenues in the polytechnic subsector came from tuition fees; in 2003, this particular source of revenues only accounted for 10% of all the funding received by polytechnic institutes. Among universities, the relative weight of tuition fees in the total revenues obtained increased by 6-7 percentage points over the period under analysis.[8]

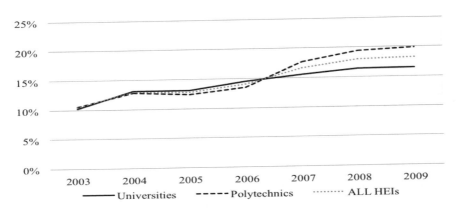

Figure 1. Share of total revenues obtained from tuition fees (Portugal, 2003-09), public HEIs.

In Table IV, we provide some descriptive statistics for the dependent and independent variables included in the empirical model. Comparative statistics for public universities and public polytechnics confirm that significant differences exist between the two subsectors: the former are larger, have a greater proportion of postgraduate students, a more qualified academic staff, a more diversified programmatic offer, and are located in regions where purchasing power tends to be higher on average. Given such differences between subsectors, we conduct our empirical analysis separately for universities and polytechnics. The statistics also include the within and between variation for each variable, confirming that institutions under scrutiny are very dissimilar – between variation is always larger than within variation. For this reason, using an empirical method able to account for both within and between variation – as random effects panel data models – is essential (Greene, 2002, p. 295; Baltagi, 2005, p. 17).

Empirical Results

Table V presents the empirical results obtained from the estimation of random effects panel data models. In our analysis we conducted separate analysis for universities and polytechnics in order to reflect the specificities of both sectors and to see to what extent those would have an impact on the revenues generated through tuition fees. In Model 1, we include all the explanatory variables previously discussed and described. In Model 2 we use forward and backward selection methods to obtain the smallest number of significant explanatory variables, so as to provide a parsimonious model.

	n	Mean values	Overall std dev.	Between variation	Within variation	U	P
Share of revenues from tuition fees **	210	0.1473	0.0486	0.0371	0.0320	0.1427	0.1518
Total undergraduate enrolled students (1000)	210	8.2673	5.5722	5.6250	0.5628	10.5703	5.9643
Share of postgraduate students in total enrolments	210	0.0723	0.0792	0.0637	0.0484	0.1257	0.0189
Subject mix	180	0.5128	0.1897	0.1876	0.0421	0.5214	0.5042
Share of PhDs in total academic staff	180	0.3318	0.2214	0.2171	0.0568	0.5325	0.1311
Regional purchasing power (NUTs 3) (Country=1)	210	0.9953	0.2998	0.3004	0.0473	1.1028	0.8879

*Data for the variables Subject Mix and Share of PhD professors in total academic staff are only available for 2003-2008.
**Share of revenues from tuition fees is the dependent variable in our estimations.
U stands for Universities; P stands for Polytechnics.
Subject mix is measured by the normalised diversification index computed with data on enrolments at HEIs across eight disciplinary fields (education; humanities and arts; social sciences, business and law; science; engineering, manufacturing and construction; agriculture; health and welfare; services). For methodological details about the computation of diversification index, please see Teixeira et al (2012, 2013).

Table IV. Descriptive statistics (Portugal, 2003-09)*.

The results confirm that significant differences exist among universities and polytechnics regarding the characteristics that influence their relative reliance on tuition fees revenues. Among universities, few determinants besides time effects are found to be strongly significant. Revenues from tuition fees seem to be relatively more important in smaller and less diversified (or, in other words, in more specialised) universities. In contrast, larger and more diversified universities in terms of programmatic offer may be able to collect funds from other sources (e.g. research funding and/or larger transfers from the European Union [EU] and the rest of the world), so the income gathered through tuition fees is less important in total annual revenues, although it may be larger in absolute terms. The relative importance of tuition fees and cost-sharing mechanisms is also slightly greater in universities with a more qualified academic staff, although the effects are weakly significant and possibly reflect the general improvement of staff qualifications in the university subsector in recent years.

Regarding the polytechnic subsector, the results show that polytechnics with a stronger dependence on revenues from tuition fees are those with more students, with a more specialised programmatic offer, those less endowed with highly qualified staff and located in regions with lower purchasing power. These are probably the institutions with poorer ability to collect revenues from other sources than public funding and tuition fees.

	Universities				Polytechnics			
	Model 1		Model 2		Model 1		Model 2	
Total undergraduate |enrolled students	-0.0031 (0.0017)	*	-0.0028 (0.0017)	*	0.0039 (0.0016)	**	0.0041 (0.0016)	**
Share of postgraduate students	-0.0432 (0.0762)				-0.1936 (0.1271)			
Subject mix	-0.0896 (0.0416)	**	-0.0987 (0.0437)	**	-0.0957 (0.0269)	***	-0.0877 (0.0280)	***
Share of PhDs in total academic staff	0.0876 (0.0666)		0.0926 (0.0537)	*	-0.1807 (0.0899)	**	-0.1941 (0.1012)	*
Regional Purchasing Power (NUTs3)	0.0002 (0.0002)				-0.0006 (0.0003)	**	-0.0638 (0.0258)	**
Constant	0.1242 (0.0342)	***	0.1453 (0.0349)	***	0.1973 (0.0261)	***	0.1938 (0.0253)	***
R^2 within	0.7599		0.7592		0.8358		0.8309	
R^2 between	0.6444		0.5982		0.6423		0.6249	
R^2 overall	0.6605		0.6194		0.7619		0.7520	
Number of observations	90		90		90		90	
Rho (fraction of variance due to HEIs' unobserved heterogeneity)	0.8310		0.8153		0.5239		0.5710	
Breusch-Pagan test for random effects	122.87	***	123.59	***	46.46	***	48.88	***

[a] The period covered in estimations was restricted to 2003-08 as no data were available on HEIs' subject mix and academic staff for the year 2009. *, ** and *** mean significant at 10%, 5% and 1% levels, respectively. The values in brackets correspond to standard errors robust to heteroskedasticity. Time dummies were included in all specifications. We do not report the coefficients to save space, being available upon request from the authors. Using 2003 as the reference year, all the coefficients were positive and statistically significant.

Table V. Multivariable analysis of the share of revenues from tuition fees – random effects panel data models (Portugal, 2003-08)[a].

Overall, the results highlight that revenues from tuition fees have been particularly important for those HEIs with lower research-intensity (or, alternatively, more teaching-intensive institutions) and with a more specialised programmatic offer. Under the increasing pressures for revenue diversification and a greater autonomy of public HEIs from the government, these institutions are thus becoming more dependent on enrolments than ever. This may be also the result of the fact that those institutions are less likely to obtain additional funding through research activities from public and private sources.

Discussion and Concluding Remarks

The expansion of public higher education over recent decades has created important financial challenges, especially due to the limitations that many governments face in the aftermath of the current financial and economic crisis. In this chapter we analysed the factors that may explain the ability of public HEIs to accumulate revenues from students' tuition fees other than the number of enrolments. Our analysis of the relative share of revenues coming from tuition fees does not suggest a kind of Matthew effect in the institutional distribution of these revenues, similar to that one detected many years ago in research production. Accordingly, those institutions that have more and better resources – for instance, better qualified academic staff – do not seem to be more successful in generating more revenues, in relative terms, from tuition fees. This may be also the result of the fact that those institutions are more likely to obtain additional funding through other sources such as EU funding, selling services to the public and private sector, and, even more significantly, through research activities. Thus, they tend to be less reliant on students' tuition.

For institutions less focused on research, reliance on revenues from students makes them vulnerable to shifts in the students' demand. The demographic decline and the rising levels of graduate unemployment have dented the confidence that used to exist in Portugal about the high returns associated to a higher education degree. Moreover, recent data have indicated a growing inequality among graduates regarding the returns of their degrees (Figueiredo et al, 2013), with less prestigious polytechnics and universities apparently showing a greater decline in the premium to a higher education degree than more prestigious institutions. The data on the number of applicants to higher education for the academic years 2012-13 and 2013-14 indicate a decline in the number of candidates, especially in areas that have seen major hikes in graduate unemployment and affecting unevenly the higher education sector (with peripheral and less prestigious institutions being left with a large number of unfilled student places). Thus, among the institutions strongly reliant on tuition revenues, some may be facing significant challenges in the near future.

To those less reliant on tuition fees revenues, especially those with better qualified staff and greater emphasis on research, important challenges are also looming. Until recent years, being a research intensive institution seemed to pay off in the Portuguese higher education system. Public funding for research increased steadily and significantly and institutions could also cross-subsidise research activities due to the fact that a significant part of the time of their faculty was being paid through general funding for teaching. However, the cuts in research funding and in staff numbers have made it more difficult to pursue that model further. Thus, this group of institutions may be tempted to rethink its strategy in terms of funding, resulting in more intense competition for students. Since funding for teaching is still essentially determined by enrolments, they may be tempted to increase their intake to compensate for the funding cuts. This may pose a significant threat to weaker institutions, but also, on the long term, to the research credentials of research intensive institutions.

The analysis is also significant regarding certain equity aspects in the higher education system. The development of cost-sharing was accompanied by a debate about the mechanisms of student support and the loan system that eventually was developed. However, the loan system was developed rather late and its impact has been restricted by the financial constraints of recent years. This is even more significant since the cuts in public expenditure and the pressure on institutions to diversify their revenues have constrained the institutional capacities to channel resources for the existing mechanisms of student support. A greater pressure on revenue diversification through tuition fees poses additional risks regarding inequalities in the access and completion of degrees of students from families with lower incomes.

Overall, our results indicate that the Portuguese higher education system faces important challenges and that the trends that coalesced over the last two decades may be reaching a turning point. With major pressures upon public expenditure, especially due to the current bailout agreement signed with the EU, the European Central Bank and the International Monetary Fund (and valid for the period 2011-14), public higher education has been struggling to find other revenues that may alleviate their financial constraints. Thus, it is not a surprise that cost-sharing has become a significant revenue stream for many institutions, especially for those less capable of finding other sources of funding. However, it is questionable how this pattern may be pursued further as the economic and social situation deteriorates and the demand for higher education suffers accordingly. Hence, the current Portuguese experience begs for reflection about the effects of a policy emphasis on tuition revenues as a sustainable solution to deal with the increasing cuts in public funding to higher education.

Notes

[1] Institutions in these sectors will find it hard to contain costs because their workers expect their salaries to follow the increase in living costs, which is being pushed by those sectors experiencing greater productivity increases (Geiger, 2004). The rising premium for qualified labour that took place in many advanced economies has certainly exacerbated these trends.

[2] There are signs that in many European institutions additional investment has been poured into enhanced research capability and especially in the

qualification of their academic and non-academic staff, often due to increasing competition and benchmarking. This has inevitably increased the labour costs of higher education, which in many institutions represent three quarters or more of the total running costs (Zhang & Ehrenberg, 2010). Other factors such as rising costs for libraries, information and technology and other equipment have added to this trend (see, for instance, Geiger, 2004; Lenton, 2008).

[3] The colleges are smaller and more specialised institutions than their university and polytechnics counterparts. To achieve a university or polytechnic status, institutions need to cover a minimum of a number of diverse scientific fields.

[4] Until 2008, institutions, especially public universities, were rather autonomous in the establishment of new programmes. They had to inform the Directorate-General of Higher Education which tended to check for formal compliance. In 2008, a new agency was established for the accreditation and quality assurance, following the guidelines defined in the European Standards and Guidelines, and the approval of new programmes became far more demanding regarding scientific and educational criteria.

[5] It is interesting to note that there was no major political resistance to the introduction of the loan system from students or HEIs. On the one hand, this came at a later stage, when tuition fees were already largely integrated in the system. Thus, they were not regarded so much as part of that process, but rather as an instrument to increase the opportunities given the small budget allocated to grants within the student support mechanism. On the other hand, several of the reasons mentioned in the previous section on tuition fees also played a role. The political context was not favourable to students' activism and these were regarded as a rather privileged group within a very unequal society regarding income and life opportunities.

[6] Most studies have indicated that price sensitiveness seems not to be very significant in the European context (Barr & Crawford, 2005; Vossensteyn, 2005; Johnstone & Marcucci, 2009).

[7] Connolly (1997), in her analysis of public and private funding of universities, has found that additional funding from public sources and private donors enhances the amount provided by the other over time, and that external sponsors seem willing to allocate funding to those universities that do the highest quality research. Besides, funding from either source seems to be perceived by them as a signal about quality of the receiving university.

[8] The remaining sources of revenues other than tuition fees include the funding received from the government budget (which still represents the major income source among public HEIs) and other non-public revenues (namely, revenues from proprietary rents, transfers from private entities, non-profit institutions, European Union and the rest of the world, as well as revenues from the provision of goods and services).

References

Ali, M.M., Bhattacharyya, P. & Olejniczak, A.J. (2010) The Effects of Scholarly Productivity and Institutional Characteristics on the Distribution of Federal Research Grants, *Journal of Higher Education*, 81, 164-178.

Archibald, R.B. & Feldman, D.H. (2010) *Why Does College Cost So Much?* New York: Oxford University Press.

Baltagi, B.H. (2005) *Econometric Analysis of Panel Data*, 3rd edn. Chichester: John Wiley & Sons.

Barr, N. (2004) Economics of the Welfare State, 4th edn. Oxford: Oxford University Press.

Barr, N. & Crawford, I. (2005) Financing Higher Education – answers from the UK. London: Routledge.

Barreto, A. (1996) The Social Situation in Portugal. Lisbon: Instituto de Ciências Sociais (ICS). (In Portuguese.)

Cerdeira, L. (2009) *The Funding of Portuguese Higher Education: cost-sharing*. Coimbra: Almedina. (In Portuguese.)

Clotfelter, C. (1996) *Buying the Best – cost escalation in higher education*. Princeton: Princeton University Press.

Connolly, L.S. (1997) Does External Funding of Academic Research Crowd Out Institutional Support?, *Journal of Public Economics*, 64, 389-406.

Figueiredo, H., Teixeira, P. & Rubery, J. (2013) Unequal Futures? Mass Higher Education and Graduates' Relative Earnings in Portugal: 1995-2009, *Applied Economics Letters*, 20(10), 991-997.

Geiger, R. (2004) *Knowledge and Money*. Stanford: Stanford University Press.

Greenaway, D. & Heynes, M. (2003) Funding Higher Education in the UK: the role of fees and loans, *Economic Journal*, 113(February), 150-166.

Greene, W.H. (2002) *Econometric Analysis*, 5th edn. Upper Saddle River, NJ: Prentice Hall.

Herbst, M. (2006) *Performance Based Funding*. Dordrecht: Springer.

Johnstone, B. & Marcucci, P. (2009) *Financing Higher Education Worldwide. Who Pays? Who Should Pay?* Baltimore: Johns Hopkins University Press.

Lenton, P. (2008) The Cost Structure of Higher Education in Further Education Colleges in England, *Economics of Education Review*, 27, 471-482.

Merton, R. (1973) *The Sociology of Science*. Chicago: University of Chicago Press.

Rosa, M.J., Amado, D. & Amaral, A. (2009) Funding Allocation and Staff Management: a Portuguese example, *European Journal of Education*, 44(1), 127-140.

Simão, V., Santos, S. & Costa, A. (2002) *Ensino Superior: Uma Visão para a Próxima Década*. Lisbon: Gradiva.

Teixeira, P., Johnstone, B., Rosa, M. & Vossensteyn, J. (2006) *A Fairer Deal? Cost-Sharing and Accessibility in Higher Education*. Dordrecht: Springer.

Teixeira, P., Rocha, V., Biscaia, R. & Cardoso, M.F. (2012) Competition and Diversity in Higher Education: an empirical approach to specialization patterns of Portuguese institutions, *Higher Education*, 63(3), 337-352.

Teixeira, P., Rocha, V., Biscaia, R. & Cardoso, M.F. (2013) Competition and Diversification in Public and Private Higher Education, *Applied Economics*, 45(35), 4949-4958.

Teixeira, P., Rocha, V., Biscaia, R. & Cardoso, M.F. (2014) Revenue Diversification in Public Higher Education: comparing the university and polytechnic sectors, *Public Administration Review*, 74(3), 398-412.

Vossensteyn, H. (2005) *Perceptions of Student Price-responsiveness*. Enschede: Center for Higher Education Policy Studies, University of Twente.

Zhang, L. & Ehrenberg, R.G. (2010) Faculty Employment and R&D Expenditures at Research Universities, *Economics of Education Review*, 29, 329-337.

CHAPTER 3

France: a low-fee, low-aid system challenged from the margins

NICOLAS CHARLES

ABSTRACT In France, the vast majority of programmes are not free of charge, even though higher education programmes are generally inexpensive. Student funding has long been characterised by low up-front fees and limited support for students, aiming at ensuring social justice. Yet, the French system has partly failed to address inequalities of access to higher education and has recently been subject to the international movement towards cost-sharing. Thus the status quo is relatively fragile. While national policy reforms do not propose new tuition fee instruments, some higher education institutions have recently renewed their practices, especially by implementing variable fees. These institution-based instruments have not challenged so far the overall predominance of the French *service public* logic, where higher education is expected to be inexpensive and the cost of studies is to vary according to parental income. However cost-sharing has nonetheless recently taken a major step in France, along with the state laissez-faire in a context of economic crisis and subsequent decreasing public funding, even though it may lead to increasing inequalities.

Introduction

All developed countries are subject to cost-sharing rationales in one way or another (Johnstone & Marcucci, 2010). France seems to resist this trend insofar as student funding, including fees and support, relies on two driving principles: free tuition and the financial responsibility of the family (Chevaillier & Paul, 2006). Similarly, in a comparative perspective, France is considered as a country where public universities do not charge tuition fees (Marcucci & Johnstone, 2007). Based on the analysis of recent tuition policy changes carried out by higher education institutions, this chapter provides evidence that this analysis is increasingly far-fetched and should be challenged. To what degree and through what means has the French higher education system, a statist system historically free of tuition fees, been incorporating cost-sharing in recent years? Are the new instruments for increasing fees accompanied by social justice rationales and do they result in specific outcomes in terms of access to higher education?

Firstly, we show that French student funding can adequately be characterised as a low-fee, low-aid system. Despite the existence of severe inequalities and challenges to the free-tuition principle, French national regulation has not undergone significant reforms and the status quo – in favour of low registration fees – still prevails in universities.[1] Secondly, we highlight the influence of cost-sharing through an overview of major trends in tuition policy shaped by higher education institutions themselves. We show that these developments do not challenge the predominance of the French *service public* rationale, that is, higher education is to be inexpensive for low-income families. Thirdly, we show that this rising cost-sharing phenomenon has benefited from a laissez-faire state policy in the current context of economic crisis, even though it might lead to higher inequalities in the future.

A Stable though Fragile Low-fee, Low-aid Student Funding System

In order to understand the French higher education system, we must first set the stage in terms of institutions. In 2010, the major programmes taught in universities (bachelor's, master's and PhD) accounted for approximately 57% of 2.32 million students in France (Direction de l'Evaluation, de la Prospective et de la Performance [DEPP], 2012). In addition, the universities also host two-year vocational 'technical' courses (*Instituts universitaires de technologie*) whose students account for approximately 5% of the total student population. Outside universities, two-year programmes with a stronger emphasis on vocational training (*sections de technicien supérieur*) are taught in upper secondary schools and account for approximately 10% of higher education students. In parallel of university programmes, French higher education has an elite track. It starts with two-year, highly selective programmes (*classes préparatoires*) (approximately 3% of students). These programmes lead to selective institutions (*grandes écoles*), such as business schools (about 5%) and engineering schools (approximately 6%). A variety of institutes and schools, often less prestigious and mostly private, complete the picture of French higher education. All these institutions can either be public – four-fifths of the student population – or private.

Teaching 75% of students in 1970 and 68% in 1980, 63% in 1990, 59% in 2000 and 57% in 2010, public universities are certainly a major player, but no longer dominate French higher education. The other public institutions, whose diversity is described above, have been quite stable over the past decades. In contrast, the position of private institutions has become ever more powerFful, increasing its share of the student population from

13% in 1990 to 18% in 2010. In particular, enrolments in business schools nearly tripled between 1990 and 2010 (DEPP, 2012).

Rather than a no-tuition fee system, French higher education is better characterised by a low-fee, low-aid scheme (Johnstone & Marcucci, 2010), as well as a strong dispersion of tuition levels among institutions and programmes. Indeed, the general principle is that students are charged for registration but not for tuition (Chevaillier & Paul, 2006). The majority of university students must pay €181 to enrol in a bachelor's programme, €250 for a master's degree and €380 for a PhD (figures correct in 2012). In other higher education institutions, the level of tuition varies greatly depending on the status of the institution: public or private, non-profit or for-profit, etc. (see Table I). For example, programmes in *sections de technicien supérieur* and *classes préparatoires*, taught in state-led upper secondary schools are free.[2] But when the same programmes are offered by private secondary schools, fees are high. As for *grandes écoles*, on one end of the spectrum, some of the students are granted the status of civil servants and, thereby, get paid by the central state while they study.[3] On the other end of the spectrum, certain schools charge fees of up to about €15,000 per year. Apart from the limited change concerning the *classes préparatoires* – that is students in such programmes must enrol in a university and pay the corresponding registration fees – the law on higher education passed in July 2013 did not address the issue of funding despite its stated objective to 'improve the student success rate'.

Institution type	Status	Annual total (tuition/registration) fees
Classes préparatoires	Public	Free (currently being reformed towards a mandatory registration in a university)
	Private under contract*	From €1000 to €2000
	Private, no contract	Up to €8500
Instituts Universitaires de Technologie (IUT)	Public	€183
Sections de Technicien Supérieur (STS)	Public	Free
	Private under contract*	Around €1000
	Private, no contract	Around €5000
Universities	Public	From €183 to about €600
	Specific status (private, Catholic, *Grand établissement*, etc.)	From €1000 to €6000
	Medical studies	From €183 to about €600; progressive compensation from the sixth year

Business schools	Private – tied to the local chamber of commerce and industry	From €7000 to €12,000 (in general for three years)
	Other non-profit or for-profit private institutions	From €4000 to €8000 (in general for three to five years)
Engineering schools	Public	From €200 to €1200; as future civil servants, some students get compensation from the state
	Private – tied to the local chamber of commerce and industry	From €3000 to €6000
	Other private institutions	From €4000 to €8000
Schools preparing students for the high civil service (Polytechnique, other military schools, Écoles Normales Supérieures, etc.)	Public	In some schools, students get paid as civil servants, in others they pay fees of a few hundred euros
Other schools: paramedical, journalism, architecture schools, etc.	Various	Various

*Some private institutions have a contract with the state. It means that they will comply with an educational state framework. They can charge tuition fees in so far as they remain low. They also get as much public funding for human resources as public institutions.

Table I. Tuition fees in different types of institutions in France.
Sources: Websites *Ministère de l'Éducation nationale* [4], *ONISEP* [5] and the *Conférence des grandes écoles* [6] (accessed September 10, 2013).

Student support programmes mainly consist of means-tested grants. The level of support depends on parental income – except if the student is married or has children – and on other criteria like the distance from the place of study and the number of children in the care of the student's parents. As of 2012, students are ranked on a scale from 0 to 6 corresponding to the amount of financial support (0 indicates the lowest level of eligibility for support, 6 the highest). To obtain the grant, students must be under the age of 28 and make academic progress. Aside from the grant itself, grant-holders in public institutions are generally not required to pay registration fees. In 2012, 26% of the student population in France was awarded a grant. About 620,000 grants were allocated, ranging from the mere reimbursement of registration and social insurance fees up to €4697 per year (DEPP, 2012). In 2008, parallel to these means-tested grants, the central state also devised a system of guaranteed (though not subsidised) bank loans for students of public institutions, both universities and non-university institutions (with interest rates between 3.8 and 4.5%, up to €15,000 and accessible to all).[7]

If direct public support (grants and loans) is limited, the French model for financing students also includes significant indirect social benefits. In 2011, public loans and grants for students amounted to 30% of the total state spending for student welfare (€5.9 billion) (DEPP, 2012, p. 357). Housing support (29%) is another direct aid. Other more indirect types of aid include, notably, fiscal aid for student parents (24%), support for the student health system (9%), and contribution to the *Cnous* for investments in higher education facilities (6%).

The French system of student funding has remained stable because it relies on a strong social justice rationale. Fee-wise, higher education is not entirely free of charge, but low fees are part of the ideal that free education should run through compulsory schooling. This principle – studies should be free or almost free – was affirmed in 1984 (*Loi Savary*) and has never really been called into question. Since then, registration fees have just been rising along with inflation. The student grant public policy has been more or less generous according to various periods, but grants have depended on parents' income since the 1950s. Education, including higher education, is legally and socially considered as a service of general interest (*service public* in French), including the objective of a nationally-fixed, 'reasonable' price. The notion of *service public* is the French interpretation of the long dominant representation in Europe of higher education as a public good.[5] In a sense, if fees have been kept at such a low level, it is because of the high political stakes at play (Musselin, 2010). Although – or maybe because – the *service public* logic does not encompass all higher education programmes in France, it remains a relatively strong rationale in the French case.

Such a rationale could have led to a high-aid framework as in the Nordic countries, but it did not: direct support for students in France is limited and mainly means-tested. Students are targeted on the basis of their parents' income because France has a partly conservative welfare state, where families are expected to play a significant role in the destiny of their children. Less than in southern Europe (Italy or Spain for instance), but a lot more than in northern Europe (Great Britain, Sweden, etc.), parents are expected to financially support their children, including after they reach 18 years old. That is why French students often heavily depend on their parents' financial support, and it is generally considered that the state should only intervene in the case of family failure to guarantee support. Social justice rationales in the French case result from a tension between a family-based social model and the assumption that low fees would guarantee low levels of social inequalities.

Given that education is almost free, the support system, therefore, focuses on a small section of students; those from the poorest families. Overall, the French rationale is based on the idea that a low-fee, low-aid system would lead to fair access, as high tuition fees may deter candidates from entering higher education.

This funding system faces several challenges. First, inequalities of access to higher education are rather high. As far as social origin is concerned, France seems to be an 'exclusive system', where students from low education backgrounds are under-represented, and those from high education backgrounds are strongly represented in comparison to other European countries (Orr et al, 2011). In particular, the most academically selective institutions are also the most socially elitist. Thus, compared to their share of the overall student population (35%), children of managers and professionals are over-represented in *classes préparatoires* (53%) and the various prestigious *grandes écoles* (54% in *grands établissements*, 53% in the engineering programmes, 52% in business schools), and 65% in the *écoles normales supérieures*. Statistics are inversely proportional for children of blue-collar backgrounds (see Table II). Furthermore, given that student support is strictly a youth outreach programme – support is only provided for students under the age of 28 – students aged 30 or older represented only 8.8% of the entire student population in France in 2008, a significantly lower figure than the average of 16% in Europe and of over 30% in Nordic countries (Eurydice, 2012, p. 146), where social justice also includes providing a second chance for adults.

In addition, the French funding system is challenged by students' multiple financial difficulties, as shown in the 2010 study of the *Observatoire national de la vie étudiante* (Galland et al, 2010). Over the academic year, students said they restricted spending (52%), dipped into savings (48%), faced bank overdrafts (32%), asked family members for exceptional financial help (24%), worked overtime to make ends meet or to cope with unexpected events (16%), asked friends for exceptional financial help (8%), borrowed from the bank (6%), asked for additional emergency public support exceptional benefits (6%), and faced refusal of bank credit (2%) (Cordazzo & Tenret, 2011).

The limited scope and scale of student aid in France contribute to accounting for the financial troubles of students. The French student support system is strongly redistributive – students whose parents have not more than a lower secondary school education get more support than the socially more advantaged students – but it provides a very low absolute amount of aid in comparison to universal student support systems such as in England or Sweden (Charles, 2012). On the one hand, a larger share of students receive public support in Sweden (86%) and in England (86%) than in France (65%). On the other hand, the absolute monthly sums paid in public support for more disadvantaged students proves to be higher in Sweden

(€665 purchasing power parity [PPP] [9]) and England (€533 PPP) than in France (€362 PPP).

	Managers and Professionals (%)	Blue-collar Workers (%)
Universities (except IUT)	35.2	11.4
Instituts universitaires de technologie (IUT)	30.0	15.2
Sections de technicien supérieur (STS)	16.8	22.4
Classes préparatoires	52.7	6.5
Grands établissements	54.0	4.1
Engineering programmes	53.1	5.7
Business schools	52.0	3.0
Ecoles normales supérieures	65.0	2.9
Total	34.4	12.7

Notes: Based on Institut national de la statistique et des études économiques (INSEE) social classification. Data do take into account non-responses.

Table II. Percentage of students from two different social groups (managers/professionals and blue-collar workers) in different higher education sectors. Source: DEPP, 2011. Except for grands établissements (DEPP, 2010).

Overall, this has weakened the credibility of the French student funding system. During the 2012 French presidential campaign, political parties debated higher education issues, which is unsurprising given the sector's massive reforms over the last ten years. The two most important French think tanks, the Institut Montaigne and Terra Nova, respectively 'politically independent' liberal and progressive, urged decision-makers to raise fees and direct support for students towards 'fairer and more effective' student funding, i.e. a high-tuition, high-aid system. However, the main right- and left-wing parties have not considered any major student funding reform so far.

Despite both challenges, the status quo prevails. Very low registration fees tend to persist in universities. The elaborate administrative and legal framework that monitors universities partly prevents attempts to change their practices. A 2007 law enhancing university autonomy [10] temporarily favoured a context in which extra fees could be instated through institution-based policies, but the law did not give more actual autonomy to universities on this specific matter. Up until now, an annual decree has determined registration rates for the three most common university programmes (the bachelor, master, and doctoral degrees). This is why the law has not triggered the possibility of additional fees. Indeed, since 2005 – a few years before the application of the law – each year, the largest student union (the Union nationale des étudiants de France [Unef]) has released an annual report denouncing the illegal fee collection practices of public higher education institutions. Such a statement has generally been followed by a press release from the Minister of Higher Education stating its will to put an end to such inappropriate habits. The student union has taken legal action at several occasions, which has sometimes proved effective. According to Unef (2013), this illegal fee-setting phenomenon has been decreasing since the first report was published in 2005.

Though cost-sharing in French higher education seems on the whole to be contained, recent policy evolutions plant seeds of doubt. What are the major emerging trends and instruments for raising tuition fees? To what extent are these new policies gaining ground today and how do they impact on the still dominant social justice rationales?

Emerging Cost-sharing Trends
Framed in Strong Social Justice Rationales

The dominant no-fee policy in France masks new cost-sharing trends developing outside the universities. The diversity of fees among institutions and programmes is nothing new (Chevaillier & Paul, 2006), but this phenomenon has recently gained even greater impetus (see Table I). Fee policy of the private sector, in particular business schools, has long been characterised by cost-sharing. French business schools are best characterised by a high-tuition, high-aid scheme (Johnstone & Marcucci, 2010). These schools do not benefit from the same level of state funding as public ones. They rely on private sources of revenues, such as company sponsorships or student tuition fees. French business schools generally charge between €5000 and €10,000 a year (usually for three to four years). But the more prestigious schools are also the more expensive ones: the top five business schools in national rankings charge between €11,200 and €13,200 a year.[11] Since 2006, fees have increased by 50% and more in these top institutions, whereas they have remained stable in most other lower-tier business schools. Furthermore, business schools tend to adopt two levels of fees, one for European Union (EU) students, and a different one for non-EU students. The latter group pays higher fees; between €14,000 and €19,000 for the five most prestigious schools.[12]

Among these top-tier business schools, at least three offer significant grants beyond state grants (Cour des comptes, 2013). Additional aid is connected to the state-defined levels of support. For instance, in two of these schools, grant holders from levels 1 to 6 do not pay any fees and those at level 0 benefit from a reduction. However, the more prestigious the institution, the less socially open it is. Thus, while these schools can exempt all level 1 and higher state grant holders, less prestigious business schools cannot. Indeed, the latter schools, which are not capable of gathering the same amount of student aid, paradoxically continue to enrol more students from low social backgrounds. The business school sector seems to have turned into a kind of 'market' where pricing is a sign of the competitive relations between schools to attract the best students. As some students (and their families) are willing to spend a large amount of money for a high wage premium on the job market, the range of fees has recently been growing, giving students the opportunity to choose – at least theoretically – between high-price (high-quality) studies and lower-price (lower-quality?) programmes. Prices have been differentiated for EU and non-EU students and student support has partly followed the increase in fees.

This evolution toward cost-sharing, that is, fee increase, is also noted in some public higher education institutions. Two groups of institutions, also representing two types of tuition instruments, are particularly important: public *grandes écoles* in political science (*Instituts d'études politiques*) and public *grandes écoles* in engineering. In these public institutions in engineering [13] fees are not variable per se, but most students pay fees while state grant-holders benefit from fee discounts. Depending on the Ministry supervising their activity, registration fees are on average higher in public engineering schools than in universities. In 2012, most engineering schools, administered by the Ministry of Higher Education (but also by the Ministry of Sustainable Development) charged €596 for registration fees. Others administered by the Ministry of Economy charged €800 for the same year. State grant-holders do not pay these registration fees. However, for the past two years, some institutions have added tuition beyond registration fees. As for *grandes écoles* in management and in political science (see above), this evolution has been limited to the top-tier institutions.[14]

The *Instituts d'études politiques* are *grandes écoles* focusing on the full range of social sciences and beyond. Their students are prepared to enter a broad range of careers, but specifically fill many top positions in public and para-governmental institutions. From the 8 higher education institutions training 21,000 students in this field, the biggest and internationally best known is Sciences Po Paris. In 2004, this *grande école* introduced a specific student funding scheme: variable fees from €0-4000 depending on parental income. After annual incremental increases until 2008 (to a €6300 maximum), fees have been differentiated between the bachelor's and master's levels. As of 2013, fees are now up to €9800 for bachelor's students and €13,500 for master's students. This system is modelled on the previously discussed French logic of family financial responsibility: State grant-holders are not subjected to fees, and the variable fee programme means that families are expected to pay as much as they are able to. As an instrument, variable fees have slowly been extended to most other *Instituts d'études politiques*.[15] This instrument systematically uses the same logic to define the amount of variable fees: it relies on tax return information, that is the family's total annual income and *parts fiscales*.[16] Some of these institutions first introduced fixed fees, and some are still in the implementation process of such a funding scheme.[17] One other university, Paris Dauphine, has the particular status of being a *grand établissement* [18] and has therefore been able to also start to set variable fees (from €1575 to €4200 in 2013) for some of its master's programmes.[19] This variable-fees system is just emerging in the French context. For the moment, only about 3% of French students are affected, but it is quickly spreading to more institutions.

These cost-sharing developments may appear contradictory with the French low-fee, low-aid student funding system. But they are actually framed by the core idea of social justice rationales in France, that is, higher education should be inexpensive for low-income families in order to guarantee equality of opportunity. These strong rationales explain how fee increases in public institutions have ended up taking a specific shape in France, one that combines cost-sharing with equal access principles. Variable fees in French higher education have nothing in common with flexible fees as defined in the international literature on cost-sharing, which allows 'fees to reflect the different financial returns that students (once graduated) get depending on the institution attended and subject studied' (Jongbloed, 2005, p. 297). In France, 'variable' fees are about means-tested tuition fees, and, more specifically, fees varying with parental income. As for state grants, this system excludes older students and focuses on social background to the exclusion of ethnic, gender or spatial inequalities. The state grant rationales – family financial responsibility – and its instrument – means-tested support – are so powerful that tuition-fee increases in public institutions have been framed by the very same rationale and policy instrument.[20]

Cost-sharing has therefore been adapted to the French social justice rationale. However, the issue of timing remains: why has cost-sharing emerged so recently in France?

The State's Relative Laissez-faire Policy Despite Potentially Increasing Inequalities

Recent national governments have adopted a laissez-faire policy regarding the rise of fees. This passive role should not be under-estimated as the national government backs public institutions' fee-raising policies, often implicitly, for instance through non-intervention. Indeed, the autonomy of most public higher education institutions is so limited that they cannot raise their fees without at least implicit state approval. Along with structural arguments for cost-sharing, the current economic crisis is of utmost importance to explain this situation.

The first structural argument in favour of cost-sharing is the increase of competition between higher education institutions when fees are at stake. The institutions discussed earlier in the chapter partly set their prices based on a comparative norm (Ward & Douglass, 2006; Musselin, 2010). Business schools compete with each other to attract students. Top-tier institutions face international competition, while less prestigious schools compare themselves to other French institutions. In both cases, pricing is increasingly about setting a price theoretically equivalent to the quality of the programme. 'The more you pay, the more you get' is the logic at play. To a lesser extent, some regional *Instituts d'études politiques* are also copying their prestigious Parisian counterpart, Sciences Po Paris, and raising their tuition fees, although to a lesser degree. This may also be the case for engineering schools.

The second structural argument for cost-sharing relies on the impact of rising fees on income redistribution (Jongbloed, 2005, p. 272) as 'it can be questioned whether a further subsidization of higher education is an equitable policy, as it implies an income transfer from the average taxpayer to tomorrow's well-off'. This pro-fee argument means that it would not be fair to aggravate a specifically French equity concern, that is, the most highly subsidised students also get the highest wages thanks to their education. In the light of the few cases of cost-sharing that exist in France, state non-interference seems to be addressed only to prestigious programmes providing graduates with a high earnings premium. It does not concern mass university courses and have strictly been implemented in the most reputed *grandes écoles*. Aside from public *grandes écoles* in engineering and political science, the clearest illustration of this logic is the Université Paris Dauphine, which has set variable fees (from €1575 to €4200 in 2013) for part of its master's programmes, particularly for degrees generating a high graduate earnings premium, meanwhile openly comparing itself to a much higher publicly-funded institution in the same field, Sciences Po Paris.

Cost-sharing can be advocated for many reasons, but none of them seemed to be decisive in the French case – such arguments are not new and could have been made for years. The real trigger behind the emergence of cost-sharing in France is to be found in the current strong concern for reducing public debt. This policy of non-interference by recent French governments on higher education institutions' tuition policies holds insofar as it articulates equity concerns, that is, it enables fee increases in the case of high earnings premium, with economic realism, that is, it trades fee increases with decreasing public funding. The recent political context led the national government to reconsider public funding, especially for prestigious, highly-funded institutions. French institutions have mainly raised their tuition fees in order to, as Musselin puts it (2010, p. 86), 'compensate the increase in budget and the decrease in public funding'. Top-tier business schools have dramatically increased their fees as a means of coping with European and international competition and vanishing traditional funding sources, particularly public ones. Indeed, whether we look at funding from chambers of commerce [21] (*chambres de commerce et d'industrie*), which in 10 years has fallen from 35% to 11% of school total budgets, at uncertainties regarding the apprenticeship tax (*taxe d'apprentissage* [22]), which represented 10% of the total budget in 2011, or at the low level of direct public funding (3%), the conclusion remains that business schools no longer benefit from generous public support. In the public sector, the new balance can roughly be summed up as follows: public funding has remained stable in universities, but has decreased slightly in most other institutions (DEPP, 2012, p. 347).[23] Therefore, directors of *grandes écoles* in engineering and political science have recently blamed static and even decreasing public funding to justify tuition fee increases. This development is the consequence of a long-standing inequality between under-funded universities and other far better off sectors, especially public *grandes écoles*. But the state has not chosen to diminish public funding without offering any compensation, that is, turning a blind eye on fee increases.

This relative laissez-faire is far from being harmless when it comes to access inequalities. It is difficult to assess the impact of tuition fees on inequalities in access for an individual institution. Some of the cost-sharing evolutions described occurred within the last several years, and researchers lack the perspective and data necessary to evaluate these moves. But even for business schools, which are far more expensive than other programmes, there is no evidence that social reproduction is higher than in other prestigious *grandes écoles* (see Table II).[24] Reviewing existing research on the subject of student demand, Jongbloed (2005) suggests that students are on average not very responsive to price. Needless to say, such studies have been conducted in countries where tuition fees have been introduced sometimes a long time ago, which also explains the limited impact of higher tuition fees on student demand. French students, in particular those coming from families with disadvantaged socio-economic backgrounds, might be much more price sensitive, and in particular much more debt averse.

While it is possible to measure the general impact on inequalities of opportunity in higher education when a global change in student funding occurs, it is more difficult to analyse the impact of a new tuition policy in specific institutions. On the whole, these recent evolutions in tuition fees contribute to an increase in fee dispersion in French higher education, which were already at a high level. This could lead to an ever more divided system between no-tuition universities at one end of the spectrum and high-tuition *grandes écoles* at the other. Above all, the issue at hand is inequality of access, which is already high in *grandes écoles* (see Table II). Indeed, the more prestigious the institutions tend to be, the more the system has provided unequal access to students over the last 30 years (Albouy & Wanecq, 2003).

Conclusion

The main arguments of this chapter can be summarised as follows:

First, we have challenged the idea of France being a no-fee country and we have explained how the French student funding system has remained stable while facing criticism. Administrative rules have set low and stable fees to cover the costs of student registration. Such a scheme still prevails in universities in spite of high inequalities of access to higher education and various challenges to the tuition principle. Except for the growing but still comparatively minor private sector, it is no wonder that cost-sharing has so slowly been introduced in France, since some student unions, such as Unef, have been very efficient 'watchdogs', closely monitoring cost-sharing instruments and keeping them under control.

Second, we have explored the dynamic process of cost-sharing in the French context. Fees have been gradually introduced in private institutions, but also in some public *grandes écoles*. This growing tendency towards cost-sharing in public institutions may be seen as a play in three acts. The first step is a tuition fee increase (except for state grant-holders) beyond registration fees. Some *grandes écoles* in engineering have recently moved in this direction, following *Institut d'études politiques*. The second step consists of drastically increasing the maximum amount of tuition while determining fee rates according to parental income. After a short period of fixed tuition, the *Instituts d'études politiques* are now one by one turning their student funding scheme into a variable fee system. The third step may be the introduction of student loans. Variable fees mean that students may be charged thousands of euros a year. Deferred fees are thought as an adequate way of tackling the issue. The main instrument currently under discussion is income-contingent loans (Charles, 2012). Repayment of this type of loan, taken out by the student, is characterised by deferral until the income of the graduate reaches a certain level. This system was recommended by economists (see for instance Courtioux & Gregoir, 2010) and think tanks, but has not yet been implemented by any institution. There may be a long road ahead, but the *Instituts d'études politiques*, along with engineering *grandes écoles*, might be leading the way. Setting fixed fees may just be one step before implementing a variable-fee system. Income-contingent loans might become, finally, the third step along the French path towards cost-sharing.

Third, we have highlighted the circumstances in which cost-sharing has recently taken a major step in France, even though it has not yet fundamentally transformed social justice rationales. Fee increases come from the institutions themselves and are not the result of national reforms in France. In the current economic crisis, the relatively passive role played by recent governments results of decreasing public funding in some public institutions. Successive governments have implicitly approved institutions' tuition increases, at least for those where graduate earnings premiums are high, and on the condition that they stick to the French social justice rationale, that is affordable fees for low-income families. If the French social justice rationale is safe, it does not mean that the system is free from inequalities. As always in French student funding, inequalities may not come from the student support scheme itself, but rather from increasing, evolving fee and support dispersion in a two-tier system including tuition-free universities and high-tuition *grandes écoles*.

Cost-sharing has become a pervasive trend in France. Influenced by the booming private institutions, fees are increasing from the margins of the public sector, but it might not remain on the margins of the universities. In particular, the very specific trend of variable fees according to parental income could become the most acceptable cost-sharing instrument. Additional research is needed to evaluate the impact of such a scheme on inequality of opportunity, on price responsiveness, and on debt aversion among French students, in particular from low-income families. Also, higher education pricing strategies could be the object of more in-depth analyses that would provide a better understanding of the connections between national reforms and institutional evolutions, beyond the current economic difficulties that provide governments an opportunity to consider fees as a pragmatic public policy option.

Notes

[1] In this chapter, the term 'universities' refers to the major part of universities, that is public ones. A few other universities, accounting for 40,000 students, are private institutions, and therefore can set tuition fees more freely.

[2] The only change concerning tuition fees in the law on higher education voted in July 2013 in France limits free education for programmes in secondary schools. The law stipulates that students in *classes préparatoires* shall now also register at a university and pay the fees pertaining to this registration. But this evolution has nothing to do with cost-sharing. It was brought in so that students on the elite track would contribute financially to higher education funding at the same level as university students.

[3] Needless to say, only a small number of students benefits from this status. The wages can be substantial (up to €2000 a month).

[4] http://www.enseignementsup-recherche.gouv.fr/cid20195/frais-d-inscription-pour-la-rentree-universitaire-2014.html

[5] www.onisep.fr

[6] www.cge.asso.fr/

[7] This newly devised system replaced loans offered by the national centre for student welfare (*Cnous*) (interest-free, up to €3800, selection based on social criteria).

[8] The distribution of a public good is not systematically considered and administrated as a *service public*. However, higher education as a public good in France is steeped in the notion of *service public*.

[9] Purchasing power parity (PPP) is used for comparing economic data in different currencies. It takes into account the effective purchasing power of a given currency.

[10] Loi relative aux libertés et responsabilités des universités (LRU).

[11] Hec (€11,900), Essec (€13,200), Escp (€11,200), Emlyon (€12,200), Edhec (€12,300). Figures for 2012-13 or 2013-14. Average of the three years of the traditional programme Grande école after two years of classes préparatoires.

[12] Hec (€17,500), Essec (€19,000), Escp (€15,900), Emlyon (€15,700), Edhec (€14,000).

[13] Many engineering schools are private and charge high tuition fees (see Table I).

[14] *Ponts et Chaussées* charged an additional €706 in 2012, *Telecom Paris* and *Lille* €584 and *Mines Nantes* €380. *Agro ParisTech* charges €1400 and *Mines Paris* will charge an additional €440 starting in 2013. In 2014, the nine schools 'Telecom' and 'Mines' will charge €1850. In most of these institutions, grant-holders do not pay the fees. http://www.legifrance.gouv.fr/affichTexte.do?cidTexte=JORFTEXT0000283 87723 (accessed January 23, 2014).

[15] Bordeaux (since 2013, up to €6300 [bachelor's] and €6615 [master's] in 2013); Lille (since 2013, up to €3200); Lyon (since 2012, up to €1650 in 2013); Rennes (since 2009, up to €3800 in 2013); Strasbourg (since 2012, up to €3000 in 2013); Toulouse (planned in 2014, up to €3000).

[16] In order to evaluate income tax, the French administration considers the family as a whole, calculating *parts fiscales* (on the basis of adults and children in the family) and dividing the total income by this family fiscal index. The more *parts fiscales* in a family, the smaller the tax burden. The idea behind this system is to provide extra benefits for 'official' families and their children.

[17] Aix (€812 in 2013), Grenoble (between €940 and €1300, depending on level of studies, in 2013).

[18] *Grand établissement* is an administrative status with slightly more autonomy than the universities. This status mostly includes prestigious public *grandes écoles*. For the complete list of institutions, see http://www.legifrance.gouv.fr/affichTexte.do?dateTexte=20081028&cidTexte =JORFTEXT000000764812 (accessed September 9, 2013).

[19] Some private, Catholic-run universities (Institut catholique de Paris, Université catholique de Lyon, Université catholique de Lille), accounting for around 40,000 students in France in 2012, do have such variable tuition schemes and differentiate fees according to programmes and income of students' families.

[20] From a French point of view, it may be surprising that many other countries with means-tested support (for example, England or the USA) have not applied this principle to tuition fees (Jongbloed, 2005).

[21] The local chambers of commerce are historically involved in the development of many business schools in France.

[22] This tax is paid by private companies with more than 10 employees and is used for developing vocational training programmes. Business schools are allowed to receive such funding directly from companies.

[23] Without any clear decision, but according to the rationale that universities are the key players in higher education systems worldwide, successive French governments have balanced public funding more equally over the last 10 years. However, French universities remain under-funded.

[24] However, social reproduction may benefit different students. Business school students clearly tend to come from backgrounds with more economic-capital, while in some public *grandes écoles*, students come from the cultural and political elites.

Nicolas Charles

References

Albouy, V. & Wanecq, T. (2003) Les inégalités sociales d'accès aux grandes écoles, *Economie et Statistique*, 361, 27-52.

Charles, N. (2012) Income-contingent Student Loan Repayment: a higher education payment system importable into France?, *Revue française de sociologie*, 53(2), 193-233.

Chevaillier, T. & Paul, J.-J. (2006) Accessibility and Equity in a State-funded System of Higher Education. The French Case, in P. Teixeira, D.B. Johnstone, M.J. Rosa and H. Vossensteyn (Eds) *Cost-Sharing and Accessibility in Higher Education: a fairer deal?*, pp. 295-316. Dordrecht: Springer.

Cordazzo, P. & Tenret, E. (2011) L'économie étudiante, in O. Galland, E. Verley & R. Vourc'h (Eds) *Les mondes étudiants. Enquête Conditions de vie 2010*, pp. 217-225. Paris: La documentation française.

Cour des comptes (2013) Les écoles supérieures de commerce et de gestion (ESCG): un développement à réguler, *Rapport public annuel 2013*, pp. 305-380.

Courtioux, P. & Gregoir, S. (2010) Les propositions de l'EDHEC pour réformer l'enseignement supérieur: les contrats de formation supérieure. EDHEC Position Paper, Nice.

Direction de l'Evaluation, de la Prospective et de la Performance (DEPP) (2010) *Repères et références statistiques sur les enseignements, la formation et la recherche – édition 2010*. Paris: Ministère de l'éducation nationale, Ministère de l'enseignement supérieur et de la recherche.

Direction de l'Evaluation, de la Prospective et de la Performance (DEPP) (2011) *Repères et références statistiques sur les enseignements, la formation et la recherche – édition 2011*. Paris: Ministère de l'éducation nationale, Ministère de l'enseignement supérieur et de la recherche.

Direction de l'Evaluation, de la Prospective et de la Performance (DEPP) (2012) *Repères et références statistiques sur les enseignements, la formation et la recherche – édition 2012*. Paris: Ministère de l'éducation nationale, Ministère de l'enseignement supérieur et de la recherche.

Eurydice (2012) L'espace européen de l'enseignement supérieur en 2012: rapport sur la mise en œuvre du processus de Bologne, *Rapport thématique*, 138.

Galland O., Verley E. & Vourc'h R. (Eds) *Les mondes étudiants. Enquête Conditions de vie 2010*, Paris: La documentation française.

Johnstone, D.B. & Marcucci, P.N. (2010) *Financing Higher Education Worldwide. Who Pays? Who Should Pay?* Baltimore, MD: Johns Hopkins University Press.

Jongbloed, B. (2005) Tuition Fees in Europe and Australasia: theory, trends and policies, in J.C. Smart (Ed.) *Higher Education: handbook of theory and research*, vol. xix, pp. 241-310. Amsterdam: Kluwer.

Marcucci, P.N. & Johnstone, D.B. (2007) Tuition Fee Policies in a Comparative Perspective: theoretical and political rationales, *Journal of Higher Education Policy and Management*, 29(1), 25-40.

Musselin, C. (2010) Universities and Pricing on Higher Education Markets, in D. Mattheou (Ed.) *Changing Educational Landscapes. Educational Policies,*

Schooling Systems and Higher Education – a comparative perspective, pp. 75-90. Amsterdam: Springer.

Orr, D., Gwosc, C. & Netz, N. (2011) Social and Economic Conditions of Student Life in Europe. Synopsis of Indicators. Final Report. Eurostudent III 2008-2011. Eurostudent.eu

Union nationale des étudiants de France (Unef) (2013) Frais d'inscription, sélection illégale: 36 universités hors-la-loi. Dossier de presse. http://unef.fr/wp-content/uploads/2013/07/DOSSIER-DE-PRESSE-UNEF-2013-FII-11.pdf

Ward, D. & Douglass, J.A. (2006) Higher Education and the Spectre of Variable Fees: public policy and institutional responses in the United States and the United Kingdom, *Higher Education Management and Policy*, 18(1), 1-28.

CHAPTER 4

The Rise and Fall of Student Fees in a Federal Higher Education System: the case of Germany

OTTO HÜTHER & GEORG KRÜCKEN

ABSTRACT Germany is a highly interesting case concerning tuition fees. While broader transnational trends like New Public Management and marketisation shape its higher education system, the widespread trend towards tuition fees is not mirrored in Germany. We identify several factors for this outcome, among which the federal system is of particular importance. The introduction of tuition fees cannot be decreed by a central government, but must be decided and implemented by 16 federal state governments on a case-by-case basis. Based on the low level of legitimacy in the political discourse and the fact that elections in the 16 states take place at different times, tuition fees, therefore, have become a permanent and too risky election campaign issue for its proponents. Due to shifting coalitions and political risk aversion, the few states that introduced tuition fees later abolished them.

Introduction

Germany, like many other European countries, has seen a great variety of reform initiatives in the higher education sector during the last 20 years (Braun & Merrien 1999; Amaral et al, 2003; Krücken et al, 2007a; Paradeise et al, 2009). Degree courses, for example, were changed to the bachelor's and master's system nationwide as part of the Bologna process (Brandle, 2010). At the same time, the remuneration of professors changed with the introduction of performance-related components (Herzog & Kehm, 2012). Furthermore, the governance structures of universities have also changed with, as in other countries, the orientation towards the so-called New Public Management Model (Kehm & Lanzendorf, 2006; de Boer et al, 2007). For Germany, this means that the position of the university presidents and the deans is strengthening, while the academic committees are losing influence

(Hüther, 2010). Simultaneously, competition between universities and individual researchers is increasing. Examples include the 'Excellence Initiative' or the increasing level of external funding (Münch, 2006; Schubert & Schmoch, 2010). In addition, the relationship between universities and the corporate sector has become much closer in the last 20 years through a wealth of political reform measures and the activities of entrepreneurial scientists (Krücken et al, 2007b). The German higher education system is therefore currently in a phase of rapid change (Hüther & Krücken, 2013).

In the course of these changes, there is at least a tendency that the international trend towards New Public Management and marketisation has played, and still does play, a significant role in Germany. Nevertheless, one distinguishing feature is that currently, or more precisely, in the immediate future, publicly-funded higher education institutions do not, or will no longer, charge tuition fees. There are private universities with tuition fees in Germany, but their relevance is low in international comparison (Ertl, 2005, p. 210). In addition, the reputation of private universities in Germany is not as high as in other countries. The German higher education system is therefore to be regarded as predominantly free of charge – at least for the first degree completed within the prescribed time frame. Germany's higher education institutions are therefore – in contrast to the United Kingdom (UK), the USA and Australia for example – financed almost exclusively through direct or indirect funds by the state (Bundesministerium für Bildung und Forschung [BMBF], 2012b; Organisation for Economic Cooperation and Development [OECD], 2012, p. 251).

There was, however, an attempt to introduce tuition fees in Germany. From 2006 students had to pay general tuition fees of around €500 per semester in several federal states (Ebcinoglu, 2006; Hadamitzky et al, 2008). But since 2008, all the federal states concerned have either abolished tuition fees or will shortly do so. The question is, therefore, how can we explain this development? While there is a trend towards marketisation in Germany, it was not politically possible to introduce tuition fees. Our hypothesis is that a combination of factors is responsible. First, the strong orientation in Germany towards the welfare state which turns the subject of tuition fees into a highly-charged political question. Arguments of social justice are decisive in this context. Second, there was the issue of uncertainties about the effects of tuition fees, which the media repeatedly focused on. A third factor is the federal structure of the German higher education system. The combination of these factors leads to tuition fees not being viewed as legitimate in Germany, resulting in a 'liability of newness' effect as described in innovation and organisational research (Stinchcombe, 1965; Freeman et al, 1983). This 'liability of newness' explanation accentuates how difficult it is to permanently establish something new. The results show that the institutionalisation of tuition fees did not succeed. The failure of institutionalisation occurred as a dynamic reaction to the social systems of politics, science and education, and mass media.

To explain these connections we will first describe the process of introducing and abolishing tuition fees in Germany. We will then focus on the central pro and contra arguments of the debate about tuition fees in Germany. The next step will be to examine the actual effects of tuition fees and how they were treated in public discourse. Finally, we will discuss the effects of Germany's federal structure.

Tuition Fees in Germany 1960-2013

Tuition fees and lecture fees were traditionally part of university funding in Germany. In the 1960s they were between 120 and 150 Deutsche Mark (DM) per semester and they were only abolished in the winter semester of 1970-71. The aim of abolition was to better integrate previously disadvantaged population groups into the higher education system (e.g. Müller-Böling, 1995; Berger & Ehmann, 2000, pp. 258-266). The cost-free higher education system in Germany is therefore closely bound up with the concepts of equity and social justice.

After abolishing tuition and lecture fees in the 1970s, the federal state of Baden-Württemberg reintroduced tuition fees of €511 per semester in 1997. However, these were not levied on all students, only on 'long-term students', who were defined as students who were more than four semesters over the prescribed time for completing a degree course (on average nine semesters). In 2003 and 2004 similar fees were introduced in Bavaria, Hesse, Lower Saxony, Saarland, Saxony-Anhalt and Thuringia.[1] With hindsight, the fees for long-term students can be considered as the introduction of tuition fees 'through the back door' (Ertl, 2005, p. 223). They reduced the number of registered students and were seen by some politicians as a success. The number of students who had been matriculated for more than 15 semesters dropped by around 87,000 between the winter semester of 2003 and the winter semester of 2004 (Statistisches Bundesamt, 2004, 2005). These figures indicate that a significant number of students had been enrolled at German universities who were no longer seriously studying or had enrolled on a second degree course in order to maintain their student status and its privileges.[2]

The introduction of tuition fees for long-term students in Baden-Württemberg and the increasingly heated discussion about tuition fees which we will focus on below prompted the national government in 2002 to legislate against the introduction of tuition fees for a first degree in the Sixth Amendment to the Framework Act for Higher Education. According to the German constitution, the federal states are responsible for higher education institutions. However, due to an amendment to the constitution in 1969, the national government received the power to enact framework legislation for higher education institutions. This was mainly implemented by means of the Framework Act for Higher Education, which, in this case, was used to prevent tuition fees.

This legislation was highly disputed and six federal states brought the case before the constitutional court. The court decided in its verdict on 26 January 2005 that the ban on tuition fees by the national government was unconstitutional and therefore invalid (Bundesverfassungsgericht [BVerfG], 2005). The national government had overstepped its powers to set the framework legislation for higher education, unconstitutionally restricting the rights of the federal states. This opened the way for the federal states to introduce general tuition fees for first degrees. Consequently, 7 of the 16 federal states introduced general tuition fees between 2006 and 2007 (see Table I).

In most federal states, students had to pay €500 per semester, i.e. €1000 per year. Within each state, fees were, on the whole, the same at all universities. There were two exceptions. In Bavaria, higher education institutions could set their own fees between €100 and €500. In North Rhine-Westphalia, higher education institutions were even free to decide if they wanted to set fees at all. If they did, the fees were not allowed to exceed €500.[3]

	Decision to implement	Implementation	Decision to abolish	Abolition
Lower-Saxony	December 2005	WS 2006	December 2013	WS 2014
Hesse	October 2006	WS 2007	July 2008	WS 2008
Saarland	July 2006	WS 2007	February 2010	SS 2010
Hamburg	June 2006	SS 2007	September 2011	WS 2012
North Rhine-Westphalia	March 2006	WS 2006	February 2011	WS 2011
Bavaria	May 2006	SS 2007	April 2013	WS 2013
Baden-Württemberg	December 2005	SS 2007	July 2011	SS 2012

WS: winter semester; SS: summer semester.

Table I. General tuition fees in the federal states.

After a peak number of seven federal states had introduced tuition fees by 2007, Hesse decided to abolish them again as early as 2008. Saarland followed in 2010, and Hamburg, North Rhine-Westphalia and Baden-Württemberg in 2011. Bavaria decided in April 2013 in favour of abolition. In Lower-Saxony they will be abolished for the winter semester of 2014 (see also Alecke & Mitze, 2012, p. 360).

The Development of the Debate on Tuition Fees in Germany

The first question is, why were tuition fees introduced in Germany? It is generally accepted that there was a crisis in the German university system in the 1990s (e.g. Glotz, 1996; Stölting & Schimank, 2001; Baker & Lenhardt, 2008). This is primarily to be seen as a crisis of funding. It is important here to note that the federal states are not just responsible for providing higher education institutions, but are also responsible for the largest part of their funding. Although the number of students increased (Ertl, 2005), the federal states could not increase funding, partly due to the costs of German reunification. There were even funding cuts in some states (König, 2006). At the same time, teaching quality was being criticised (e.g. Dohmen, 2004) because of overflowing seminars and lectures, a lack of practical orientation of the courses, high drop-out rates, and the long duration of a degree course in international comparison. In view of these observations, the introduction of tuition fees promised financial relief on the one hand and additional funding to improve teaching quality on the other.

The serious debate about tuition fees started in 1995, with an internal debate within the German Rectors' Conference (HRK). At the end of this debate in July 1996, the HRK passed a resolution not to come out in favour of tuition fees at that point in time. Despite the rejection, the debate at the HRK established tuition fees as a realistic political option. In 1998, the Stifterverband für die deutsche Wissenschaft [4] and the Centrum für Hochschulentwicklung (CHE) presented a so-called *Studienbeitragsmodel* (model for a financial contribution to the cost of a degree course) in a joint publication (Stifterverband für die Deutsche Wissenschaft and CHE, 1998), further enflaming the debate. Furthermore, in 2004, the German Employers' Association *Bundesvereinigung der Deutschen Arbeitgeberverbände* (BDA) presented a model for tuition fees (BDA, 2004). In the same year, the HRK demanded that tuition fees should be made possible. They should be used exclusively as 'external funding' for teaching in order to raise the quality of university teaching. From 1995 onwards we can therefore see a debate about tuition fees as part of the academic and educational policy discourse, in which the central actors moved slowly towards an acceptance of tuition fees.

Tuition fees were not only a subject of heated debate within the science and education arena, but also featured in the media. Figure 1 shows how often articles with the term 'tuition fees' in the main text appeared in the leading 'serious' national media, as well as the frequency of the term in the title of articles.[5]

As can be seen from the anaylsis in Figure 1, the term 'tuition fees' was used much less frequently before 1995. There is a first recognisable peak in the debate between 1995 and 1998. In particular, the coverage of the fee model proposed by the Stifterverband and the CHE, but also the student protests about the low quality of teaching and the critical financial situation of universities in 1998, led to increased coverage. Though not intended by the protesting students, some saw tuition fees as a solution for this double-edged problem. Between 1999 and 2001, the topic loses relevance for the media, but stays above the 1995 level. From 2002 onwards, the coverage increases, coinciding with the verdict of the constitutional court and the introduction of tuition fees in 2006 and 2007. The coverage reaches its peak in 2008, the year with the first abolition of tuition fees in Hesse. Thereafter, coverage decreases and in 2012 it reaches the level of 1998 and 2002. The analysis shows that tuition fees became a permanent topic in the media after 2002 and were still being discussed after their introduction in 2006. The continuing discussion after their introduction indicates their controversial nature, their perceived lack of legitimacy and that they were not viewed as self-evident and beyond question – that is, they did not become institutionalised.

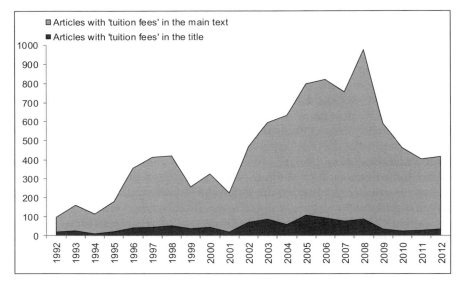

Media analysed: Der Spiegel, Die Zeit (from 1994), Süddeutsche Zeitung, and Frankfurter Allgemeine Zeitung.

Figure 1. Coverage of tuition fees in leading German media.

Overall, increasing debate in academia and educational policy, as well as among the general public, about the purpose of tuition fees takes place from 1995 onwards. In the following we will reconstruct the main arguments for and against tuition fees and use these as a basis for examining the question of legitimacy and related problems of institutionalisation.

The Formation of Political Battle Lines
and the Arguments in the Tuition Fee Debate

From the start the subject of tuition fees was ideologically charged and proponents and opponents could be relatively clearly placed into the market liberal vs welfare state camps. Tuition fees thus became a symbolic topic, whose proponents and opponents could usually be placed clearly into different political camps. Whereas the Conservatives (Christian Democratic Union [CDU] and Christian Social Union [CSU]) and the Liberals (Free Democratic Party [FDP]) wanted to introduce tuition fees, the Social Democrats (Social Democratic Party [SPD]), the Greens and the Party of Democratic Socialism (PDS, later known as 'die Linke' or 'the Left') were against it. It was Chancellor Schröder's government, a coalition between the SPD and the Greens, who used the Framework Act for Higher Education to ban tuition fees. The ultimately successful legal challenge against this ban was introduced by federal states governed either by the CDU alone (in Bavaria, the CSU) or by a coalition of the CDU and the FDP. Consequently, tuition fees were introduced only in states that were governed either by the CDU or the CSU alone or in a coalition of the CDU and the FDP. Federal states governed by the SPD did not introduce tuition fees.

The central argument against tuition fees was that they would increase social selectivity. Tuition fees would prevent young adults from low-income and underprivileged backgrounds from attending higher education institutions (e.g. Duz Magazin, 1996; Reiter, 1997; Berger & Ehmann, 2000). According to the opponents, the great achievement of free access to higher education institutions since the 1970s was at stake. As in other countries, it is therefore social justice arguments that play a central role in the German debate. Studies from the USA showing that increased tuition fees cause higher social selectivity (e.g. Kane, 1994; Björklund & Jäntti, 1997; Carneiro & Heckman, 2002) played an important part in the debate (e.g. Hartmann, 2006).

Although problems of social selectivity connected with tuition fees are also a permanent point of debate in other countries, the debate in Germany was particularly charged around the year 2000. The reason was the so-called 'PISA Shock' (e.g. Fahrholz et al, 2002; Loeber & Scholz, 2003; Schwager, 2005). The Programme for International Student Assessment (PISA) study showed that in international comparison a firm link exists in Germany between a family's socio-economic status and the type of school [6] their children attend and the level of the child's competencies. In addition to the critical results of German pupils overall, the PISA results also showed that social selectivity is particularly high in Germany (Artelt et al, 2001; Deutsches PISA-Konsortium, 2001). Furthermore, the internationally comparative Progress in International Reading Literacy Study (PIRLS) from 2001 again highlighted the high selectivity of the German school system. According to this study, children from upper middle-class families have a 4.5 times higher chance of moving onto a *Gymnasium* after primary school than working-class children. For middle-class children the chance is 2.7 times higher than for working-class children (Becker, 2011, p. 116). This is important for the question of social selectivity as the *Gymnasium* is the first and foremost path to higher education institutions.

The quota of those eligible to study at higher education institutions also shows the high selectivity of the German school system. Although the quota has increased over time, in international comparison it is still very low. Between 1995 and 2005, for example, only 36% to 43% of 18 to 21 year olds attained the formal qualification necessary to attend higher education institutions (BMBF, 2012a). There are further selective effects during the transition into higher education. Young adults from low-income and underprivileged families are less likely than their counterparts from middle-class families to go directly to higher education institutions, even if they have the formal qualification to do so (Schindler & Reimer, 2010; Quast et al, 2012). This effect stems from the dual system of vocational training in Germany. For many, this offers an attractive alternative to a university degree, since within a shorter time, with less risk, and at lower cost, an occupational qualification can be obtained. Since early financial independence and short training times are more important for young adults from low-income and underprivileged families than for their middle-class counterparts, the dual system 'deflects' these young adults from aspiring for university degrees (e.g. Müller & Pollak, 2007; Becker & Hecken, 2008; Quast et al, 2012). The results of the selectivity of the school system and the deflection towards the dual system are very significant: in 2000, only 12% of the children with a working-class father start university enrolment, compared with 37% of the children with a white-collar worker as father and 72% of the children with a civil servant as father (Schnitzer et al, 2001).

From an academic point of view, the results about social selectivity in the year 2000 were not really a surprise and had already long been known (e.g. Brake, 2003). What changed in 2000 was that the media picked up the topic and a public debate about the quality and selectivity of the German school and higher education systems ensued. Long-known findings from education research were now brought to light by the media, forcing politicians to enter this debate. What was destroyed in this debate was the myth of equal opportunities, which had been perpetuated since the 1970s (Geißler, 2004).

For the opponents of tuition fees it was a given that even small increases in the costs of a university degree would result in an increase in the previously described social selectivity in the higher education system. It is thus not surprising that in the models of the BDA and the CHE and Stifterverband, and the HRK resolution, avoiding an increase in social selectivity is a central issue. The constitutional court also emphasised that tuition fees have to be socially acceptable and must not discourage children from low-income families from attending university (BVerfG, 2005, 2013).

However, the high selectivity of the German higher education system was also used as an argument in favour of tuition fees. The following arguments were advanced: without tuition fees, the poor are financing the education of the rich via their taxes; whereas kindergarten, which is far less socially selective, charges fees, universities do not; precisely because, in contrast to kindergarten, children from low-income and underprivileged families rarely attend university, tuition fees are socially acceptable – these fees ensure that the better-off pay for their own education (e.g. Krämer, 1999; Ederer et al, 2000; Biffl & Isaak, 2002).

A further argument in favour of tuition fees were various studies which showed that the costs of a degree course were not recouped by more tax paid later. Graduates achieve a net gain, but its size depends on the degree course (e.g. Grüske, 1994; Borgloh et al, 2008). If a degree were financed exclusively via taxes, all taxpayers would pay for the foundation of the graduates' later gains. The proponents of fees saw this as a social injustice that could at least be partially rectified by the introduction of tuition fees (e.g. Krämer, 1999; Dohmen, 2004).

Many arguments in the debate point towards the marketisation of the higher education system (e.g. Schwanitz, 1999; Zöllner, 1999; Butterwege, 2009; Lieb, 2009). Students who pay for their degrees become consumers. Tuition fees therefore also change the relationship between teachers and students. The proponents assumed that students could then formulate demands for the quality of their education that would lead to quality improvements. The opponents on the other hand saw the Humboldtian community of teachers and students as endangered. The proponents also expected that different levels of tuition fees would promote competition between universities. Competition forces universities to implement innovative solutions which contribute to improving the quality of the education.

Further arguments for the introduction of tuition fees were the chronic underfunding of universities and the previously mentioned problems of quality. Tuition fees were expected to increase the overall funding for universities, leading to a greater funding diversification. The opponents doubted this effect. They rather feared that the federal states would, at least in the medium term, use the additional funds generated by tuition fees to further reduce their contribution to university funding (Dilger, 1999; Zöllner, 1999). Funding diversification would occur, but no increase in overall funding. Without more funding there would be no increase in quality.

During the debate between 1995 and 2005 the proponents slowly gained the upper hand in the media (Krause, 2008). The reason for this change in public opinion around the year 2000 is certainly the shift towards neo-liberalism in Germany. In the relationship between the state and the market, market solutions were clearly being favoured in the public debate. Germany was viewed as the 'sick man of Europe' and a strong need for reform was perceived. Competitiveness and individual responsibility took centre stage in the reform debate, in contrast to previous debates where the emphasis had been on the welfare state. Examples include the loosening of banking controls, but also the far-reaching reform of the labour market that was associated with a fundamental new orientation of the German welfare state.

A shift towards strengthening individual responsibility and cutting back welfare spending was visible not just in the media, but also in public opinion. Whereas in 1994 only 9.8% of the population were in favour of cutting welfare benefits, this number rose to 20.2% in 2000 and 23.2% in 2004 (Terwey & Baltzer, 2012, p. 379). There was also a shift in opinions towards tuition fees. Surveys from 1998, 2000 and 2003 show that 54%, 57% and 64% of those questioned were in favour of tuition fees if they were paid directly to the universities and used to improve study conditions. But 70% (1998), 74% (2000) and 72% (2003) of those questioned were against tuition fees if the money raised went to the federal states (forsa Gesellschaft für Sozialforschung und statistische Analyse mbH [FORSA], 2003). We can see an increasing acceptance of tuition fees under certain conditions, but also a strong rejection if those conditions are not met.

Overall, the debate about tuition fees shows that in the media and among the general public they were only viewed as legitimate under certain conditions. It is these conditions we will investigate now.

The Effects of Tuition Fees and the Question of Legitimacy

Tuition fees are only considered legitimate by the media and large sections of the population if the revenue increases overall university funding, if the additional income is only used to improve the quality of education, and, simultaneously, effective measures to prevent increased social selectivity are established. The controversial nature of tuition fees has also meant that their effects are the subject of permanent scrutiny. The media and opponents of fees are constantly checking whether the legitimacy requirements are being met.

Such scrutiny results in an advantage for the opponents: uncertainty about the effects of measures that have not yet been institutionalised can relatively easily be used to undermine their legitimacy. Uncertainty about the effects of new measures is, however, much harder to utilise for building or maintaining legitimacy. The proponents therefore had to rely on the actual fulfilment of the legitimacy requirements in the eyes of the media and the general public. For the opponents, on the other hand, uncertainty in the eyes of the general public and the media about the effects was sufficient to keep the controversy alive.

The legitimacy of tuition fees could only be ensured if, in both the media coverage and public perception: (a) no reduction of state funds occurred; (b) tuition fees were only used for improving teaching and the overall quality of higher education; and (c) the selectivity of higher education did not increase.

We will now examine whether and how these three necessary conditions were fulfilled and, secondly, whether the legitimacy of tuition fees was confirmed in public discourse.

Were State Funds Reduced after the Introduction of Tuition Fees?

Whereas in the 1990s and up until the middle of the 2000s funding for higher education institutions hardly increased or was even cut, which resulted in serious funding problems, the situation changed drastically from 2007 onwards. Figure 2 shows a significant increase in expenditure by universities and universities of applied science. In addition to the funds for the 'Excellence Initiative' which aims at fostering top-level research at universities (about €4.6 billion between 2006-17), there were also funds from the Quality Pact for Teaching (€2 billion until 2020) and the Higher Education Pacts which are intended to create additional places for students (over €20 billion from 2007-18). After the introduction of tuition fees, the federal states therefore increased both baseline and external funding and did not reduce them. In particular, the federal states that introduced tuition fees did not reduce baseline funding for higher education after their introduction (Statistisches Bundesamt, 2012b, p. 123). A delegitimisation of tuition fees by a simultaneous reduction in funding is not evidenced by the figures and also played no part in public discourse after the introduction of tuition fees.

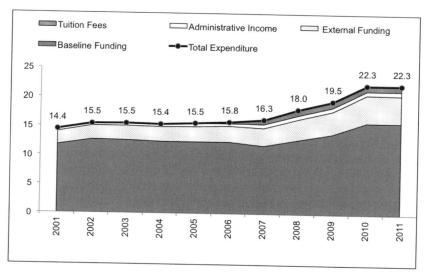

Figure 2. Expenditure and income of universities (without medical institutions) and universities of applied science between 2001 to 2011 in billion euro.
Source: Statistisches Bundesamt, 2001-2012.

However, we assume that the better overall financial situation led to a delegitimisation of tuition fees, since one of the arguments for their introduction – chronic underfunding – loses some of its relevance in the media and public perception. Due to the increase in funding, universities' financial hardship was to a lesser extent perceived as such a pressing problem and the proponents lost one of their main arguments in favour of tuition fees. This perception is also strengthened by the fact that the financial impact of tuition fees has been relatively small in comparison with the programmes implemented from 2006 onwards. The contribution of tuition fees to the overall funding of universities is only 4% to 5% in the years 2007 to 2012. The role of tuition fees for the overall funding of universities was hardly ever significant, even at the time when at least seven federal states were levying them.

The relatively small effects on funding and the overall improvement in the financial situation of universities meant that in the public eye tuition fees were no longer viewed as an absolute necessity. This is a key factor in the abolition of tuition fees. This effect is reinforced by the fact that after the abolition of tuition fees the lost revenue has been at least partially replaced by the state. In effect, but also in the public debate, the abolition of tuition fees had hardly any effect on the financial resources of universities.

Were Tuition Fees Used for Improving the Quality of University Teaching and Did They Lead to an Improvement?

According to law, tuition fees could only be used for improving teaching quality. However, it is difficult to measure positive effects of tuition fees on the quality of teaching. In response to a parliamentary request for information from the Green Party in 2012, the national government answered that 'no data for changes in the quality of higher education were available which could solely be attributed to the introduction of tuition fees' (Deutscher Bundestag, 2012, p. 15). The problem of measuring the effects of tuition fees on teaching quality is a result of the simultaneous conversion of the degree course system to the bachelor's and master's system and the additional resources of the Quality Pact for Teaching and the Higher Education Pacts. The effects of tuition fees, the conversion of degree courses, and of the increased funding on the quality of teaching cannot be separated. Even if teaching quality has improved, the effects of tuition fees alone cannot be identified. Proponents can therefore not legitimise the introduction of tuition fees by positive effects on teaching quality. Opponents, however, may point out that the effects of tuition fees are not measurable and thus the usefulness of a controversial measure remains to be proven. Precisely this discussion can be found in the media (e.g. *Hannoversche Allgemeine*, 2012; *Spiegel Online*, 2012).

In addition, the strong association between tuition fees and improving the quality of higher education teaching is slowly dissolving in the public debate. Instead, the question of teaching quality is increasingly discussed in the context of the introduction of bachelor's and master's degree courses. It is no longer the question of whether tuition fees should be introduced or not that is regarded as crucial for teaching quality, but whether or how the bachelor's and master's degree courses are being implemented.

Furthermore, since the introduction of tuition fees, a number of media reports surfaced suggesting a misappropriation of the income from tuition fees by the universities (e.g. *Der Stern*, 2007; *Telepolis*, 2010; *Der Tagesspiegel*, 2010; *Spiegel Online*, 2011a, 2011b; *Süddeutsche.de*, 2011). There are, for example, reports that universities did not spend the money, but saved it instead. In addition, tuition fees were partly used for construction projects, for the repayment of loans or for financing the central administration, not necessarily measures that lead to an improvement in teaching quality. Even if the vast majority of universities used their tuition fees for improving teaching quality, a suspicion of misuse remains in the public perception.

Overall, it can be said that an improvement in teaching quality is not measurable and that this fact is discussed in the media. At the same time, the media repeatedly report the misappropriation of funds. Consequently, it is questionable whether improving teaching quality, the condition that was associated with the introduction of tuition fees, is being met. The legitimacy of tuition fees is therefore being undermined.

Has Social Selectivity Increased Because of Tuition Fees?

Thus far we have established that the two main arguments for the introduction of tuition fees in Germany – improving the financial situation and improving teaching quality – have lost much of their driving power since the mid-2000s. Could at least the most important counter-argument – increasing social selectivity – then be rebutted?

In this context, it is first necessary to examine the situation of students and those starting a degree course in Germany since the introduction of tuition fees. Both the number of students and the number of new students in Germany have increased significantly in recent years (see Figure 3). However, there are slight drops in 2006 and 2007 in the number of new students and those already at university. These declines coincide with the introduction of tuition fees. After that we see a continuous increase despite tuition fees. Since this takes place in federal states with and without tuition fees, it can be concluded that they have had no negative effect on the student numbers, at least after 2007.[7]

Undeterred by the relatively low impact on student and new student numbers, there has been a fierce debate about the effects in terms of social selectivity. One trigger was the models of tuition fees that were introduced. In all federal states where they were levied, tuition fees had to be paid immediately. In other words, in general all states introduced 'up-front tuition fees' (Marcucci & Johnstone, 2007).[8] We also find elements of the 'deferred tuition fee' system. All students have the right to get interest-charging loans which have to be paid off under varying conditions after graduation. Despite this deferred tuition fee element, the increased costs for a degree course were due and felt immediately.

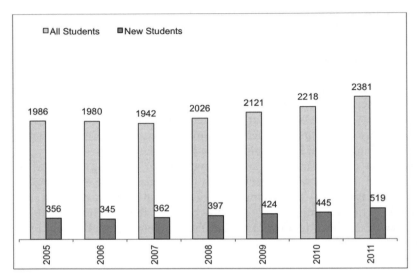

Figure 3. Number of students and new students in Germany (in 000s).
Source: Statistisches Bundesamt, 2012a.

To counteract excessive student debt, the federal states limited the total amount of debt a student would face. Included in this ceiling were tuition fees and government loans for living expenses during a degree course.[9] The debt ceiling was between €10,000 and €17,000 (Ebcinoglu, 2006) and was meant to prevent students from low-income families from being discouraged to start a degree course due to the fear of high debts. Despite this ceiling, the cost of a degree course increased, also for students who already received a government loan. A general exemption from fees based on low income of the student or their parents had not been envisaged; only hardship clauses were introduced.[10] In addition, unlike other countries, there were hardly any scholarships to finance tuition fees.[11]

Although the tuition fee models introduced by the federal states did contain elements to counteract increased social selectivity, significant deficits remained: the charges were in general up-front, students who already received state support had to pay tuition fees, and there was no well-developed system of grants. All this enabled the opponents to plausibly claim that tuition fees increase social selectivity. Already at the model level there are aspects which are detrimental to the legitimisation of tuition fees. Furthermore, the empirical data concerning social selectivity do not lead to clear findings in this respect.

On the basis of surveys of young people qualified to study at a university, Heine et al (2008) point out that the tuition fee debate on the whole caused uncertainty. The consequence is a drop in the propensity to study from 2005 to 2006. This decrease is particularly strong amongst women and young people from disadvantaged backgrounds. Quast et al (2012) also find that tuition fees have an effect of global uncertainty leading to a decreased propensity to study among certain groups. However, the decrease is no greater in federal states with tuition fees than in those without them. It is important to mention that the effects measured in the studies are rather small, but against the background of the selective school system in Germany, they are nonetheless still relevant.

In contrast to the two previous empirical studies, Baier and Helbig (2011) find no effect of tuition fees on the general propensity to study, nor did they find any effects on women and young people from disadvantaged families. Interestingly, all three studies use the same data set, but come to different conclusions. Also due to this fact, the discussion of the different results shifted towards methodological issues that were barely comprehensible to the general public. It should be noted that the impact of tuition fees on social selectivity has remained controversial even in view of empirical studies. This also implies that the central argument against tuition fees retained its prominent role in the public debate on tuition fees in Germany.

The Legitimacy Problems of Tuition Fees

Overall, it can be said that the legitimisation of tuition fees after their introduction presented significant problems. First, the central counter argument that they reinforce social selectivity could not be invalidated. Second, no positive effects on teaching quality could be measured, but there was a suspicion of misappropriation of funds. Third, the financial problems of the German higher education system have eased significantly since 2006.

It can be assumed that it was less the scientific research (e.g. concerning social selectivity) that was responsible for the delegitimisation of tuition fees, but rather how they were presented in the media. As shown above, tuition fees remained a frequent topic in the media even after their introduction. The peak media coverage from 2008 was only reached two years after the legislation for their introduction was passed (see Figure 1). The ongoing public debate necessitates a continuous defence of tuition fees, while the arguments of the proponents lost some of their relevance, and were partly not supported by empirical data. In addition, students repeatedly organised boycotts and demonstrations against tuition fees. This also meant that tuition fees were constantly debated and their legitimacy was constantly being challenged.

Another factor relevant to the legitimisation problems is the significant shift in the political climate in Germany since 2005. Whereas neo-liberalism clearly dominated public discourse in the period between 1995 and 2005, this was changing gradually from 2005 and rapidly after the financial crisis of 2008. Aspects of the welfare state and regulation by the state were again being more strongly emphasised, while market solutions were being viewed more critically. This can be seen in the proportion of the population in favour of cuts in social benefits: the figure dropped from 23.2% in 2004 to 12.5% in 2010 (Terwey & Baltzer, 2012, p. 379).

However, problems of legitimation of new political measures are not unusual and do not necessarily lead to their abolition. The labour market reforms in Germany have also been highly controversial, yet are still in place. Problems of legitimation of tuition fees are not a specifically German phenomenon. We can also find an ongoing discussion at least about the level of tuition fees and also intense student protests in other countries too. The above-mentioned legitimation problems are to be viewed as only a necessary, but not a sufficient condition for the abolition of tuition fees in Germany. Germany's federal structure is in fact a crucial aspect that we will now consider.

The Effects of the Federal System

We have already pointed out that it is the federal states in Germany that are responsible for higher education. The first effect of federalism is the fact that only seven states introduced tuition fees. This in itself hindered the institutionalisation of tuition fees because they were not generally accepted in the overall German political system, but their introduction depended on each federal state. At the same time, the legitimacy of tuition fees was eroded because their partial non-implementation made them not appear to be a necessity.

But federalism influences the institutionalisation and legitimacy of tuition fees in other ways too: at the federal state level, Germany is in a constant election campaign. This is caused by the fact that elections in the federal states take place at different times. Between 2006 and 2012, there were 27 such elections in the federal states on 17 different dates. This means that there are nearly four election campaigns per year on average. Due to the clear political fronts on the question of tuition fees, they are a permanent issue in many election campaigns and the controversy is constantly being renewed. Whereas in centralised systems a consolidation phase is possible between taking a major decision and the next election, this is not the case in Germany. We rather find a permanent debate about tuition fees, which constantly challenges their legitimacy.

The federal structure in combination with the clear political positioning of the proponents and opponents also leads to a relatively long period of uncertainty within the higher education system. Thus, there was the possibility that tuition fees could be introduced or abolished following a change of government. A final decision is therefore never reached, but has to be taken anew each time and then legitimised again.

Finally, although no new tuition fees have been introduced since 2006 due to a change of government at the federal state level, five of the seven decisions for abolition took place after a change of government (North Rhine-Westphalia, Baden-Württemberg, Hamburg, Lower Saxony, Saarland). Except for in the Saarland, a CDU-led government was voted out in each of them and the new governments of the SPD or a coalition of the SPD and the Greens abolished tuition fees, usually as one of the first official acts. The promptness of the decision to abolish shows once again the symbolic importance of the subject in the political arena. The CDU only stayed in power in the Saarland, although tuition fees were also abolished after an election. However, the previous CDU–FDP coalition was replaced by one comprising the CDU, the FDP and the Greens. The abolition of tuition fees was then a concession to the Greens.

In Hesse and Bavaria we find different scenarios and abolition is not accompanied by the formation of a new government. In Hesse, the CDU suffered severe losses in the 2008 election, but there was no clear majority and it was not possible to form a government. However, the votes of the SPD, the Greens and the Left – all of whom were against tuition fees – were sufficient to decide on the abolition of tuition fees in the state parliament. To exclude the controversial topic of tuition fees from the 2009 election, the CDU promised that they would not reintroduce tuition fees if they won the election. The constellation in Hesse is considered particularly relevant for the abolition of tuition fees because Hesse was the first federal state to abolish them. After abolition in Hesse it was clear that abolition was possible, which in turn led to an increased mobilisation of opponents. It also became clear that the CDU wanted to avoid this controversial topic whenever the party perceived a danger of losing an election because of it. This effect was also seen in Bavaria in 2012. Here, a referendum against tuition fees was initiated. After the necessary majority for a referendum was reached, and opinion polls suggested that 72% of the Bavarian population were against tuition fees (*Süddeutsche.de*, 2013), the CSU–FDP government was facing a defeat shortly before the 2013 federal state election. To prevent this and to increase the chances of winning the election, the controversial topic was removed from the election campaign by abolishing tuition fees before the election. To summarise, in Hesse and Bavaria it became obvious that tuition fees do not necessarily decide elections, but were nevertheless increasingly viewed by proponents as a risky election campaign issue. In political constellations where the election results are expected to be close, the CDU and the CSU responded by abandoning their support for tuition fees.

The abolition of tuition fees in the federal states can therefore be explained by different case scenarios and situational factors. The federal structure of the German higher education system means that the controversial nature of tuition fees is constantly being put in the foreground, frequent election campaigns provide the opportunity to abolish tuition fees, and tuition fees are increasingly viewed by their proponents as a risky campaign issue.

Summary and Discussion

Our chapter has been concerned with the question of why, in contrast to many other countries, there has been no universal introduction of tuition fees in Germany, and why, in the federal states they were introduced, they were abolished again. This is an anomaly within the German higher education system in so far as that since the late 1990s it has been subject to comprehensive New Public Management reforms and equally comprehensive processes of marketisation. In our chapter we have identified three distinct but closely related causes which in their interaction are responsible for this initially puzzling development.

First, tuition fees enjoy only limited legitimacy in the political and media discourse in Germany due to a broad-based welfare state tradition. The window of opportunity created by a wider acceptance of neo-liberal ideas in society in the late 1990s allowed the introduction in individual federal states, but closed again in the wake of the financial and banking crisis.

Second, this discourse has been shaped by studies from the social sciences focusing on the socially selective effects of the German education system as a whole. In the wake of the 'PISA shock', the social selectivity that had been highlighted by educational researchers since the 1970s shifted into the broader focus of politics and the general public.

Third, the federal system is of particular importance, since the introduction of tuition fees cannot be decreed by a central government, but must be introduced by 16 federal state governments on a case by case basis. Thus the subject of tuition fees became a permanent issue in political communication and turns into a politically risky election campaign issue several times a year for its proponents.

Finally, we would like to mention four perspectives, two concerning the conceptual level of research on tuition fees and similar subjects and two concerning the empirical level of comparisons and future developments.

First, our analysis suggests that the interweaving of the social systems of politics, education and science, and mass media played a central role in the rise and fall of tuition fees in Germany. The question here is how to grasp this interweaving conceptually (see also Weingart, 2001, 2002). On the one hand, the internal logic and diversity of the respective social systems would have to be understood more accurately. This means working out the specifics of scientific knowledge, mass media attention and political decisions in order to conceptually capture the fault lines and necessary translations between these systems. On the other hand, close linkages between these different systems are visible. Only these linkages produced the result that we analysed here. It is also important in view of the much-discussed 'crisis of the social sciences' to point out that it was education research – a social science – that in many ways shaped public discourse and political debate on tuition fees.

Second, the rise and fall of tuition fees can be seen as a failed institutionalisation process. From a neo-institutionalist perspective, institutionalisation can be understood in accordance with Berger and Luckmann (1966) as a process in which new practices gain legitimacy in order to become established as self-evident and unquestioned practices in society. This process also implies the deinstitutionalisation of existing practices. However, the institutionalisation of new practices failed due to different but connected causes, ranging from the low legitimacy within the institutional framework of welfare state culture, to the critical role of scientific research on the subject, and to the mechanisms of a federal system. But here there is also a need for conceptual effort beyond pure observation, an effort which takes account of the perspective provided by the interconnectedness of these factors and considers the processes of institutionalisation and deinstitutionalisation equally.

Third, and more aiming at the empirical level, is the question of the link between politics, science and education, and mass media, as well as of the institutionalisation and deinstitutionalisation of tuition fees in the higher education systems of other countries. The international perspective is particularly interesting from an empirical point of view because we can observe, in international comparison, an asynchronicity between marketisation developments. Thus, marketisation is not to be seen as an all-inclusive package, but allows multiple strategies to adapt to national contexts, which lead, for example, to tuition fees, unlike many other elements of marketisation, not becoming part of the German way.

Fourth, there is also the question of the future development of tuition fees in Germany. Considering the openness of societies to future options, which hardly allows for far-reaching predictions, it is hard to give an assessment here. Germany is a particularly good example because German reunification in 1990 and its impact on the development of the higher education system had not been anticipated by either politicians or by social scientists. However, tentative suggestions about the main diverging tendencies in the coming years are possible. On the one hand, the aspects described in our chapter will continue to hinder the institutionalisation of tuition fees in Germany. On the other hand, financial restrictions arising from the global financial crisis, the Euro crisis and the constitutional constraints of fiscal consolidation could create a situation in which tuition fees are again viewed – and this time maybe permanently – as a viable and potentially sustainable policy option.

Notes

[1] Other federal states (Bremen, North Rhine-Westphalia, and Rhineland-Palatinate) introduced so-called study account schemes, which also led to a fee of about €500 after exceeding a prescribed time limit.

[2] For example: discounts on public transport, privileges in social insurance, free health insurance via their parents, child benefit.

[3] The vast majority of universities in North Rhine-Westphalia decided on tuition fees of €500 (Hadamitzky et al, 2008; Hubner, 2012).

[4] The Stifterverband is private not-for-profit association for the German science system. Members of the Stifterverband are mainly business companies like BASF, Siemens or Deutsche Bank.

[5] The most influential and prestigious 'serious' national daily and weekly journals in Germany are: *Der Spiegel, Die Zeit, Süddeutsche Zeitung, Frankfurter Allgemeine Zeitung* (Wilke, 1999).

[6] After primary school, which all children attend, the German school system is divided into three branches: *Hauptschule, Realschule* and *Gymnasium*. Consequently, children are usually separated at the age of ten and then sent to one of the three school types, although considerable variation between the different federal states exists.

[7] It should be noted that since 2007 the number of new students also increased as a result of shortening the duration of schooling required to attain the *Abitur* (the usual qualification for higher education) from 13 years to 12 years. Consequently, there were 'double cohorts' of students in a number of federal states starting a degree course. But even after considering this effect, the adjusted number of young people starting a degree as a proportion of their cohort rose from 36.8% to 50.9% between 2007 and 2011 (BMBF, 2012c).

[8] This was also true for Hamburg until the winter semester of 2008-09. After that deferred fees of €375 were introduced.

[9] Students from families on low income can apply for funds for living expenses. Half the money is given as a loan and the rest as a grant that does not have to be paid back.

[10] Furthermore, most states had exemptions under certain circumstances. Students with children were usually exempt, although the age limit for the children varied between 8 and 14 years (Baden-Württemberg: 8 years; Bavaria: 10 years; Hamburg and Lower Saxony: 14 years; Saarland: 'students with small children'). Students with a disability were also exempt from tuition fees. In most cases an exemption was also possible if siblings were studying at a university with tuition fees (Ebcinoglu, 2006; Strate & Meyer, 2006).

[11] Universities did have the option to wave tuition fees for students with exceptionally good results (Ebcinoglu, 2006; Strate & Meyer, 2006).

References

Alecke, B. & Mitze, T. (2012) Studiengebühren und das Wanderungsverhalten von Studienanfängern. Eine panel-ökonometrische Wirkungsanalyse, *Perspektiven der Wirtschaftspolitik*, 13(4), 357-386.

Amaral, A., Meek, L.V. & Larsen, I.M. (Eds) (2003) *The Higher Education Managerial Revolution?* Dordrecht: Kluwer.

Artelt, C., Baumert, J., Klieme, E. et al (2001) *PISA 2000: Zusammenfassung zentraler Befunde*. Berlin: Max-Planck-Institut für Bildungsforschung.

Baier, T. & Helbig, M. (2011) War all die Aufregung umsonst? Über die Auswirkung der Einführung von Studiengebühren auf die Studienbereitschaft in Deutschland. Discussion Paper, Social Science Research Center Berlin (WZB), Forschungsschwerpunkt Projektgruppe bei der Präsidentin.

Baker, D.P. & Lenhardt, G. (2008) The Institutional Crisis of the German Research University, *Higher Education Policy*, 21(1), 49-64.

Bundesvereinigung der Deutschen Arbeitgeberverbände (BDA) (2004) *Studienbeiträge und die Reform der Studienfinanzierung. Ein Modellvorschlag*. Berlin: BDA.

Becker, R. (2011) Entstehung und Reproduktion dauerhafter Bildungsungleichheiten, in R. Becker (Ed.) *Lehrbuch der Bildungssoziologie*, pp. 87-138. Wiesbaden: VS Verlag.

Becker, R. & Hecken, A.E. (2008) Warum werden Arbeiterkinder vom Studium an Universitäten abgelenkt? Eine empirische Überprüfung der „Ablenkungsthese von Müller und Pollak (2007) und ihrer Erweiterung durch Hillmert und Jacob (2003), *KZfSS Kölner Zeitschrift für Soziologie und Sozialpsychologie*, 60(1), 3-29.

Berger, D.J. & Ehmann, C. (2000) Gebühren für Bildung – ein Anschlag auf die Chancengleichheit. Auswirkungen der Abschaffung und der Erhebung von Gebühren im deutschen Bildungswesen, *Recht der Jugend und des Bildungswesens*, 48(4), 356-376.

Berger, P.L. & Luckmann, T. (1966) *Social Construction of Reality: a treatise in the sociology of knowledge*. Garden City, NY: Anchor Books.

Biffl, G. &Isaak, J. (2002) Should Higher Education Students Pay Tuition Fees?, *European Journal of Education*, 37(4), 433-455.

Björklund, A. & Jäntti, M. (1997) Intergenerational Income Mobility in Sweden Compared to the United States, *American Economic Review*, 87(5), 1009-1018.

Bundesministerium für Bildung und Forschung (BMBF) (2012a) Datenportal. Anteil der Studienberechtigten an der 18- bis 20-jährigen Bevölkerung (Studienberechtigtenquote) nach Art der Hochschulreife. http://www.datenportal.bmbf.de/portal/Tabelle-2.5.85.html

Bundesministerium für Bildung und Forschung (BMBF) (2012b) Datenportal. Relative Anteile öffentlicher und privater Ausgaben für Bildungseinrichtungen nach Bildungsbereichen und Staaten. http://www.datenportal.bmbf.de/portal/Tabelle-2.1.6.html

Bundesministerium für Bildung und Forschung (BMBF) (2012c) Datenportal. Studienanfänger/-innen im 1. Hochschulsemester und Studienanfängerquoten nach Geschlecht und Land des Erwerbs der Hochschulzugangsberechtigung.' http://www.datenportal.bmbf.de/portal/Tabelle-2.5.73.html

Borgloh, S., Kupferschmidt, F. & Wigger, B.U. (2008) Verteilungseffekte der öffentlichen Finanzierung der Hochschulbildung in Deutschland: Eine Längsschnittbetrachtung auf der Basis des Sozioökonomischen Panels, *Jahrbücher für Nationalökonomie und Statistik*, 228(1), 25-48.

Brake, A. (2003) Worüber sprechen wir, wenn von PISA die Rede ist?, *Zeitschrift für Soziologie der Erziehung und Sozialisation*, 23(1), 24-39.

Brandle, T. (2010) *10 Jahre Bologna-Prozess: Chancen, Herausforderungen und Problematiken*. Wiesbaden: VS Verlag.

Braun, D. & Merrien, F.-X. (Eds) (1999) *Towards a New Model of Governance for Universities? A Comparative View*. London: Jessica Kingsley.

Butterwege, C. (2009) Hochschulen im Wettbewerbswahn: Wo bleibt die gesellschaftliche Verantwortung der Wissenschaft?, in K. Himpele & T. Bultmann (Eds) *Studiengebühren in der gesellschaftlichen Auseinandersetzung. 10 Jahre Aktionsbündnis gegen Studiengebühren (ABS). Rückblick und Ausblick*, pp. 25-31. Marburg: BdWi-Verl.

Bundesverfassungsgericht (BVerfG) (2005) 2 BvF 1/03 vom, January 26.

Bundesverfassungsgericht (BVerfG) (2013) 1 BvL 1/08 vom, May 8.

Carneiro, P. & Heckman, J.J. (2002) The Evidence on Credit Constraints in Post-secondary Schooling, *Economic Journal*, 112(482), 705-734.

de Boer, H., Enders, J. & Schimank, U. (2007) On the Way Towards New Public Management? The Governance of University Systems in England, the Netherlands, Austria, and Germany, in D. Jansen (Ed.) *New Forms of Governance in Research Organizations. Disciplinary Approaches, Interfaces and Integration*, pp. 137-152. Dordrecht: Springer.

Der Stern (2007) Mit Studiengebühren Kredite bezahlt. February 22.

Der Tagesspiegel (2010) Kritik an Verwendung von Studiengebühren: Studierende bezahlen den Bachelor. August 18.

Deutsche Universitätszeitung (Ed.) (1996) *Studiengebühren Pro und Contra*. Bonn: Raabe.

Deutscher Bundestag (2012) Drucksache 17/8301. http://dipbt.bundestag.de/dip21/btd/17/083/1708301.pdf

Deutsches PISA-Konsortium (2001) *PISA 2000. Basiskompetenzen von Schülerinnen und Schülern im internationalen Vergleich*. Opladen: Leske & Budrich.

Dilger, A. (1999) Quo vadis, Studiengebühren? Kritische Anmerkungen, *Forschung & Lehre*, 6(8), 403-404.

Dohmen, D. (2004) Hochschulfinanzierung zwischen Gutscheinen und Studiengebühren, *Das Hochschulwesen*, 52(4), 130-137.

Ebcinoglu, F. (2006) *Die Einführung allgemeiner Studiengebühren in Deutschland*. Hannover: Hochschul-Informations-System (HIS).

Ederer, P., Kopf, C., Schuler, P. & Ziegele, F. (2000) *Umverteilung von unten nach oben durch gebührenfreie Hochschulausbildung: Materialsammlung*. Gütersloh: Centrum für Hochschulentwicklung (CHE).

Ertl, H. (2005) Higher Education in Germany. A Case of 'Uneven' Expansion, *Higher Education Quarterly*, 59(3), 205-229.

Fahrholz, B., Sigmar, G. & Müller, P. (Eds) (2002) *Nach dem Pisa-Schock: Plädoyers für eine Bildungsreform.* Hamburg: Hoffmann und Campe.

Forsa Gesellschaft für Sozialforschung und statistische Analyse mbH (FORSA) (2003) *Akzeptanz von Studiengebühren. Ergebnisse einer forsa-Umfrage in der Bevölkerung und bei Studierenden.* Berlin: FORSA.

Freeman, J., Carroll, G.R. & Hannan, M.T. (1983) The Liability of Newness: age dependence in organizational death rates, *American Sociological Review*, 48(5), 692-710.

Geißler, R. (2004) Die Illusion der Chancengleichheit im Bildungssystem von PISA gestört, *Zeitschrift für Soziologie der Erziehung und Sozialisation*, 24(4), 362-380.

Glotz, P. (1996) *Im Kern verrottet? Fünf vor zwölf an Deutschlands Universitäten.* Stuttgart: Deutsche Verlagsanstalt.

Grüske, K.-D. (1994) Verteilungseffekte der öffentlichen Hochschulfinanzierung in der Bundesrepublik Deutschland. Personale Inzidenz im Querschnitt und Längsschnitt, in R. Lüdeke (Ed.) *Bildung, Bildungsfinanzierung und Einkommensverteilung*, pp. 71-147. Berlin: Duncker und Humblot.

Hadamitzky, A., Geist, A. & von Blanckenburg, K. (2008) Studiengebührenmodelle in der Praxis, *Das Hochschulwesen*, 56(1), 6-11.

Hannoversche Allgemeine (2012) Studiengebühren bringen keinen Qualitätsgewinn. January 24.

Hartmann, M. (2006) Chancengleichheit trotz Studiengebühren: Die USA als Vorbild?, *Aus Politik und Zeitgeschichte*, 48, 32-38.

Heine, C., Quast, H. & Spangenberg, H. (2008) *Studiengebühren aus der Sicht von Studienberechtigten. Finanzierung und Auswirkungen auf Studienpläne und -strategien.* Hannover: Hochschul-Informations-System (HIS).

Herzog, M. & Kehm, B.M. (2012) The Income Situation in the German System of Higher Education. A Rag Rug, in P.G. Altbach, L. Reisberg, M. Yudkevich, G. Androushchak & I.F. Pacheco (Eds) *Paying the Professoriate: a global comparison of compensation and contracts*, pp. 145-154. London: Routledge.

Hubner, M. (2012) Do Tuition Fees Affect Enrollment Behavior? Evidence from a 'Natural Experiment' in Germany, *Economics of Education Review*, 31(6), 949-960.

Hüther, O. (2010) *Von der Kollegialität zur Hierarchie? Eine Analyse des New Managerialism in den Landeshochschulgesetzen.* Wiesbaden: VS Verlag.

Hüther, O. & Krücken, G. (2013) Hierarchy and Power: a conceptual analysis with particular reference to new public management reforms in German universities, *European Journal of Higher Education*, 3(4), 307-323. http://dx.doi.org/10.1080/21568235.2013.850920

Kane, T.J. (1994) College Entry by Blacks Since 1970: the role of college costs, family background, and the returns to education, *Journal of Political Economy*, 102(5), 878-911.

Kehm, B.M. & Lanzendorf, U. (2006) Germany – 16 länder approaches to reform, in B.M. Kehm & U. Lanzendorf (Eds) *Reforming University Governance. Changing Conditions for Research in Four European Countries*, pp. 135-185. Bonn: Lemmens.

König, C. (2006) Verhandelte Hochschulsteuerung. 10 Jahre Zielvereinbarung zwischen den Bundesländern und ihren Hochschulen, *die hochschule*, 15(2), 34-54.

Krämer, W. (1999) Falscher Ruf nach Gerechtigkeit. Ohne Studiengebühren bezahlen Arme den Reichen das Studium, *Forschung & Lehre*, 6(8), 401-402.

Krause, Norbert (2008) *Die Debatte um Studiengebühren. Systematische Rekonstruktion eines rapiden Meinungswandels.* Wiesbaden: VS Verlag.

Krücken, G., Kosmützky, A. & Torka, M. (Eds) (2007a) *Towards a Multiversity? Universities between Global Trends and National Traditions.* Bielefeld: Transcript Verlag.

Krücken, G., Meier, F. & Müller, A. (2007b) Information, Cooperation, and the Blurring of Boundaries – technology transfer in German and American discourses, *Higher Education*, 53(6), 675-696.

Lieb, W. (2009) Studiengebühren und unternehmerische Hochschule, in K. Himpele & T. Bultmann (Eds) *Studiengebühren in der gesellschaftlichen Auseinandersetzung. 10 Jahre Aktionsbündnis gegen Studiengebühren (ABS). Rückblick und Ausblick*, pp. 55-63. Marburg: BdWi-Verl.

Loeber, H.-D. & Scholz, W.-D. (2003) Von der Bildungskatastrophe zum PISA-Schock. Zur Kontinuität sozialer Benachteiligung durch das deutsche Bildungssystem, in B. Moschner, H. Kiper & U. Kattmann (Eds) *Perspektiven für Lehren und Lernen. PISA 2000 als Herausforderung*, pp. 241-286. Hohengehren: Schneider-Verlag.

Marcucci, P.N. & Johnstone, D.B. (2007) Tuition Fee Policies in a Comparative Perspective: theoretical and political rationales, *Journal of Higher Education Policy and Management*, 29(1), 25-40.

Müller-Böling, D. (1995) *Deutscher Studienfonds zur Qualitätssicherung der Hochschulen.* Gütersloh: Centrum für Hochschulentwicklung (CHE).

Müller, W. & Pollak, R. (2007) Weshalb gibt es so wenige Arbeiterkinder in Deutschlands Universitäten?, in R. Becker & W. Lauterbach (Eds) *Bildung als Privileg*, pp. 303-342. Wiesbaden: VS Verlag.

Münch, R. (2006) Wissenschaft im Schatten von Kartell, Monopol und Oligarchie. Die latenten Effekte der Exzellenzinitiative, *Leviathan*, 34(4), 466-486.

Organisation for Economic Cooperation and Development (OECD) (2012) *Education at a Glance 2012.* Paris: OECD.

Paradeise, C., Bleiklie, I., Ferlie, E. & Reale, E. (Eds) (2009) *University Governance: Western European comparative perspectives.* Dordrecht: Springer.

Quast, H., Spangenberg, H., Hannover, B. & Braun, E. (2012) Determinanten der Studierbereitschaft unter besonderer Berücksichtigung von Studiengebühren, *Zeitschrift für Erziehungswissenschaft*, 15(2), 305-326.

Reiter, M. (1997) Studiengebühren – Abschied von der offenen Universität. Argumente wider Studiengebühren, *Kurswechsel*, 12(2), 125-133.

Schindler, S. & Reimer, D. (2010) Primäre und sekundäre Effekte der sozialen Herkunft beim Übergang in die Hochschulbildung, *KZfSS Kölner Zeitschrift für Soziologie und Sozialpsychologie*, 62(4), 623-653.

Schnitzer, K., Isserstedt, W. & Middendorff, E. (2001) Die wirtschaftliche und soziale Lage der Studierenden in der Bundesrepublik Deutschland 2000. 16. Sozialerhebung des Deutschen Studentenwerks durchgeführt durch Hochschul-Informations-System (HIS). Bonn: Bundesministerium für Bildung und Forschung (BMBF). Source: GESIS - Social Indicators Monitor (SIMon), German System of Social Indicators (accessed 13 September 2014).

Schubert, T. & Schmoch, U. (2010) Finanzierung der Hochschulforschung, in D. Simon, A. Knie & S. Hornbostel (Eds) *Handbuch Wissenschaftspolitik*, pp. 244-261. Wiesbaden: VS Verlag.

Schwager, R. (2005) PISA – Schock und Hochschulmisere. Hat der deutsche Bildungsföderalismus versagt?, *Perspektiven der Wirtschaftspolitik*, 6(2), 189-205.

Schwanitz, D. (1999) Symbolisches oder reales Kapital? Zur Frage der Studiengebühren, *Forschung & Lehre*, 6(8), 396-398.

Spiegel Online (2011a) Studiengebühren: Blindflug bei der Verteilung. January 7.

Spiegel Online (2011b) Verwendung von Studiengebühren: Geld für Googeln und Geschenke. April 26.

Spiegel Online (2012) Ratloses Bildungsministerium: Nützen Studiengebühren? Keine Ahnung. January 24.

Statistisches Bundesamt (2001-2011) *Bildung und Kultur. Finanzen der Hochschulen.* Wiesbaden: Statistisches Bundesamt.

Statistisches Bundesamt (2004) *Bildung und Kultur. Studierende an Hochschulen.* Wiesbaden: Statistisches Bundesamt.

Statistisches Bundesamt (2005) *Bildung und Kultur. Studierende an Hochschulen.* Wiesbaden: Statistisches Bundesamt.

Statistisches Bundesamt (2012a) *Bildung und Kultur. Studierende an Hochschulen.* Wiesbaden: Statistisches Bundesamt.

Statistisches Bundesamt (2012b) *Bildungsfinanzbericht 2012.* Wiesbaden: Statistisches Bundesamt.

Stifterverband für die Deutsche Wissenschaft, and Centrum für Hochschulentwicklung (CHE) (1998) *Modell für einen Beitrag der Studierenden zur Finanzierung der Hochschulen (Studienbeitragsmodell).* Gütersloh, Essen: CHE und Stifterverband.

Stinchcombe, A.L. (1965) Social Structure and Organizations, in J.G. March (Ed.) *The Handbook of Organizations*, pp. 153-193. Chicago: Rand McNally.

Stölting, E. & Schimank, U. (Eds) (2001) *Die Krise der Universitäten.* Wiesbaden: Westdeutscher Verlag.

Strate, G. & Meyer, S. (2006) *Studienfinanzierung – Modelle und Möglichkeiten. Studiendarlehen, Studienkredite, Bildungsfonds, Studiengebührenausnahmeregelungen und Stipendiendatenbanken. Info-Brief / Wissenschaftliche Dienste des Deutschen Bundestages.* Berlin: Deutscher Bundestag.

Süddeutsche.de (2011) Bayerns Hochschulen sollen Millionen horten. December 13.

Süddeutsche.de (2013) Mehrheit gegen Studiengebühren. January 9.

Telepolis (2010) Studiengebühren, ein Wintermärchen. December 23.

Terwey, M. & Baltzer, S. (2012) *ALLBUS 1980-2010. Variable Report.* Cologne: GESIS.

Weingart, P. (2001) *Die Stunde der Wahrheit? Zum Verhältnis der Wissenschaft zu Politik, Wirtschaft und Medien.* Weilerwist: Velbrück Wissenschaft.

Weingart P. (2002) The Loss of Distance: science in transition, in G.E. Allen & R.M. MacLeod (Eds) *Science, History and Social Activism: a tribute to Everett Mendelsohn*, pp. 167-184. Dordrecht: Kluwer.

Wilke, J. (1999) Leitmedien und Zielgruppenorgane, in J. Wilke *Mediengeschichte der Bundesrepublik Deutschland*, pp. 302-329. Cologne: Böhlau.

Zöllner, J.E. (1999) Wettbewerbsverzerrend und wissenschaftsfeindlich, *Forschung & Lehre*, 6(8), 399-400.

CHAPTER 5

Access to Dutch Higher Education: issues of tuition fees and student financial support

HANS VOSSENSTEYN

ABSTRACT This chapter analyses access and study success in Dutch higher education with relation to developments in tuition fees and student financial support. The long-standing tradition of cost-sharing in Dutch higher education through tuition fees and a system of 'direct support to students' with a growing reliance on student loans provides an interesting case to estimate the impact of financial incentives on student choice and study behaviour. Particularly since 1986, public policies have sought a right balance between private and public responsibilities with regard to higher education financing, as well as setting incentives for efficient study behaviour. In this respect, tuition fees have been continuously increased since 1986 and the system of student financial support has been altered many times, e.g. by introducing a public transport card, performance requirements, reducing grants, increasing loans, etc. This chapter will explore whether and how this has had an impact on the demand for higher education and the choices students make within a wider context of access policies. The overall conclusion is that gradual changes in the financial conditions for students do not have a strong impact on access, and that, while stronger financial shocks may stimulate risk and debt aversion, they appear to only have temporary effects on access. The first section provides a brief overview of Dutch higher education and entrance routes into the system. The succeeding sections will discuss tuition policies, student financial support arrangements and the impact of both on access and study success. The chapter ends with broader conclusions.

Higher Education in the Netherlands

Until the mid-1980s, Dutch higher education consisted only of traditional research universities. The system was transformed in 1984 into a binary system by upgrading former upper secondary professional schools into a sector of non-university professional higher education institutions (*hogescholen*), now called Universities of Applied Sciences (UAS). Currently there are 13 traditional research universities. The research universities include nine general universities, three universities specialising in engineering and one in the area of agriculture. The research universities prepare students for independent scientific work in an academic or professional setting. Additionally, a number of small 'designated institutions' are part of the university sector: a private university for business administration (Nijenrode), four institutes for theology, a humanist university, as well as several international education institutes. These are formally part of the system, but are usually not included in educational statistics.

The UAS sector consists of 39 institutions, including teacher training institutions, colleges of art, technical schools and more comprehensive professional institutions (Kaiser & Vossensteyn, 2005). The UAS sector has been an answer to the massification of higher education since the mid-1960s and primarily had a teaching and no research function. They also offer more part-time and professional programmes that fit the labour market's needs and the Dutch economy in general. In order to make the *hogescholen* efficient and effective, the previous 350 vocational schools were merged in two waves resulting in only 39 publicly funded ones currently.

In addition to the universities and the UAS institutions, students can follow publicly funded tertiary education at the Open University (OU). The OU offers a wide range of courses which may lead to both formal university and higher professional education degrees. Furthermore, the Netherlands has a large number of private teaching institutes and organisations that offer recognised certificates, diplomas and degrees in various professional fields such as accountancy and business administration. Quite often these are structured as 'external studies' in the sense of correspondence and/or distance learning courses with limited face-to-face interaction.

Pathways to Higher Education

In the Netherlands, access to higher education is organised through a number of secondary education pathways including a few levels and orientations. The minimum access requirement to enter a bachelor's programme at one of the UAS is either a HAVO diploma (Hoger Algemeen Vormend Onderwijs, a five-year general upper secondary education diploma) or an MBO diploma (Middelbaar Beroepsonderwijs, a four-year secondary vocational education diploma). Disciplinary programmes may require some pre-knowledge. Both types of school leavers can also enter the relatively new associate degree programmes at one of the UAS institutions, which are short cycle two-year programmes that lead to a professional qualification, as well as access to the final two years of a related UAS bachelor programme.

To enter the more academically oriented university bachelor's programmes students require a six-year VWO diploma (Voorbereidend Wetenschappelijk Onderwijs, a six-year pre-university diploma) or a completed first year (60 credits) of a bachelor's programme at one of the UAS. The VWO diploma also grants access to UAS institutions.

As an exception to the rule, prospective higher education students of 21 years or over may be admitted to higher education after passing a special entrance examination (*colloquium doctum*) which tests if other previously acquired competences enables them to enter higher education.

All master's programmes require a bachelor's degree in one or more specific and connected disciplines, in some cases in combination with other requirements, like a high grade point average for 'research master's'.

The OU admits all applicants of 18 years and over regardless of their previous qualifications. As such, the OU is regarded as providing 'second chance' education, though most of the OU students already hold a higher education degree.

In general, access to Dutch higher education is based on the principle of 'open access'. This means that all students with the right entrance qualification can attend the study programme and institution they prefer. However, there are a few limitations to this rule. Firstly, any higher education programmes require students to have completed one of the four specific subject clusters of courses (*profiles*) in secondary education. Secondly, there are a few programmes with a limited number of study places. These so-called *numerus fixus programmes* – such as medicine, veterinary medicine, dentistry, life sciences, architecture, journalism and physiotherapy – have a maximum number of first-year students to be admitted and generally select their students. The maximum quota can be set at national or institutional level. Selection takes place through a central admissions system in which grade point average, a weighted lottery, as well as institutional soft selection criteria – such as motivation letters and intake interviews – play a role.

All in all, the general policy context has been inviting institutions to attract large numbers of students. Financial incentives – to be discussed in the next section – stimulate institutions and students to successfully complete their studies within a limited time frame with quality being guaranteed through a long-standing well-elaborated quality assurance system including programme and institutional accreditation (Vossensteyn & Westerheijden, 2013). In times when many countries show decreasing student numbers, the Netherlands has a still growing higher education system, both in absolute and relative terms.

Tuition Fee Policies

Tuition fees are a part of the general funding philosophy of higher education in the Netherlands. Since the existence of universities, students have had to pay a contribution to the costs of education, though the government generally pays the largest share of the costs.

Public universities and UAS institutions receive public funding for the provision of accredited and recognised study programmes and for research. The total national budget for higher education is annually set by the Minister of Education, Culture and Science, with separate budgets for the UAS sector and for universities. The latter budget is subdivided into a part for teaching (1/3) and a part for research (2/3). In 2011, one universal funding model for teaching replaced the previously different systems for universities and UAS institutions. The funding principles have remained roughly the same (since 1993) with allocating funds for students that are within the nominal duration of a programme and for the successful completion of bachelor's and master's degrees. Institutions thus can increase their budget by increasing their market share of students, by stimulating study progress and by high completion rates. If one considers the policy of open access, one can imagine that it is particularly interesting for higher education institutions to expand participation of underrepresented groups. Funding takes the form of block grants which can be spent by higher education institutions at their own discretion.

The Netherlands represents the very few countries with a long history of tuition fees. Since the establishment of universities, full-time students in publicly funded higher education have had to pay a statutory universal tuition fee, regardless of the costs related to different study programmes. Having students pay part of the costs could always count on wide political support, as long as fees would not harm access. These fees apply to all Dutch and European Union (EU) full-time students who study for the nominal duration (plus 1 year) of a degree programme and who start before the age of 30. The government annually sets the level of the statutory fees by law, leading to an annual increase in line with the consumer price index or slightly higher. The statutory tuition fee is €1835 for the academic year 2013-14. Tuition fees account for between 15% and 22% of the teaching costs, which in both universities and UAS are around €8000 per year (as calculated by the Centraal Planbureau [Netherlands Bureau for Economic Policy Analysis; CPB], 2013). Students pay their fees directly to the institutions, who can then use these revenues according to their own priorities. Students can pay their fees in one amount at the beginning of the academic year or spread the payments in four or even twelve instalments throughout the year.

The developments in the level of tuition fees are shown in Figure 1. The time series starts in 1945 to demonstrate the clear policy changes that took place over time. The real value of the tuition fees declined in the 1945-1971 period because the nominal fee rate was kept stable at 200 Dutch Guilders (NLG) (€91) per academic year. It gradually became a sort of a symbolic private contribution to the costs of higher education. In 1971, the government proposed several reforms to make higher education better serve the needs of students and the labour market. It was also proposed to raise tuition fees to a more substantial and realistic level representing better the shared interests of society and students, as well as to help pay for the continuously increasing higher education costs resulting from the strong growth in student numbers. As such, the fees were increased to NLG 1000 (€454) in 1972-73. However, the government could not agree on a student financial support system that would guarantee more equal access. This led to massive student protests and political pressure claiming that it was unacceptable to strongly increase study costs while hardly any students would be financially compensated through scholarships. Therefore the tuition level was halved to NLG 500 (€227) between 1974 and 1980. Since then, tuition levels have gradually increased to €1835 in 2013-14.

Figure 1 shows that except for the tuition shock in 1972 – followed by a 50% reduction in 1974 – tuition fees have gradually increased over time, particularly in the period since 1986. If one bears in mind that, over time, the inflation rate in the Netherlands varies between 1-2.5% annually, one can read from this graph that tuition increases in various years were bigger than inflation. As a result, a larger share of the cost of higher education has gradually been shifted to students. Most of the ongoing policy debate has been about government proposals to increase tuition fees, while student unions and some political parties – particularly the Labour Party – have argued to abolish or reduce tuition fees (Vossensteyn, 1997, 2002).

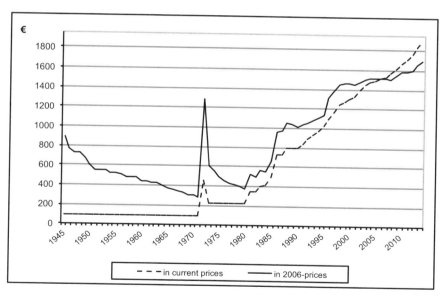

Figure 1. Changes in tuition fees (€, in current and real prices).
Source: My calculations based on official data (Annual announcements by the Ministry of Education; Ministerie van Onderwijs en Wetenschappen, 2013). Real prices are based on consumer price index (2006).

Particularly during the 1980s, the then Christian Democratic government argued that tuition fees constitute a 'fair' private contribution to the costs of higher education, which brings individual students considerable future rewards (monetary, as well as non-monetary). Given the economic recession, there was a strong political call for public budget reductions. In addition, it was argued that higher socio-economic groups are heavily overrepresented in higher education. Therefore higher education subsidies concern a societal transfer of the 'poor' to the current and future rich in society. But the opponents of fees continuously argued that additional fees would harm access, particularly for those from lower socio-economic backgrounds (Vossensteyn, 1997). Also during the 1990s, this led to many heated political debates on how to finance the continuously growing higher education system. As a good Dutch tradition, such debates generally end in compromises that include moderate tuition increases accompanied by full compensation for lower-income students through means-tested grants and loans (Vossensteyn, 2005, 2013). Regardless of the continuous discussions about the potential negative impact of tuition fees (and student loans) on access, the Dutch government continued its policy of gradual tuition increases. As will be explained in following sections, participation in higher education continued to increase.

Differential Tuition Fees

Other major discussions related to a potential introduction of differential tuition fees, particularly when an inter-ministerial working group explored this issue in 2002-03 (Interdepartementaal Beleidsonderzoek [IBO], 2003). The government wanted to allow institutions to charge higher contributions in return for enhanced quality programmes, and to make particular subjects like science, engineering and teacher training more attractive by possibly reducing tuition fees. However, again, opponents feared that this would harm access for poor students and it was questioned – particularly by labour-oriented parties – whether abandoning the equity principle, not to mention the public costs involved, could be justified by the expected number of extra students attracted to the desired programmes. For example, it was found that abolishing fees for science and engineering would increase student numbers by only a few hundred, while costing the state millions of Euros (Felsö et al, 2000; Van den Broek & Voeten, 2002).

Different Fee Regimes for Specific Target Groups

In contrast to the uniform statutory tuition fees for regular full-time students, part-time students are required to pay higher tuition fees, ranging between €1835 and €5000 per year, depending on the programme and institution. Students who are not eligible for student financial support, as well as non-EU foreign students, may have to pay up to the full costs of education, with tuition fees of up to €15,000 per year. This is also the case for the more recently established professional master's programmes at UAS institutions.

Together with the new funding model for teaching in 2011, it was decided to charge students who exceed the nominal duration of a study programme by more than one year a penalty fee of €3000 extra per additional year studied – the so called *Langstudeerdersboete* (Tweede Kamer der Staten Generaal, 2011). This regulation was introduced on 1 September 2012. For these students the institutions would receive €3000 less public funding. Though many students really speeded up to complete their studies 'in time', many others failed to do so and had to pay the additional €3000. However, from the start, many students complained about mistakes made by the institutions leading to study delays. University councils supported these students which resulted in various costly compensation arrangements for universities and UAS institutions. Therefore, heavy political pressure led to the withdrawal of the *Langstudeerdersboete* from 1 January 2013. The envisaged public savings since then are planned through transforming the basic grants given to all full-time students into loans, as will be discussed in the next section.

Student Financial Support Policies

The developments in student financial support resemble a similar pattern as the developments in tuition fees that, particularly since the mid-1980s, reflect the political preferences towards a situation of cost-sharing. Since 1945, successive Dutch governments have developed an increasingly sophisticated system of student support, though with a change of focus over the following six decades (Regt, 1993; Vossensteyn, 2013). In the period until the mid-1980s, the major aim of student support was to open up opportunities for small numbers of talented low-income students through limited bursary and loans programmes which became available to a slowly increasing number of recipients. Financial support consisted mainly of indirect support via tax benefits and family allowances for the parents of students.

However, during the 1970s, student unions argued in favour of more financial independence for students, and with the 1984 government coalition, the new envisaged Minister of Education – Deetman – would only take office if he could 'finally solve the student financing issue' (Vossensteyn, 1997). As such, in 1986, he implemented a new and relatively generous system of student financial support by means of the Student Finance Act (WSF). This system transformed all indirect support like tax benefits and family allowances into direct financial support to students themselves. The system established a compromise between access, students' financial independence, system transparency and simplicity, and affordability for the government (Hupe & Van Solm, 1998). The major characteristics of the system – that is still largely in place today – are reflected in the following basic elements: (a) a basic grant (*basisbeurs*) for all full-time students; (b) a means-tested supplementary grant for about 30% of the students (students from wealthier families are supposed to receive this in the form of 'parental contribution'; (c) loans that can be taken up on a voluntary basis, carrying a below-market interest rate; and (d) a certain annual amount that students can earn before they lose part of their grant entitlements. All components together add up to the normative budget that the Ministry annually calculates as the amount students need for their study and living costs. From this perspective, no (full-time) student should face financial barriers to participate in higher education. However, the government budget has been under continuous pressure and participation in higher education continuously increased (in absolute and relative numbers). This resulting financial pressure, as well as the wish to link student support to study success, triggered a host of changes made to the original system (Vossensteyn, 1997, 2002, 2005, 2008). The major changes to the system can be clustered around the following themes: (a) a straightforward development towards cost-sharing; and (b) a development towards performance orientation.

Development Towards Cost-sharing

Along with the tendency to gradually increase tuition fees and make students pay a larger share of the cost of higher education, the level of basic grants has also been reduced several times, particularly in 1991 and in 1996. In addition, the duration of grants was also reduced in two successive steps (1991 and 1996) from the nominal duration of courses plus two years to the nominal duration only. This remained the same with the implementation of the bachelor—master structure in 2002 in the Netherlands. All increases in tuition fees and decreases in basic grants – as well as inflation corrections – have been compensated by increasing the supplementary grants (to guarantee access for students from disadvantaged backgrounds) or by increasing the amount and share of student loans. In addition, the government started to charge interest on student loans in 1991 as many students just used student loans to gain interest over their own savings accounts. The loan take-up rate immediately decreased from 80% to 20% in 1991. Currently, about 60% of students take up a loan; others would rather undertake part-time employment (Vossensteyn, 2013). Since 1995, students have been permitted to replace the (assumed) parental contributions with student loans if parents do not contribute. In 2007, the student support system was expanded with an additional loan facility through which students could also borrow their tuition fees (*collegegeldkrediet*). This tuition credit was a real top-up and remedied the fall in the real value of financial support that took place over the preceding years (Vossensteyn, 1997, 2008). It also solved the long-standing issue that the Dutch government had to provide basic grants to mobile EU students to compensate them for the Dutch tuition fees (Vossensteyn, 2008).

Implementation of Performance Requirements

To make the system more efficient and stimulate students to perform better, the minister introduced performance requirements within the student financial support system in two successive steps. This would push inactive students ('no-show' students) out of the system and would make other students study faster and more successfully. As such, in 1993, the so-called 'progress-related grant' (*Tempobeurs*) was introduced which regulated that students who would not pass 25% of the annual study credits would see their grants being converted into interest-bearing loans (Hupe & Van Solm, 1998). In 1996, the system was intensified through the 'performance-related grant' (*Prestatiebeurs*). Since then, all grants have been awarded initially as loans, and only if students pass 50% of the exams in the first-year and complete their degree within the nominal duration of the programme plus two years, will their initial loans will be converted into a grant. This fitted very well with the logic of public funding to universities which since 1993 allocated 50% of the teaching funds based on the number of degrees conferred.

The Current Student Financing System

The developments in the previous decades resulted in the following student financial support system for Dutch students under the age of 30 years enrolled in accredited or recognised full-time higher education programmes in the Netherlands or abroad. All student support is administered by a central agency, called *Dienst Uitvoering Onderwijs* (DUO).

All full-time students receive the basic grant regardless of parental income. Students living away from their parents receive a higher amount than students living at their parents' house (€272.46 and €97.85 per month respectively in 2013). In addition, all students can take up a voluntary interest-bearing loan up to the maximum of €288.66 per month, as well as a special tuition fee loan (*collegegeldkrediet*) of €152.92 per month. The supplementary grant is means-tested which implies that only students from lower income parents are entitled to it (around 30% of the student population) with a maximum of €252.17 per month. Students who are not eligible for the supplementary grant, or a part of it, are expected to receive the remaining share from their parents. If parents are not willing to contribute, the student may take out this part as a loan as well. When students lose their entitlements to grants, such as if they exceed the nominal duration of studies, they can take all support in the form of loans for a maximum period of 36 months. All students eligible for financial aid are entitled to a public transport pass (a personalised smart card), giving unrestricted free travel on public transport throughout the Netherlands either during working days or during the weekend.

Students are allowed to earn a gross income of €13,530.90 (correct as of 2013) from employment without their grants being affected. However, if their income exceeds this amount, they will have to repay (part of) their grants. Students can prevent such a claim by not applying for financial support that year. As discussed above, the basic grant and supplementary grant are performance-dependent (*Prestatiebeurs*) and are initially paid out in the form of a loan. If a student graduates within 10 years, the loan is converted into a non-repayable grant.

In principle, all student debt must be repaid. All loans accumulate interest from the moment students take them out. The interest rate is the rate the Dutch government pays to the National Bank plus a small administrative surcharge. This normally results in a very low interest rate (in 2012 and 2013 only 0.6%; in the previous decade on average around 3.5%). After graduation, graduates have a 'grace period' of two years in which they do not need to make any repayments. After that, repayment is spread out over a period of 15 years according to a mortgage-style repayment schedule with fixed monthly instalments and a minimum monthly amount of €45. If graduate income is low, one can annually apply for a temporary repayment reduction including a means test. All remaining debt after 15 years repayment is cancelled. In total, about 3% of outstanding debt is not repaid (Centraal bureau voor de Statistiek [CBS], 2012).

Towards a System of 'Social Loans'

The current student support system is under debate. Due to the financial crisis, the Dutch government set severe budget reduction targets in 2012. Most political parties agreed to change the student financial support system through replacing grants with 'social loans' with an income-based repayment scheme. The first idea was to introduce such social loans for all master's students from 1 September 2012. However, due to the fall of the government in spring 2012, the implementation was postponed. However, the massive protests against the *Langstudeerdersboete* and its successive abolishment (see the previous section) put the political debate on 'social loans facility' in a new and different perspective. The new minister in early 2013 proposed a system that would replace all basic grants for bachelor's and master's students with loans and an income-related repayment scheme following the examples of Australia and England (Tweede Kamer der Staten Generaal, 2013). As expected, a strong public debate followed, focusing on the potential harm to access for students from weaker socio-economic backgrounds. However, most stakeholders, including students, were mainly discussing what requirements are necessary to make a system of social loans acceptable. Regardless of the fact that many political parties supported such a measure, the political power battles in Parliament and the Senate about the various proposals on reducing public spending made the minister postpone the implementation of a full social loans system (Apperloo, 2013). It now is envisaged to implement a 'social loans system' in 2015.

Overall, taking into account the long-term developments in tuition fees and student financial support, one can conclude that there has been a gradual shift towards increased cost-sharing in the Netherlands. Tuition fee rates have gradually increased, both in nominal and real terms. In addition, though in 1986 a relatively generous system of student financial support was introduced, over time there has been a shift from grants to loans and performance requirements were introduced. As such, based on general claims that cost-sharing may harm access, one would expect that these changes constituting deteriorated financial conditions for students have had a negative impact on access and participation, particularly for students from disadvantaged backgrounds. This will be explored in the following sections.

The Impact of Financial Incentives on Students

Analysing the impact of financial incentives like tuition fees, grants and loans can be done in various ways. In this chapter, we will look at general participation patterns, access of students from various backgrounds and study success in terms of study progress and completion for different groups of students.

Impact on Participation in General

As discussed in the previous sections, the emphasis on private contributions to the costs of higher education by students and their parents has gradually increased in the Netherlands resulting in a clear example of cost-sharing which has negatively affected the financial position of students. One would expect this to lead to problems of access to higher education. As in other countries, potential access problems related to tuition fees and student financial support have been popular topics for public and political debates in the Netherlands. However, participation in higher education has continuously increased, both in absolute numbers and in terms of transition ratios and participation rates. In the academic year 2012-13, 662,840 students were enrolled in Dutch public higher education, 241,321 at the 13 research universities, and 421,519 at the 39 UAS (CBS, 2013). Figure 2 shows enrolment in Dutch higher education since 1950 as the proportion of all 17-22 year-olds.

Figure 2 shows some interesting developments. Between 1950 and 2012, the number of higher education students increased tremendously both in absolute numbers and as a proportion of the relevant age group (17-22 year olds). Figure 2 also shows that the UAS sector has always been larger and hosts over 60% of all higher education students. The growth of the UAS sector became steeper than in the university sector since the UAS sector was officially recognised as higher education in 1984. The ambition to expand and widen higher education by offering a 'cheap' alternative to university education has been achieved. The Committee on the Future Sustainability of Dutch Higher Education confirmed this success as it stated that the UAS sector plays a crucial role in educating large numbers of highly qualified professionals that are strongly appreciated in the labour market (Veerman et al, 2010).

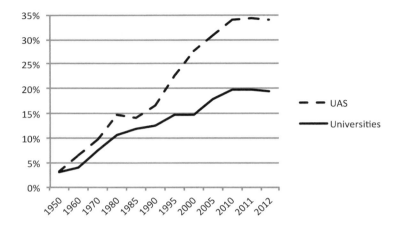

Figure 2. Total enrolment in Dutch higher education since 1950 (x1000 and as % of 17-22 year olds). *Source*: CBS, 2013.

Relating these data to the information presented on the developments in tuition fees and student financial support, one can argue that the development towards cost-sharing has not had a major impact on access to higher education. During the first wave of massification in the 1960s and 1970s, students did not receive generous financial support. Participation patterns also do not show any reaction to the 'tuition shock' in 1972. After financial support was made much more generous in 1987, participation kept on growing, particularly in the UAS sector, but, surprisingly, less strong in the university sector. Actually, the slope of the university participation curve shows an interesting tendency in the 1990s: a slight decrease in absolute numbers and stabilisation in the participation rate – the latter particularly since 1994. This stabilisation can be partially explained by student financing policies. With the introduction of performance incentives in the allocation of basic grants (see previous section), university students started to study faster which reduced the total volume of students. In addition, the 1996 performance related grant also made students more cautious in their choices: many university qualified students opted for study programmes at one of the UAS as they were perceived to be 'easier' and thus generated less financial risk. Some other students postponed their choice for a year and students enrolling in university, but not actively studying, just left the system. However, after a few years, traditional study choice patterns became re-established (Vossensteyn, 2005).

Since 2010, the number of enrolments has stabilised, both in universities and UAS. This has happened due to demographic developments and the fact that most qualifying students already attend higher education. Growth can hardly be found among traditional groups anymore. However, in 2013, the number of applicants increased by 6% compared to previous years. One of the explanations is that prospective students anticipate the change in student financing towards a 'social loan' system, which will no longer entitle them to basic grants. Students, who would normally take a year off to travel or work, may now opt for enrolling in higher education immediately. However, no hard research data are available on this issue yet.

All in all, statistical data cannot demonstrate a clear relationship between student financing and participation in general. The introduction of generous support in 1987 did not boost participation, nor did the gradual development towards cost-sharing, by growing fees and less favourable student support since 1990, result in decreased access and participation. However, substantial changes to the system, like the introduction of performance requirements in 1996, as well as the anticipated introduction of a full-loans system (social loans in 2014 or 2015), can have a temporary effect on the choices students make.

It is interesting to add here that longitudinal survey research through the Student Monitor indicated that students are debt averse (Van den Broek et al, 2011). However, in practice growing numbers of students take up loans and accumulate higher debt. The number of borrowers and the actual average student debt have increased substantially in recent years from 20% in 1992, to 40% in 2000, and about 60% currently (Vossensteyn, 2005, 2013). The average total debt of graduates with a study debt was about €8000 in 2007, €12,000 in 2010 and €15,000 in 2012 (CBS, 2013). At the same time, students have also increased their involvement in part-time paid jobs, often to avoid taking up loans (Van den Broek et al, 2011).

Impact on Students from Different Backgrounds

A second and more detailed way to look at the impact of financial incentives on student choice behaviour is to specify the impact on students from different backgrounds. In this respect, Dutch research pays most attention to the potential negative impact of cost-sharing on access for students from disadvantaged backgrounds – students from ethnic minority backgrounds, from lower income and lower educated families, and with lower entrance qualifications.

Ethnicity. Looking at ethnicity, a general distinction is made between native Dutch students, non-native Western students (first or second generation non-natives coming from European countries [excluding Turkey], North America, Oceania, Indonesia and Japan) and non-native non-Western students (first or second generation non-natives coming from other countries,

123

who mostly have Dutch nationality). Within Dutch society, the non-native non-Western students are regarded as the weaker socio-economic group, often being the descendants of 'blue collar immigrants'. Table I presents the number of new entrants from the different groups in Dutch higher education between 1995 and 2012. These statistics show that the majority of Dutch higher education students are native Dutch students, though this proportion declined from 80% in 1995-96 to 67% in 2012-13 (CBS, 2013). In universities, this decline was much stronger (to 62%) compared to the change in the UAS sector (to 72%). In both sectors, the proportion of non-native non-Western freshmen increased from about 6%to about 15% of the total intake between 1995 and 2013. The number of non-native Western students doubled in the university sector from 9% to 18%, while this proportion remained stable in the UAS institutions at around 8%.

Year	1995-96	2000-01	2005-06	2010-11	2011-12	2012-13
Total population	15,4241,22	15,863,950	16,305,526	16,574,989	16,655,799	16,730,348
Natives	.	83%	81%	80%	79%	79%
Non-natives (total)	.	17%	19%	20%	21%	21%
Non-natives (Western)	.	9%	9%	9%	9%	9%
Non-natives (non-Western)	.	9%	10%	11%	11%	12%
Higher education total	85,428	10,4681	11,4429	13,4099	13,5001	13,3614
Natives	80%	73%	73%	69%	68%	67%
Non-natives (Western)	8%	8%	10%	13%	12%	12%
Non-natives (non-Western)	6%	10%	13%	15%	15%	14%
Unknown	6%	9%	4%	4%	5%	6%
Universities total	29,946	32,871	42,292	52,452	52,826	51,997
Natives	81%	78%	72%	65%	63%	62%
Non-natives (Western)	9%	10%	12%	17%	17%	18%
Non-natives (non-Western)	6%	9%	13%	14%	14%	13%
Unknown	4%	4%	4%	4%	6%	7%
UAS total	67,304	85,315	88,850	100,103	98,884	96,933
Natives	80%	73%	75%	72%	72%	72%
Non-natives (Western)	7%	8%	9%	9%	9%	9%
Non-natives (non-Western)	6%	10%	13%	15%	15%	15%
Unknown	6%	10%	4%	4%	4%	4%

Table I. First-year students by ethnic background (as a % of total).
Source: CBS, 2013.

Table I shows the proportion of non-native persons in the total population – which unfortunately is only available from the year 2000 onwards. If these are compared to the proportions of students from non-native backgrounds, then we conclude that non-native students are relatively well represented with about 25% of all students (CBS, 2013). Surprisingly, among them also the non-native non-Western students are also very well represented, particularly in the UAS sector. In general, this tendency can be related to the successful integration of non-natives into Dutch society and that higher education opened up to ethnic minority groups, particularly the large minority groups in Dutch society from Turkish, Moroccan, Surinam and Dutch Antilles backgrounds. This also implies that the tendency of increasing tuition fees and the deterioration of student financial support conditions did not prevent these students from accessing higher education.

Parental income and entrance qualification. A recent study explored the relationship between pre-qualification, parental income, participation and study success (Kazemier, 2013; see also Figure 3). This study shows the higher education status of students on 31 August 2011 for youngsters from different parental income groups who on 1 October 2005 were enrolled in various pre-qualifying secondary education tracks. The major outcome of the study was that educational qualification has a stronger impact on participating in higher education than parental income. About 93% of pupils with pre-university education went on to higher education. For those with upper secondary general education, this figure is 85%, and of those with vocational qualifications about 45% went on to higher education. Within these groups, students from richer families go on to higher education more often than those from lower income backgrounds. The participation of students within the pre-university qualifications is 96% for the 10% highest income group vs 90% for the 10% lowest income group. For the other qualification groups the pattern is similar. This implies that parental income does have only a moderate impact on the likelihood to participate in higher education. The relatively high transition rates demonstrate in a different way that the costs of higher education may not be that important for students who directly qualify for higher education. Nevertheless, children from lower income families normally show lower education attainment scores and thus qualify for higher education less often or particularly through vocational education.

The data presented above are mainly confirmed by biennial student surveys conducted through the Student Monitor (Van den Broek et al, 2011). We will summarise the most important findings that add to the argument made so far. The proportion of pre-university qualified students from lower income groups (based on parental income) is starting to increase. Students in the UAS are more frequently from lower-income groups than students in universities and more often have lower entrance qualifications. This implies that higher education has gradually opened up for students from lower socio-economic backgrounds and that these students are not withheld by issues of cost-sharing. Nevertheless, the imbalance in net monthly parental income remains stable. Both in 2000 and 2007, parents of university students earn about €500 net more per month than parents of UAS students (€3656 and €3082, respectively in 2007). Though students in universities generally come from higher socio-economic backgrounds than UAS students, these differences slightly decrease, probably as a result of the growing group of middle income families and rising education attainment levels. However, if we take into consideration that participation in the UAS has been growing, the development towards cost-sharing can hardly have had a negative impact on the accessibility of higher education for lower socio-economic groups, regardless of the often strong political debates on this issue.

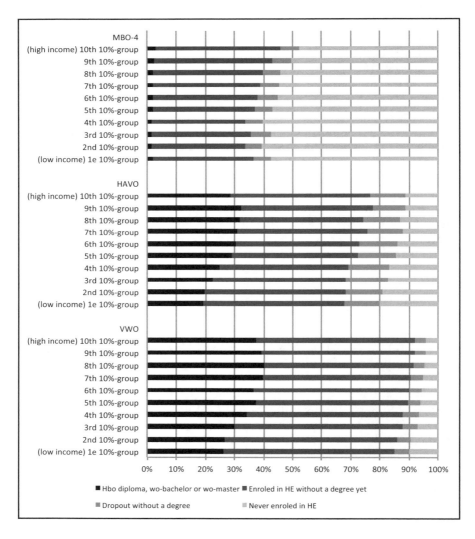

Figure 3. Enrolment in higher education on 1 August 2011 by entrance qualification on 31 October 2005 and parental income level. *Source*: Kazemier, 2013.

The Impact of Financial Incentives on Study Success

The final area to study when looking at the impact of cost-sharing on students is study success. Because tuition fees, loans and performance requirements are said to stimulate students to make well-considered study choices and to study faster, it is interesting to see whether there are signs that students can really be triggered by financial incentives, as the evidence presented above suggests that financial incentives have only a very limited impact on access to higher education. Study success is an important issue in Dutch higher education with a lot of attention for retention, dropout, study progress, completion rates and time-to-degree. In general, UAS students show higher study progress than university students, e.g. they pass more courses per year. Students from non-native non-Western backgrounds generally show lower progress than native students. But students from different parental income and education groups hardly show any differences in study progress. As expected, students who put more effort into their studies also show higher progress rates than their colleagues. An interesting given is that between 2001 and 2009 students substantially increased the number of hours per week they spent on their studies. In total, UAS students increased from 28 to 37 hours per week and university students from 22 to 33 hours per week. They all spent on average about 10 hours per week on paid work (Van den Broek et al, 2011).

Another important finding is that study success is influenced by entrance qualifications. For example, Kazemier (2013) shows that VWO-qualified students are more successful, both at university and at UAS institutions, than students with other entrance qualifications. Students with a vocational entrance qualification (MBO) have the highest likelihood to drop out. Also students from the lowest income groups drop out almost twice as often as those from the highest income groups. This suggests that socio-economic status does have an impact on the likelihood to withdraw from higher education, however no direct relationships have been found with tuition fees, student loans or grants.

Closely linked to the data on dropouts are the data on completion rates and particularly also the average duration to complete a programme. Cohort analysis by Statistics Netherlands (CBS, 2013) show that the proportion of students getting a degree within a certain number of years differs between students from various ethnic backgrounds. Native students show overall the highest completion rates and non-native non-Western students the lowest completion rates. Overall, university students have higher completion rates than UAS students (HBO raad, 2008-2012). But what is most interesting, is that CBS cohort analysis shows that university students that started after 1996 – thus after the introduction of the performance related grants – decreased their time to complete from 6.4 years on average to 5.8 years. However, this probably cannot be fully attributed to the changes in student financing because the general funding regime for universities became more performance oriented from 1993. But it demonstrates that financial instruments, together with a higher interest of institutions to make students successfully complete, can have some influence.

Finally, recent analysis by the Universities' Association (Vereniging van Universiteiten [VSNU], 2012, 2013) reveals that the proportion of university students getting a bachelor's degree has increased recently. One of the reasons is the introduction of a Binding Study Advise which, since 2012, defines that students need to pass a minimum number of credits before they are admitted to the second study year. Another reason is the implementation of a 'Hard Cut' between the bachelor and the master, implying that no student can be admitted to a master's programme without a fully completed bachelor's degree since 2010. But it appears that the €3000 tuition penalty for those who study longer than the nominal duration plus 2 years – as was discussed in the section on tuition fees – made many students increase their study tempo and complete in time. However, it was said to have such a strong impact because many students then were 'catching up'. Unfortunately, the cancellation of the tuition penalty does not allow us to evaluate the real impact of such a tuition measure. But as with the implementation of the performance requirements, it definitely had a short term impact, but now on more students completing their bachelor's degrees faster.

Conclusions

Over time, Dutch policies regarding tuition fees and student financial support demonstrate a development towards cost-sharing. Tuition levels have increased in absolute and real terms. Furthermore, the focus of the support policies has shifted: from opening up opportunities for lower income groups until the mid-1980s, followed by creating a basic income provision for all students in 1986, after which the system reverted once again to mainly supporting underprivileged students. The relatively generous support system in 1986 in first instance was claimed to boost access and participation in higher education. However, this effect was never proven causally as participation patterns did not really change and many contextual factors may have also had an impact (Vossensteyn, 1999). From the early 1990s onwards, student support became less generous, parents and students had to bear a larger share of the costs of study, and grants were made dependent on performance requirements. This chapter has demonstrated that, regardless of the expectation that monetary incentives can influence the behaviour of students, the Dutch experiences with tuition fees and student financial support indicate that fees and loans do not necessarily harm access. Steadily growing tuition rates have never hindered students' participation in higher education. Nevertheless, fees have always remained a political issue and the political debate has often focused on the negative impact fees may have on access for students from lower socio-economic backgrounds. The same goes for student loans. Even though students, particularly those from disadvantaged socio-economic backgrounds, repeatedly indicate that they dislike student loans, they increasingly take up loans. Loans are not a preventing factor for enrolment in higher education. It may affect the choice of the type of programme or institution to enrol in, but to a very limited extent.

Only certain systemic shocks, a huge increase in tuition fees and the introduction of performance requirements, may have generated a temporary negative impact on accessibility. Examples of these have been the tuition shock in 1972, leading to massive student protests, and the introduction of the performance-related grants in 1993 and 1996. Students temporarily chose more often study options that were perceived easier. However, new generations of students quickly adapted to the new situation and returned to old participation patterns. The 2012 introduction of a €3000 tuition penalty for students exceeding certain time limits pushed many students to speed up. In the current debate about the transition from basic grants to 'social loans', students and political parties have heavily criticised the intentions of the minister as they again expect this to harm access. But this chapter has shown that such negative effects are not realistic to be expected, particularly not if students from disadvantaged socio-economic backgrounds are properly compensated.

A long-term observation is that a gradually intensifying focus on study success, also accommodated with financial incentives, may have helped to reduce the average duration of studies for university students. However, financial incentives in general only have a marginal impact on students' choices.

References

Apperloo, E.S. (2013) Het sociaal leenstelsel, En de verwachte effecten op de toegankelijkheid van het hoger onderwijs, Bachelor thesis, Universiteit Twente.

Centraal bureau voor de Statistiek (CBS) (2012) *Jaarboek onderwijs in cijfers*. The Hague: CBS.

Centraal bureau voor de Statistiek (CBS) (2013) *STATLINE*. Den Haag: Statistics Netherlands & CBS. http://www.cbs.nl/nl-NL/menu/themas/onderwijs/cijfers/default.htm

Centraal Planbureau (CPB) (2013) *Deelname-effecten van de invoering van het sociaal leenstelsel in de bachelor- en masterfase*. CPB Notitie. The Hague: Netherlands Bureau for Economic Policy Analysis.

Felsö, F., van Leeuwen, M. & van Zijl, M. (2000) *Verkenning van stimulansen voor het keuzegedrag van leerlingen en studenten*. Amsterdam: Stichting voor Economisch Onderzoek der Universiteit van Amsterdam (SEO).

HBO raad (2008, 2009, 2010, 2011, 2012) *Feiten en cijfers: Afgestudeerden en uitvallers in het hoger beroepsonderwijs*. The Hague: HBO raad.

Hupe, P.L. & van Solm, A.I.T. (1998) *Het Zoetermeerse labyrint, Beleidsgerichte studies Hoger onderwijs en Wetenschappelijk onderzoek 55*. The Hague: Sdu Grafisch Bedrijf.

Interdepartementaal Beleidsonderzoek (IBO) (2003) *Collegegelddifferentiatie in het hoger onderwijs*. Eindrapportage van de werkgroep collegegelddifferentiatie, Interdepartementaal beleidsonderzoek 2002-2003, No. 3, The Hague.

Kaiser, F. & Vossensteyn, J.J. (2005) Access in Dutch Higher Education: policies and trends in Ted Tapper & David Palfreyman (Eds) *Understanding Mass Higher Education, Comparative Perspectives on Access*. London: RoutledgeFalmer.

Kazemier, B. (2013) Het inkomen van de ouders en de toegang tot en de voortgang in het hoger onderwijs, Bijdrage van het CBS, *TH&MA Hoger Onderwijs*, 20(3), 31-34.

Ministerie van Onderwijs, Cultuur en Wetenschap (MinOCW) (2013) *Kerncijfers 2008-2012, Onderwijs, Cultuur en Wetenschap*. The Hague: MinOCW.

Regt, A. de (1993) Geld en gezin: Financiële en emotionele relaties tussen gezinsleden. Amsterdam: Boom.

Tweede Kamer der Staten Generaal (2011) *Nota naar aanleiding van het verslag wetsvoorstel verhoging collegegeld langstudeerders*, 32618. The Hague: Sdu Uitgevers.

Tweede Kamer der Staten Generaal (2013) *Hoofdlijnenbrief 'Toekomstbestendige studiefinanciering voor sterke onderwijskwaliteit'*, 479080. The Hague: Sdu Uitgevers.

Van den Broek, A. & Voeten, R. (2002) *Wisselstroom, Een analyse van de bèta-instroom in het wetenschappelijk onderwijs in de periode 1980-2000*. Beleidsgerichte studies Hoger onderwijs en Wetenschappelijk onderzoek, No. 93, Ministerie van Onderwijs, Cultuur en Wetenschappen. The Hague: Sdu Grafisch Bedrijf BV.

Van den Broek, A., Wartenbergh, F., Hogeling, L. et al (2011) *Tien jaar Studentenmonitor, Studiegedrag en de sociaal-economische positie van de generatie 2001-2010*. Beleidsgerichte studies Hoger Onderwijs en Wetenschappelijk Onderzoek. Den Haag: Ministerie van Onderwijs, Cultuur en Wetenschap (MinOCW).

Veerman, C.P., Berdahl, R.M., Bormans, M.J.G. et al (2010) *Threefold Differentiation: recommendations of the committee on the future sustainability of the Dutch higher education system*. The Hague: Koninklijke Broese en Peereboom.

Vossensteyn, J.J. (1997) *Student Financial Assistance in the Netherlands: a contextual report*. Report for the Eurydice Key Data 1997 project on 'the Allocation and Management of Financial Resources in Education. Center for Higher Education Policy Studies, University of Twente, Enschede.

Vossensteyn, J.J. (2002) Cost Sharing in the Netherlands. The Financial Position of Students, Tuition Fees, Student Support and Students' Reactions. Background Paper for the Project 'Soziale Wirkung Studiëngebühren' of WZI and HRZ of the Universität Kassel, Enschede, CHEPS, Universiteit Twente.

Vossensteyn, J.J. (2005) Perceptions of Student Price-responsiveness. A Behavioural Economics Exploration of the Relationships between Socio-economic Status, Perceptions of Financial Incentives and Student Choice. PhD dissertation, CHEPS (Center for Higher Education Policy Studies), University of Twente.

Vossensteyn, J.J. (2008) Country Report of the Netherlands, in A. Schwarzenberger (Ed.) *Public/Private Funding of Higher Education: a social balance*. Hannover: Hochschul Informations System.

Vossensteyn, J.J. (2013) *Widening Participation in the Netherlands: report submitted to HEFCE and OFFA*. Leicester: Higher Education Funding Council for England (HEFCE).

Vossensteyn, J.J. & Westerheijden, D.F. (2013) Higher Education Monitor: a country report, the Netherlands, Internal working document. CHEPS – international higher education monitor, Enschede.

Vereniging van Universiteiten (VSNU) (2012) *Factsheet Studiesucces, Studenten studeren sneller af*. Den Haag: VSNU.

Vereniging van Universiteiten (VSNU) (2013) *Nieuwsbericht, Fors meer diploma's op universiteiten*. Den Haag: VSNU.

CHAPTER 6

What Price University?
Rising Tuition Fees,
Financial Aid, and Social Justice
in Higher Education in the USA

R.N. NAHAI

ABSTRACT Since the 1960s, the American higher education system has become increasingly commercialized, with tuition fees and interest-bearing student debts rising sharply in the last decade. High 'sticker price' tuition fees combined with generous financial aid notionally create a Robin Hood style funding system, capable of supporting the twentieth century beliefs in egalitarian access to higher education as well as competitive market forces. This article describes key features of the US higher education sector, and examines some evidence for the claim that financial aid, which today largely equates to student loans, is an effective policy instrument for achieving social justice aims within a context of escalating higher education costs. Drawing on the University of California as a case study, it argues that financial aid has not adequately bridged the gap between what low- and middle-income people can afford and what college costs, contributing to a decline in application and enrollment by less-advantaged social groups, and raising challenges to the historic mission and character of public colleges and universities.

Introduction

Beyond national borders, the higher education sector in the USA is well-known for its persistent transition toward a market-based model of post-secondary education. Rapidly rising tuition fees at public as well as private universities, a widespread conception of students as 'consumers', and a cost-sharing approach resulting in substantial levels of student loan debt are just a few of the factors that characterize the sector's evolution away from its twentieth century notion of educational purpose and opportunity. The commercialization of higher education raises challenges to the social justice aims that underpin the mission of the country's public universities.

This chapter aims to do three things. To begin, it maps the terrain of student funding mechanisms and tuition fees in higher education in the USA at the federal and state levels. It further introduces the historical and contemporary challenge of conducting evaluative research on the links between student funding and access to higher education in a populous, decentralized, heterogenous republic, and suggests that a state-level view offers greater insight into questions of student funding and social justice. Finally, narrowing its focus to the University of California, the top level of California's three-tier public higher education system, it contextualizes the evolution of tuition fee policy at the University of California and considers the relationship of these policies to social justice aims.

Nationwide, both tuition fees and student loan debt have risen sharply over the last decade. One of the federal government's key rationales for shifting costs from institutions to students is that there is not enough federal money to subsidize student funding at higher levels. Yet consider the 2011 budget for defense versus that for higher education: $718 billion or 20% of gross domestic product (GDP) (Plumer, 2013) for defense against 2.6% of GDP for the post-secondary sector. Of the 2.6% of GDP allocated for higher education, 62% came from private sources, and only 38% from public (Organisation for Economic Cooperation and Development [OECD], 2013), diminishing the comparison further. Part of the rationale is thus, as I shall argue, predicated on ideology: individuals should work hard, said some of the original proponents of student loans, in order to help themselves (Wilkinson, 2005); part of Ronald Reagan's gubernatorial and presidential legacy is a culture resistant to 'handouts' or 'a free ride'. The position underlining the content that follows is that political priority and political will, far more than the presence or absence of budgetary resources, determines government allocation of funds for higher education.

A few pre-emptive clarifications are in order. My focus here is on public universities, which historically have a stronger social justice mission than private non-profit and private for-profit institutions. The latter two are briefly described for the sake of clarity. Further, though the topic of student loans arises on several occasions, for brevity's sake I omit a discussion of private student loans. These are issued by private corporations and are distinct from federal (central government) loans. Suffice to say here that this type of loan, used by 14% of all undergraduates in 2008, but by 42% at private for-profit colleges (Consumer Financial Protection Bureau, 2012), justifiably provokes controversy [1] largely in social justice terms. Finally, in using the term 'social justice', I rely on a minimal meaning of the term that has the advantage of being, amongst higher education researchers in diverse contexts, broadly shared: that higher education should be accessible to all, without regard to income, race, gender, or other ascriptive characteristics.

The Higher Education Sector in the USA

Since 1636, when Harvard University became the USA's first institution of higher education, the post-secondary education sector in the USA has evolved to encompass 6742 post-secondary Title IV institutions [2] (US Department of Education, 2009).

One of the strengths of the sector lies in its diversity of institutional types. It encompasses community colleges, religious colleges, liberal arts colleges, vocational schools and research universities, residential and commuter campuses, mega-campuses and small, intimate campuses. Institutions can be classed as degree granting (as the majority are) or non-degree granting. Degree granting institutions may be categorized according to the different levels of degrees they offer, from associates (two year), to bachelor's (four year), master's, and doctoral. Most public two-year (or less) community colleges have open admissions, which facilitates access for disadvantaged and non-traditional students; as do nearly half of private for-profit colleges, although for less benevolent reasons. Private non-profits (such as Yale or Princeton) tend to have the most competitive admissions processes, although some public institutions (such as the University of Pennsylvania) are highly competitive also. Colleges and universities generally seek to build up student bodies that share their core values, whether of academic excellence, civic and community participation, preservation of tradition, or social openness and diversity. Such 'mission differentiation' is an important component of the post-secondary education sector, supporting distinct identities and precluding the need for any definitive emphasis on sector-wide hierarchical rankings. Recognising that colleges have differential missions is in turn essential for understanding their different tuition fee and financial aid approaches, as well as access policies (Shapiro & Pham, 2010). It also provides a base for normatively evaluating the appropriateness of their funding models.

For a discussion on student funding, the distinction between public, private non-profit, and private for-profit higher education institutions is perhaps the most significant. Though there is substantial differentiation within each of these categories, each has a distinct historical and social context. Public institutions (numbering 1989) are generally part of a statewide 'system' of linked colleges [3] that share resources and have similar or intentionally complementary missions. Many of these colleges were founded by means of funding from the Morrill Land Grant Act of 1862, which supported education in agriculture and the 'mechanic arts' in order to serve the economic needs of states. From the outset, these colleges have borne a public service mission, which has included serving the post-secondary educational needs of state residents. Reflecting this public service aim, most public colleges have historically received a substantial portion of their funding from the state in which they are located, while being held to high public accountability standards for their budgets and activities. A hallmark of recent state fiscal policy, however, has been a significant decline in state funding for universities.

Private non-profit colleges (numbering 1809) are primarily funded by non-public money [4] and are formally registered as non-profit institutions, appropriating surplus funds for institutional rather than private purposes. Given the unique place of private non-profits between the ideologies and funding approaches of public and private for-profit institutions, questions concerning their appropriate level of accountability, and engagement with social justice issues, are ever-present (for example see Kahlenberg [2010] on legacy admissions in elite American universities). Harvard, Stanford, and the California Institute of Technology (CalTech) are examples of private non-profits, along with most small liberal arts colleges, such as Swarthmore, Wellesley, and Amherst.

Private for-profit colleges (numbering 2944) are funded primarily by private money [5] and are controlled by private corporations. Operating according to business principles, their overarching aim is to turn a profit for shareholders. Generally speaking, these colleges provide vocational education premised on enabling their graduates to advance in the labor market. However, some also offer academic subjects, such as English. Over the past 20 years, enrollment at for-profit colleges has increased by 225%, and they now enroll 12% of all US post-secondary students. Flexible scheduling, targeted curricula, online study options, and related factors have made for-profits particularly attractive to non-traditional students. However, serious concerns have been raised regarding the quality and standards of these institutions, their strategies for recruiting students (many of whom are low-income and racial or ethnic minorities), and the low employment rates of their graduates (National Conference of State Legislatures, 2013). Private for-profit institutions include the University of Phoenix, DeVry University, and Heald College.

Nationwide, tuition fees have increased significantly in the last decade. While tuition fees vary widely across institutional types, average fee trends support a picture of the increasing commercialization of higher education in the USA. The figures below refer to public four-year institutions and are in 2013 dollars. In general, US students at public universities can expect that tuition fees will rise year on year. In 2013 dollars, annual tuition fees at public universities have risen from $5900 in 2003-04 to $8893 in 2013-14 (see Figure 1). Also in 2013 dollars, tuition fees at private non-profit universities have risen from $24,071 in 2003-04 to $30,094 in 2013-14 (see Figure 2).

Averages do, of course, mask regional and institutional variations. Some public university systems have strived to keep tuition fees affordable, such as the University of Wyoming, which charges $4404 for in-state residents in 2013-14 (University of Wyoming, 2013). The University of New Hampshire, meanwhile, charges $16,496 for in-state residents in 2013-14 (University of

New Hampshire, 2013). These figures touch on the role of individual states in tuition fee policy, which is discussed in more depth below.

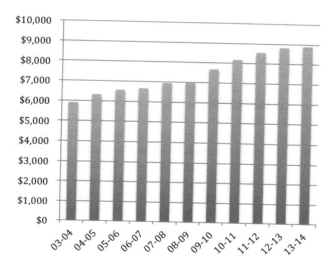

Figure 1. Tuition fees at public universities, 2003-04 to 2013-14.
Source: College Board, 2013.

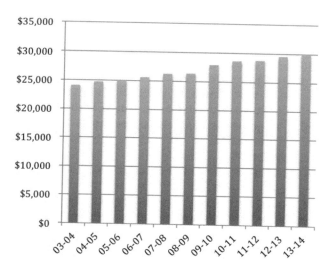

Figure 2. Tuition fees at private non-profit universities, 2003-04 to 2013-14.
Source: College Board, 2013.

The Federal Role in Tuition Fee and Financial Aid Policy

One of the factors that makes higher education costs and funding in the US so complex is that these policy areas are largely decentralized. The explicit role of the federal government in setting tuition fees is, at present, none at all; this task is left to individual states or individual colleges. Nevertheless, there is an area in which the federal government wields substantial power in higher education funding policy: federal financial aid.

The financial aid model of student funding is a primary distinguisher of US funding mechanisms from those of other countries. At its best, financial aid offsets the 'sticker price' of tuition fees, and possibly room and board (maintenance) costs, to reduce the price paid by students and their families to one they can afford. For the poorest students, this cost may be $0. The wealthiest normally pay full fees. In theory, then, a financial aid-based student funding system is a progressive one: it enables institutions to subsidize poorer students by reinvesting the surplus generated by richer students.

While the precise mix of federal financial aid programs changes over time alongside political priorities, the pillars of the system are grants, student loans, and work-study. About $150 billion is spent by the US Department of Education on these programs annually, which are intended to contribute to tuition fees as well as living costs (US Department of Education, 2013a). Federal loans and work-study are distinguished from other forms of loans and jobs because they have certain favourable characteristics not readily available on the open market (Wilkinson, 2005). Different federal aid programs have different target audiences, such as low-income families, teachers in training, or military families, and vary in their conditions in terms of, for instance, eligibility, interest rates, and repayment requirements.

Eligibility for federal aid is determined at the individual level when students submit the Free Application for Federal Student Aid (FAFSA), a form comprised of around 130 questions that aim to ascertain a family's financial circumstances. The information students enter into the FAFSA determines their Expected Family Contribution (EFC), or the amount of funding the government expects the student or their family to contribute to educational expenses. The yearly cost of tuition fees and non-educational expenses at the student's selected college(s), less the EFC, as well as institutional awards, is notionally the amount of federal financial aid for which the individual qualifies, although federal undergraduate loans do have limits attached.

The cornerstone federal grant program is the Federal Pell Grant, a non-repayable grant awarded to undergraduates from low-income families. In 2013-14, the maximum grant award annually is $5645, and the total amount of Pell Grant funding awarded has increased substantially in recent years. Although federal grants have never come near to covering tuition fees at costlier private non-profit colleges, they have been sufficient for covering fees at public colleges for poorer students. Yet while grants from all sources –

federal, state, and institutional – have, on average, risen significantly alongside tuition fees, they have not kept pace, and the funding gap has long been widening even at public institutions (see Figure 3). Thus, the increase seems merely to be plugging some of the new holes appearing in the wall of rising college costs, rather than ameliorating the situation.

Federal aid programs are administered directly by the US Department of Education. Until 2008, the majority of student loans, guaranteed by the government in the event of borrower default, were administered by private companies. However, there is strong evidence that these contracts were inefficient and more expensive than lending direct from the government (Delisle, 2008; Lucas & Moore, 2010). The US Department of Education Direct Loan Program is therefore, following the Health Care and Education Reconciliation Act of 2010, the sole originator of federal student loans, although large private corporations, most notably Nelnet and Sallie Mae, remain heavily (and controversially) [6] involved in loan servicing post-disbursement.

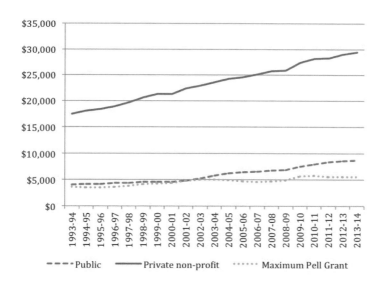

Figure 3. Inflation-adjusted maximum Pell Grant, tuition and fees (TF), and maximum Pell Grant as a percentage of TF, 1993-94 to 2013-14.
Source: College Board, 2013a.

Federal Financial Aid and Social Justice

Although grants and scholarships have existed throughout the history of higher education in the USA, the sector has not traditionally been premised on the idea of free or nearly-free college for all. Prior to the expansion of higher education in the 1940s, non-repayable money for education was generally focused on a few dedicated but needy students. Most students came from the middle and upper classes, and could either pay tuition fees outright or work their way through their studies (Wilkinson, 2005). The exception has been some state university systems, such as the University of California, which managed to establish and maintain a tuition fee-free policy for about a century.

The period following the GI Bill of 1944 [7], however, ushered in a series of policies and social programs intended to expand opportunity, establish social equality, and solidify meritocracy, and saw many policymakers shift to a social justice view of higher education opportunity. This view is reflected in the content of the 1965 Higher Education Act, which expanded financial aid programs and made provisions for establishing a general system of student loans, and was primarily justified on social justice grounds.

The 1965 Higher Education Act's major provision was for disbursement of modest student loans, allocated to cover then-manageable tuition fees, which would enable young people from more diverse backgrounds to participate in higher education. Notionally, the loans would break down barriers to college access, progressing the social justice aims that had gained political traction through the 'Kennedy legacy' of social justice advocacy, the (1955-68) civil rights movement, and the 'War on Poverty' of President Lyndon B. Johnson's Administration (Gladieux, 1995). Subsequent social justice-oriented work around access to higher education, notably by Clark Kerr through the Carnegie Commission (Douglass, 2005), as well as Alice Rivlin (1969) via the (former) US Department for Health, Education, and Welfare, strengthened the narrative of financial aid programs as instruments for social justice.

The extent to which enrollments of racial and ethnic minority students (the sometime-accurate American shorthand for 'disadvantaged') increased as a result of federal financial aid is difficult to separate from increases instigated by the general expansion of higher education from the 1940s. One argument is that, at the same time as new and expanded federal grant and loan programs were introduced, enrollment of racial and ethnic minority students also began to increase substantially, indicating a correlation. As Figure 4 demonstrates, enrollments for all major racial and ethnic groups have risen overall since 1980, although there are a few dips for all groups over the years. The figures indicate enrollment rates for all 18-24 year olds in each racial and ethnic category as a percentage of their total population in each year.

However, the correlation between early federal financial aid provision and minority student enrollment has been ultimately unclear. Consider that tuition fees also increased substantially during this timeframe; the sharp rise is thought to be a deterrent to enrollment, particularly for non-Asian minority groups. The contradiction may be partly explained through more detailed data and analyses, for instance regression-based studies that account for institutional type and different combinations of student aid. An analysis by Stampen and Fenske (1988), for example, suggests that financial aid played a significant role in increasing enrollment rates of racial and ethnic minority groups from the 1960s through the mid-1970s, when grants were the predominant form of federal aid. However, enrollment rates of Latinos and African Americans (but not Asian Americans) subsequently declined in the late 1970s as student loans superseded grants as the main form of funding. St John (2002) finds that, for a nationally representative sample of 1992 high school students, reduced federal grants exert a more substantial influence than college preparedness on the decision to attend college, contributing to a widening enrollment gap between high-income and low-income, and non-Asian minority and White students.

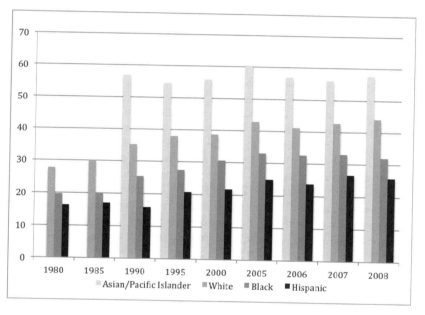

Figure 4. Percentage of 18-24-year-olds enrolled in colleges and universities, by race and ethnicity and sex, selected years, 1980-2008.
Note: Asian/Pacific Islander data is not available for 1980 and 1985.
Source: National Center for Education Statistics, 2010.

St John's conclusions bear out the aid-access narrative presented by Kane (1994), who assessed the effects of changes in public tuition fees in the 1970s and 1980s and found that higher fees correlated with lower state enrollments among Black students. Addressing some of the design weaknesses of Kane's study, Long (2004) similarly found that state tuition subsidies, or the lower in-state price public colleges charge, influence students' decision of whether to attend college and which college to attend. Dynarski and Scott-Clayton's

(2013) review of the literature on financial aid impacts indicates that cost subsidies positively impact on higher education attendance rates, choice, and attainment.

The federal government today relies on several justifications for, first, providing financial aid in the form of grants, and second, providing an increasing amount of student loans in place of grants. Grant funding plays a role in the government's drive to ensure the US has a highly educated workforce, contributing to the country's economic competitiveness and helping individuals to achieve the levels of education needed for participation in the labor market (White House, 2014). Some grants, such as the TEACH Grant, attempt to ensure that there is an adequate supply of labor for important public service jobs (US Department of Education, 2013b).

Government support for shifting the cost burden of higher education from government to individuals, in the form of student loans, is justified on more controversial grounds. For instance, one of the original justifications for student lending is that college is a good investment, leading to a career payoff (Wilkinson, 2005). This argument is increasingly contested as the amount that students borrow increases, career paths become less predictable, and the gap between college costs and lifetime earning premiums for graduates narrows, especially for those entering low-paid fields, like teaching, or volatile ones, like entrepreneurship (Shierholz et al, 2013).

Some of the rationales supporting student loans are ideological. Wilkinson (2005) highlights the historical American approval of student loans as arising from resistance to laziness or a 'free ride' (Gladieux, 1995), and conversely, from support for making one's own way. On this line of thinking, student loans are a temporary bridge to upward progress that ultimately requires borrowers to help themselves, through the hard work that subsequently enables them to repay the loans. In this sense, as Wilkinson (2005) points out, financial aid in the US paradigm can also include 'self help'.

Additionally, in theory, a system reliant on student loans is consistent with progressive ideals: those with incomes too high to qualify for grant aid should be able to afford to borrow for their education as well as repay their loans, therefore subsidising the education of the low-income individuals most in need of grants. Loans are, notionally, a way of redistributing wealth between the privileged and the needy. Thus student loans appeal to both conservative and liberal positions by supporting individualistic, self-help ideals, as well as socially progressive ones (Wilkinson, 2005). It is perhaps this dual appeal that has enabled them, over the last five decades, to evade concerted party-based castigation and develop into the widening pillar of financial aid that they are today.

The importance of student loans to student funding is, however, a key reason that their use has become so controversial. Over the last decade, higher education costs have shifted substantially from institutions to families and students, primarily in the form of repayable, interest-bearing loans. By the first quarter of 2012, federal student loan debt neared the $1 trillion mark (Federal Reserve Bank of New York, 2012). Undergraduates finish college (or fail to) with increasingly burdensome levels of loans: for the class of 2012-13, the average debt was $29,400, with 7 out of 10 college graduates emerging with student loan debt (Institute for College Access and Success, 2013). In 2012, 11.9% of graduates had loan balances of $50,000 or higher (see Figure 5).

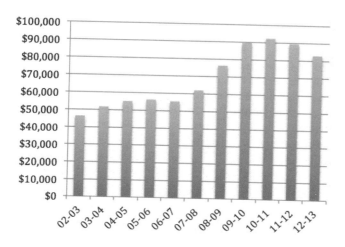

Figure 5. Total federal student loans borrowed, 2002-03 to 2012-13 (in millions, constant 2012 dollars). *Source*: College Board, 2013a.

For those with large student loan balances or who are delinquent on their repayments, the possibility of securing other types of credit – such as a loan for a car or house – may be greatly reduced. Since 2008, the number of mortgage originations by 25-30 year olds with student debt has decreased significantly in relation to their debt-free peers (Lee, 2013). Some researchers and policymakers also argue that increased provision of federal student loans (and other financial aid) encourages colleges to raise tuition fees, resulting in a vicious cycle of unaffordable education, although the long-term evidence of this is mixed (e.g. see Gillen, 2012).

Measuring the effects of US financial aid policy on access to higher education poses an ongoing challenge. Few federal financial aid policy changes are packaged as tidy amendments lending themselves to straightforward analyses. To begin, policy changes often come in quick succession, making it difficult to isolate the effects of each. Substantial legislative changes to financial aid, for instance, were enacted in the 2007 College Cost Reduction and Access Act, as well as the Ensuring Continued Access to Students Loans Act of 2008. If either impacted on access to college, identifying on a macro scale whether the impact was linked to increases in grants or in maximum student loan provisions, major provisions of the 2007 and 2008 Acts respectively, would be infeasible.

Further clouding the territory, federal legislation tends to combine a number of provisions in each Act. In the 2008 Act, for example, the changes introduced concern three different types of grants, student loan interest rates and repayment periods, the structure of the government's Federal Family Education Loan Program (FFELP), student loan forgiveness, access grants for colleges, and strengthening historically black and minority-serving institutions. Moreover, various eligibility clauses segregate potential policy winners and losers into various groups related to income level, occupation, race and ethnicity, and dates of attending university. The difficulty of disentangling the effects of centralized policymaking is therefore, to a large extent, a consequence of the sector's size and diversity, its decentralization, and the complexity of the financial aid system.

When tuition fees at some public universities began to rise in the early 1980s, there were no systematic methods in place for determining whether financial aid policies were effective in increasing or sustaining access to higher education (Hansen, 1983). Until the late 1980s, data on the distribution to different student demographics of different types of aid was not available. Despite research into the effectiveness of financial aid being carried out over the intervening decades, uncertainty remains today about the best ways to design and implement policies to maximize social justice gains (Long, 2008). Evaluations carried out by the federal government indicate a reluctance to frame enrollment pattern analyses in social justice terms, favouring instead less politically charged foci such as college preparedness (St John, 2002). The majority of analyses related to financial aid and social justice are therefore piecemeal; individual projects carried out by think tanks and academics.[8] In 2014, the available evaluations do not sufficiently demonstrate the impact of financial aid programs on access to higher education for different social groups, especially those that are underrepresented in higher education.

State and Institutional Roles in
Tuition Fee and Financial Aid Policy

It is the remit of individual states to set tuition fee levels in their public universities. In some cases, individual institutions have the right to set their own fee levels.[9] As indicated by the fee figures from the University of Wyoming and the University of New Hampshire, above, these figures vary widely across regions. In large part, the disparity in fee levels between states is determined by their political and fiscal prioritisation of public higher education, and the amount of student funding they consequently allocate. Tuition fee levels are closely linked to this figure; it is unsurprising to learn that the state of Wyoming provides over $15,000 in per-student appropriations, while New Hampshire provides $2482, the lowest per-student spending nationwide (College Board, 2013b).

At public institutions, fees are set at different levels for students residing in-state, those coming from out-of-state, and for international students. For example, at the University of California, Berkeley (UC Berkeley), there is a 'supplemental fee' for international undergraduate students in 2013-14 of $22,878, along with a baseline tuition fee about $2000 higher than resident fees, bringing total fees for the year to $37,756 (UC Berkeley, 2014). This does not include maintenance costs. The supplemental fee for out-of-state students in 2013-14 is also $22,878 (UC Berkeley, 2013), although they are subject to the same baseline fee rate as residents. Public universities do not normally extend their access missions beyond state borders, as these figures indicate; their intent remains, above all, to serve the residents of their own states. However, it is notable that as state budgets for public higher education decline, some institutions, such as the University of California, are accepting a greater proportion of out-of-state and international students in order to balance their books (Rothblatt, 2011). Private non-profit and for-profit institutions, in contrast, normally set flat rates for all students, as many expect to attract and enroll a greater proportion of students from further afield. This is especially true for elite colleges.

In most states, both states and institutions play a role in access initiatives by providing grant funding to students. State grants are more likely to be need-based and distributed according to income. While they comprise an important part of many states' higher education budgets, as with other aspects of funding for post-secondary education, the grant budget varies widely across regions. In 2011-12 in New Hampshire, it comprised 0% of the state's higher education budget, while in South Carolina, this figure was 38%. The national average was 13% (College Board, 2013b).

At the institutional level, however, different grants are often distributed according to need or academic merit. In 2012-13, an average of 51% of institutional grants in public universities were awarded on the basis of financial need, while 28% of grants awarded exceeded financial need. A further 22% were awarded in the form of athletic grants and tuition waivers (College Board, 2013). Although some social justice advocates challenge the idea of reducing costs for higher-income students for recruitment purposes, many colleges rely on merit grants as a key instrument for attracting academically bright students (Wilkinson, 2005).

Given the challenges of evaluating the aid-access relationship at the federal level, and the sector's decentralized organization, it is helpful to reduce the analytical scope of this inquiry: whether to the state, regional, or institutional level. The more focused the target, the more feasible an evaluation. For this reason, the remainder of this chapter explores tuition fees and financial aid arrangements within a particular state – California – and a particular branch of its public higher education system – the University of California.

California is in many ways an ideal site for exploring social justice in higher education given that its population of 38 million encompasses one of the country's most socially and racially diverse demographics: in 2012, it was 39.4% White, 38.2% Hispanic or Latino, 13.9% Asian, and 6.6% Black. Of those aged five or over, 43.5% speak a language other than English at home (US Census Bureau, 2013). Additionally, the University of California system is the largest public university system in the country; and from its tuition fee-free origins, it has undergone a drastic evolution in fee levels, particularly over the last decade. Each of these factors make it a fitting case study for evaluating the ability of financial aid to actually promote fair access to higher education, and achieve the social justice objectives on which this policy instrument was originally predicated.

The University of California: ideological origins and contemporary structure

The University of California was founded by means of funding from the 1862 Morrill Land-Grant Act (University of California History, 2014). The 1868 'Organic Act' that established the University as a legal entity reflected the public mission values befitting the land grant movement. Three of the ideals set out in the Act merit emphasis here. First, the agricultural and technical education aspect of the University of California embedded an early ethos of symbiosis with the economic needs of the state.[10] Second, while the Act made provision for admission and tuition fees in the University of California's early years, it specified that the University ought to be free for all residents of the state as soon as the income of the University permitted. Third, the Act established that all social groups in the state would enjoy equal representation in the University, offering an early benchmark of the University of California's pioneering commitment to social justice aims, in terms of socio-demographic diversity, which it continues to uphold today (Douglass, 2012). In these and other ways, the public character of the University of California, based on an ethos of service to the state and its residents, was established.

The postwar decades ushered in an age of expansion that called for a new strategic approach to managing demand, maintaining quality, and providing equal opportunities for higher education. In 1960, then-president of the University of California, Clark Kerr, introduced the 'Master Plan', an organizational format for systemizing equal educational opportunities while upholding academic excellence (Douglass, 2000). The Master Plan converted California's public colleges and universities into a carefully-integrated three-tier system consisting of: (1) the University of California, the research branch of the system; (2) California State University, which offers moderately-selective bachelor's, master's and vocational education, including teacher education; and (3) California Community Colleges, non-selective academic and vocational colleges centered on access and community engagement missions. Although each 'level' offers the possibility of a self-contained education, the strong transfer function between them, intended to facilitate social mobility, is a key component of the Master Plan.

The three-tier format, among other features of the state's higher education system, took seriously the social justice aims introduced in the Organic Act. It systematized the possibility of equal educational opportunity within a merit-based framework (Callan, 2009). The University of California managed to reconcile, to a notable extent, the competing demands of access and excellence, making it a model for universities in other US states and around the globe (Douglass, 2000). However, fissures began to appear in the social justice intentions of the system only a decade after the Master Plan was produced, with the onset of the Reagan era and its ideological shift away from public programs and toward an ethos of 'self help'.

Tuition Fees at the University of California

In 1960, the University of California was still tuition fee-free; the Master Plan maintained that students should not pay fees for instruction. While it made provision for incidental fees for costs not related to instruction, such as accommodation and student union fees, it specified that any fees charged should be as low as possible. Nevertheless, these types of fees had increased from $84 to $320 between 1957 and 1970, a 400% increase (Rodda, 1970). It was at this point in the evolution of fee increases that tuition fees were introduced.

In 1967, Ronald Reagan was elected governor of California. Though he had yet to fully develop the controversial economic policies that, during his time as President of the USA, would be dubbed 'Reaganomics', his policies as governor foreshadowed his later approach. These focused on lowering taxes, reducing government spending, deregulating markets, and dismantling welfare, which in 1966 he called a 'prepaid lifetime vacation plan' (Wilensky, 1975, p. 33). From the outset, Reagan was intent on challenging the progressive and, as he saw it, entitled culture at the University of California [11] whose students were then at the epicenter of the Free Speech Movement. Three weeks after his 1967 election, Reagan successfully pressured the University of California's Board of Regents to fire Clark Kerr. In swift succession, the new governor proposed cutting the University of California budget by 10%, selling rare books in the UC Berkeley's library collection, and introducing tuition fees for students. While many of his proposals met with strong opposition and failed to gain traction, variants of some manifested as policy. Tuition fees were one of these. In early 1970, California Senator Albert S. Rodda wrote to the state's Democratic legislators that 'we are now in what I have described as the "era of the politics of tuition [fees]"' (Rodda, 1970).

Tuition fees at the University of California were formally introduced in 1970. In 1971-72, tuition fees for resident undergraduates [12] were set at

$300. They remained at this rate until 1981-82 when they increased to $475. It then took nearly a decade for this rate to double. From 1998-99 through 2001-02, tuition fees actually declined from $3086 to $2716. However, in the five years to 2005-06, the rate doubled again. Then, in the five years to 2011-12, it doubled yet another time, reaching $11,160. The trend of the past decade is therefore one of tuition fees doubling every five years, with a sizeable fee increase in most intervening years (see Figure 6).

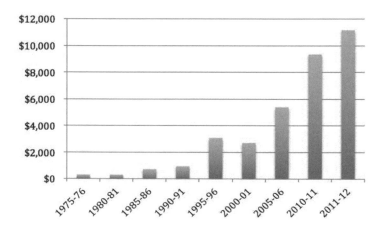

Figure 6. Resident undergraduate tuition fee levels at the University of California, selected years, 1975-76 to 2011-12.
Source: University of California Office of the President, 2011.

This fee excludes the annual 'student services fee', which has steadily risen in tandem with tuition fees and reached $972 in 2011-12 (see Figure 7). The introduction and growth of tuition fees in California has arisen in the context of the neoliberal economic policies, marked by reduced government spending and decreased taxation, that flourished during the Reagan–Thatcher years, and that took root in California during Reagan's term as governor. Indeed, the substantial tuition fee increases at the University of California have taken root alongside declining state support for the sector. Proposition 13, passed in California in 1978, marked a turning point in the trajectory of state funding for higher education: it reduced property taxes by 60% and placed severe constraints on future tax increases, cementing aspects of 'Reaganomics' ideology with negative long-term effects for student funding. The former governor's drive to minimize state support for higher education made a striking contrast to the aforementioned fervent efforts elsewhere in the mid-1960s through to the early-1970s to improve access and equity through strengthening government financial support for higher education; as well as to the ideals embedded in the Organic Act and the Master Plan.

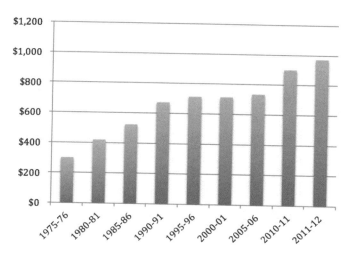

Figure 7. Student services fee levels at the University of California,
selected years, 1975-76 to 2011-12.
Source: University of California Office of the President, 2011.

Today, the University of California's primary rationale for increasing tuition
fees is that it must do so to make up the shortfall from decreasing state
funding. In turn, the state's rationale for its ongoing higher education
funding decline rests on competing, and more urgent, fiscal priorities. The
state's policy justifications therefore mirror those of the federal government –
there is not enough money – and so the trickle-down effect of political
rationales based on arguments of economic scarcity becomes evident. Yet at
the state as at the federal level, questions about which programs deserve
funding priority are not uncontroversial. California now, perhaps infamously,
spends more on prisons than on public higher education, with funding for
higher education decreasing 9% over the last decade, and that for corrections
increasing 26%. In the same period, the prison population increased by 1%,
whereas the student population of the University of California and California
State University rose by 13% (Johnson, 2012).

Higher education has absorbed a disproportionately large amount of the
state budget cuts intended to balance the (2011-12) budget deficit of $11.1
billion – at $1.8 billion, more than any other function of state government.
Of the three strategies adopted by the public university system to offset these
cuts, raising tuition fees has been the most prominent, both in terms of
budgetary contributions, and of the effects on students and their families.
Indeed, the 2011-12 fee level at the University of California made it one of
the most expensive public university systems in the country, with average
tuition fees 33% higher than those of other large public research universities
(Johnson, 2012). Figure 8 shows the importance to the UC Berkeley budget

of net tuition and other student fees, which in 2012-13 were projected to comprise 27% of its $2.16bn revenues (UC Berkeley, 2012).

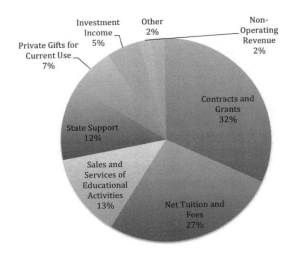

Figure 8. 2012-13 budgeted revenues: $2.16 Billion.
Source: UC Berkeley, 2012.

Financial Aid and Social Justice at the University of California

Despite sharply rising tuition fees, social justice concerns, a foundation of the 'California Idea' (Douglass, 2000) of higher education, have not been simply abandoned at the University of California. A supplementary rationale put forward to justify raising fees is that financial aid is proportionately increased and diverted to the poorest students, making the University of California's aid, like the federal system of financial aid, a progressive system. Through redistributing funds from 'rich' to poor, the University of California aims to encourage students from lower-income families to apply and enroll.

Nearly two-thirds of University of California undergraduates receive financial aid in some form, with an average annual package of around $14,000. As discussed earlier, tuition fees in the USA are often heavily mediated by financial aid in the form of grants, scholarships, work-study, and student loans, which are allocated based on either financial need or merit, or a combination of both. The 'sticker price' of tuition fees, student service fees, and room and board is therefore not the price paid by the majority of students. Beyond the external scholarships established from philanthropic gifts from individuals or organizations, the University of California itself offers three scholarships for both merit and financial need, as well as two grants. In addition, the federal Pell Grant is awarded in varying amounts to low-income students, while the state of California offers the well-funded Cal Grant. The federal government further subsidizes the cost to employers of hiring students under its work-study program, enabling some to defray educational costs through working part-time jobs (University of California, 2013a). In most cases, these funding sources cannot be expected to fully cover educational costs; they are intended instead as partial subsidies.

The primary instrument that the University of California has relied on to sustain (if not quite match) former levels of access in the face of rising tuition fees has been the statewide Cal Grant program which makes up part of its higher education budget. The number of Cal Grants awarded between 2001-02 and 2011 exceeds the number awarded in the prior 45 years combined; funding for Cal Grants rose from around $400 million in 1999-2000 to $1.2 billion in 2009 (US Senate, 2000; Quinto, 2011). This expansion reflects the growth in numbers of high school graduates over that time, driven significantly by a rising (primarily Latino) immigrant population. Thus, while tuition fees have continued to rise year on year, policymakers have aimed to ensure that the level of funding for the poorest students has kept pace. Still, the increase in high school graduates is currently outstripping the increase in Cal Grant funding (Quinto, 2011).

While there are few systematic studies on the social justice impact of the University of California grants and Cal Grants, Quinto's (2011) study, which encompasses all three of the state's higher education tiers, shows that Cal Grants have expanded higher education opportunities in the state. In particular, since the enactment of the bill SB 1644 in 2000, Cal Grants have increasingly been awarded in accordance with financial need ('entitlement grants') rather than academic merit, a contrast with the grant approaches of many other states, and have increasingly been allocated to racial and ethnic groups underrepresented in higher education. In this sense, they are achieving the historical objective of grant money for higher education which is to 'promote access to equalize higher educational opportunities for students who have historically been underrepresented' (D. Heller, quoted in Quinto, 2011, p. 80). Quinto's focus on the distribution of aid, however, precludes in this case an evaluation of the relationship between aid and access in terms of enrollment levels. It also excludes an analysis of the counterfactual: what Cal Grant recipients would have done had they not received the grant aid.

As few students have the costs of their education covered fully by either 'free money' sources or working in a job, for all but the poorest students 'financial aid' increasingly refers to student loans, which about half of the students at the University of California rely on. The average student loan amount of 2012-13 University of California bachelor's degree graduates who borrowed was $19,751 in 2011-12 (University of California, 2013b), compared to the average $29,400 in 2011-12 of the two-thirds of Americans who borrow for college (Institute for College Access and Success, 2013).

Given the substantial costs that still loom after factoring in non-repayable aid, there is little guarantee that finances will not impact on enrollment, as well as access for disadvantaged social groups. Data collected following large tuition fee hikes in 2010-11 bear this out. The rise in fees has correlated with a sharp decline in the proportion of qualified high school graduates enrolling at the University of California: from 9% in 2008 to about 7% in 2010, and 27% and 22%, respectively, of the state's most qualified high school graduates. As the number of high school graduates meeting the University of California standards and applying to the University has grown, enrollment rates have declined, suggesting a link with tuition fee increases (Johnson, 2012).

Lower enrollments may be further explained by the measure taken by the University of California to enroll more out of state and international students who pay higher fees than residents, reducing the number of places for Californians, historically and ideologically the University of California's primary constituency. In 2011, enrollment rates for undergraduates at the University did increase by 1% (California Department of Finance, 2012), but this is a small gain in relation to the lost proportion of eligible high school graduates. There is cause for further concern in that, while some young people who are eligible to study at the University of California are choosing private or out-of-state universities, one in ten are choosing to forgo higher education entirely after high school (Johnson, 2012). Enrollments at the University of California have, however, remained the steadiest of the three tiers of the state's public higher education, with California State University and California Community Colleges – the access-oriented arms of the system – experiencing the greatest enrollment declines, a trend even more worrying than the declines at the University of California (California Department of Finance, 2012; Johnson, 2012).

There are additional problems with this model. To begin with, middle-income students, who form the majority of the University of California's student demographic, tend to earn too much money to qualify for grants, and too little to pay the tuition fee sticker price outright. Most of the available grant money goes to very low income students; in 2012-13, 65% of dependent students receiving Cal Grants had family incomes of less than $35,999, with 35% of recipients above this income level. For independent students, the proportion going to the very low income is 85% (California Student Aid Commission, 2013). Furthermore, Cal Grants disproportionately benefit those attending community colleges or California State University; most of the University of California's attendees' families earn too much to make them eligible for Cal Grants. What this means, in practice, is that about half of the students who enroll at the University of California fund their education at least partly by means of federal or private student loans, contributing to the reliance on student debt financing. While the University of California administration has recognized the gap in funding for middle-income students as a problem, it has not, as yet, articulated promising solutions (UC Commission on the Future, 2010).

Also problematic is that the sheer complexity of financial aid in the USA, where federal options are interwoven with state and institutional options, and each student receives an individually tailored financial aid package and price tag for their education, deters some eligible students from applying or enrolling. The Bourdieusian perspective is apt in this instance, highlighting the ways in which differences in levels of social and cultural capital facilitate application to and enrollment in college, or the contrary. True to Bourdieu's typology, low-income prospective students in the USA, lacking the social and cultural capital of their higher-income peers, are less likely to successfully navigate the financial aid maze.

This problem has been sufficiently well-established through economics research (e.g. Bettinger et al, 2007; Dynarski & Scott-Clayton, 2008) that it comes as no surprise when the University of California financial aid website practically implores students to look into aid options before disqualifying themselves: 'Please – even if you think you won't be eligible for financial aid – take the time to explore the many options available. What you discover may surprise you' (University of California, 2013a). The administration is also concerned about the perception of the University of California as 'too expensive' that has arisen from news reports and a strengthening culture of concern over college costs (UC Commission on the Future, 2010). In this context, some low-income students who are eligible to study at the University of California may choose not to enroll in, apply to, or even explore their options for attending the University of California.

Conclusion: is financial aid enough?

This chapter has endeavored to offer the outside observer a broad overview of the structure of the higher education system in the USA, and the institutional diversity and decentralization that characterize it, as well as an insight into the US idea of financial aid as a means to social justice in higher education. In setting out some of challenges of evaluating whether federal financial aid programs achieve social justice aims, it has indicated that studies published to date suggest a positive relationship between financial subsidies and access to higher education for underrepresented social groups. The chapter has touched on an agreement amongst researchers, arising in the early 1980s and continuing to the present, that (a) understanding the effects of financial aid on access is very important, and (b) we do not yet have a systematic understanding of these effects, and must go on investigating. Amid the unremitting marketization of higher education in the USA, a contingent of committed researchers continue their efforts to make sense of the financial aid model and its links to social justice aims.

Nevertheless, this work is carried out in a context of rising tuition fee levels across all types of universities in most states, a trend that has accelerated over the last decade or so, and amid other characteristics of evident marketization in the sector. Such an environment seems likely to complicate researchers' task further. To gain perspective on these trends, this chapter narrows in on the University of California, the top tier of California's three-tier public university system, and demonstrates that the University of California's market-based tuition fee and financial aid policies have arisen from the neoliberal economic policies introduced in the late 1960s. Today, the primary justification of the University of California administration for increasing tuition fees is that they must make up the shortfall created by declining state funding; the rationale of economic scarcity thus trickles down from the federal to the state government, and to institutions themselves. A consequence is that in today's so-called 'cost sharing' arrangement of student funding, the cost burden of post-secondary education is increasingly shifted onto students and their families, and away from institutions. In combination with high tuition fees, this shift has led to a steep and rising increase in levels of student loan debt, an ascent with no cap in sight.

Though it is certain that tuition fees in the USA, and accompanying student loan levels, cannot continue rising sharply and indefinitely, there are few indications that a great repeal will take place. However, it is clear that current fee and student loan levels are unsustainable as they threaten to thwart colleges' access missions and compromise the stability of the USA's middle class. Universities recognise this: the UC Commission on the Future (2010) argues that if state funding continues to decline, the University of California will have no choice but to raise its substantial tuition fees yet again, a move that further jeopardises its historical commitment to sustaining its remarkably diverse student intake. Since this proclamation, the state of California has approved a modest increase in the University of California's funding through 2016-17, enabling it to stabilize tuition fee levels for the 2013-14 academic year (McMillan, 2013). If such a move reflects political sentiment elsewhere, there may be cause for cautious optimism.

Although liberal proponents of the financial aid system in the USA argue that it is redistributive and thus progressive, it has failed to adequately address the growing gap between available grant aid and unprecedented tuition fee levels. Affordable higher education is not the only factor that influences access, but it is an important part of the puzzle – an insufficient but necessary condition. In the pursuit of social justice aims, as Gladieux and Swail (1998) argue, 'financial aid is not enough'.

Notes

[1] The most comprehensive recent report on the private student loan sector, including its problems, is the Consumer Financial Protection Bureau's (2012) publication.

[2] A Title IV institution, briefly, is an accredited post-secondary institution eligible to participate in federal financial aid programs.

[3] A note on terminology: common parlance in the USA applies the word 'college' to all levels of higher education. While there are some formal distinctions between universities and colleges, the two are often linguistically conflated in practice. To avoid writing 'colleges and universities' time and

again, I use interchangeably 'college' and 'university' to describe all post-secondary Title IV institutions.

[4] Private non-profits may nevertheless receive substantial federal funding for research and from federal grant and loan programs. In 2010-11, federal sponsored research expenditure at Harvard amounted to $677, 711 (Harvard University, 2012).

[5] Private colleges also tend to take in substantial income from federal grant and loan programs (National Conference of State Legislatures, 2013).

[6] See Consumer Financial Protection Bureau (2012) for further insight into the practices and problems of private loan companies in education. As corporations, they answer primarily to shareholders.

[7] Formally titled the Servicemen's Readjustment Act of 1944, this bill made substantial social provisions for veterans returning from the Second World War. Its perhaps most famous provision was generous coverage of college tuition fees and living costs, which ignited the mass higher education movement in the US.

[8] For overviews of the research on the impact of financial aid, see Long (2008) and Dynarski and Scott-Clayton (2013).

[9] This is always true for private non-profit and private for-profit institutions, but only sometimes true for public institutions.

[10] In its early years, the university nevertheless grappled with the question of which subjects to emphasize and which audience to serve. In spite of the land grant funding, the primary tension concerned whether to focus on vocational or academic education. This was resolved by integrating the provision of the vocational and academic, and in the ensuing decades, the University of California remained closely aligned with the economic and social needs of the state.

[11] Or, more to the point, to 'get Berkeley' (Wilensky, 1975, p. 33).

[12] Charging higher fees to non-California residents has long been a legitimate practice. In 1971-72, California State University and community colleges charged no tuition fees to residents, but $1100 and $900 for these colleges, respectively, to non-residents. This further highlights the system's position, as a taxpayer-supported institution, toward California residents.

References

Bettinger, E.P., Long, B.T. & Oreopoulos, P. (2007) *Increasing College Enrollment among Low- and Moderate-Income Families: an intervention to improve information and access to financial aid*. New York: National Center for Postsecondary Research, Columbia University, New York.

California Department of Finance (2012) California Public Postsecondary Enrollment History, 1990-2011. http://www.dof.ca.gov/research/demographic/reports/projections/postsecondary/ (accessed December 20, 2013).

California Student Aid Commission (2013) 2012-13 Cal Grant Program Recipients. http://www.csac.ca.gov/doc.asp?ID=1162 (accessed January 6, 2014).

Callan, P.M. (2009) California Higher Education, the Master Plan, and the Erosion of College Opportunity. February. The National Center for Public Policy and Higher Education. National Center Report #09-1.

College Board (2013a) *Trends in Student Aid.* Trends in Higher Education Series. New York: College Board.

College Board (2013b) *Trends in College Pricing 2013.* Trends in Higher Education Series. New York: College Board.

Consumer Financial Protection Bureau (2012) Private Student Loans. Report to the Senate Committee on Banking, Housing, and Urban Affairs, the Senate Committee on Health, Education, Labor, and Pensions, the House of Representatives Committee on Financial Services, and the House of Representatives Committee on Education and the Workforce.

Delisle, J. (2008) *Cost Estimates for Federal Student Loans: the market cost debate.* Washington, DC: New America Foundation.

Douglass, J.A. (2000) *The California Idea and American Higher Education: 1850 to the 1960 Master Plan.* Stanford: Stanford University Press.

Douglass, J.A. (2005) The Carnegie Commission and Council on Higher Education: a retrospective. Research and Occasional Paper Series: CSHE.14.05, Center for Studies in Higher Education University of California, Berkeley.

Douglass, J.A. (2012) Poor and Rich: student economic stratification and academic performance in a public research university system, *Higher Education Quarterly*, 66(1), 65-89.

Dynarski, S. & Scott-Clayton, J. (2008) Complexity and Targeting in Federal Student Aid: a quantitative analysis, *Tax Policy and the Economy*, 22, 109-150.

Dynarski, S. & Scott-Clayton, J. (2013) Financial Aid Policy: lessons from research. NBER Working Papers 18710, National Bureau of Economic Research.

Federal Reserve Bank of New York (2012) New York Fed Quarterly Report Shows Student Loan Debt Continues to Grow, May 31. http://www.newyorkfed.org/newsevents/news/research/2012/an120531.html (accessed December 10, 2013).

Gillen, A. (2012) *Introducing Bennett Hypothesis 2.0.* Washington, DC: Center for College Affordability and Productivity.

Gladieux, L.E. (1995) Federal Student Aid Policy: a history and an assessment. http://www2.ed.gov/offices/OPE/PPI/FinPostSecEd/gladieux.html#f1 (accessed January 2, 2014).

Gladieux, L.E. & Swail, W.S. (1998) Financial Aid is not Enough: improving the odds of college success, *College Board Review*, 185 (Summer), 2-11.

Hansen, W.L. (1983) Impact of Student Financial Aid on Access, *Proceedings of the Academy of Political Science*, 35(2), 84-96.

Harvard University (2012) *Harvard University Fact Book 2011-2012.* Cambridge, MA: Office of Institutional Research. http://osp.fad.harvard.edu/content/federal-sources

Institute for College Access and Success (2013) *Student Debt and the Class of 2012.* Oakland, CA: Institute for College Access and Success.

Johnson, H. (2012) *Defunding Higher Education: what are the effects on college enrollment?* San Francisco: Public Policy Insitute of California.

Kahlenberg, R.D. (2010) *Affirmative Action for the Rich: legacy preferences in college admissions.* New York: Century Foundation.

Kane, T.J. (1994) College Entry by Blacks since 1970: the role of college costs, family background, and the returns to education, *Journal of Political Economy*, 102(5), 878-911.

Lee, D. (2013) Household Debt and Credit: student debt. Federal Reserve Bank of New York, February 28.

Long, B.T. (2004) Does the Format of an Aid Program Matter? The Effect of In-Kind Tuition Subsidies, *Review of Economics and Statistics*, 86(3), 767-782.

Long, B.T. (2008) What is Known about the Impact of Financial Aid? Implications for Policy. NCPR Working Paper, National Center for Postsecondary Education, Columbia University.

Lucas, D. & Moore, D. (2010) Guaranteed vs. Direct Lending: the case of student loans, in D. Lucas (Ed.) *Measuring and Managing Federal Financial Risk.* Chicago: University of Chicago Press.

McMillan, C. (2013) Governor Signs 2013-14 Budget. University of California. http://www.universityofcalifornia.edu/news/article/29695 (accessed January 7, 2014).

National Center for Education Statistics (2010) *Status and Trends in the Education of Racial and Ethnic Groups.* US Department of Education, NCES 2010-015. Washington, DC: US Government Printing Office .

National Conference of State Legislatures (2013) For-profit Colleges and Universities. http://www.ncsl.org/research/education/for-profit-colleges-and-universities.aspx (accessed December 20, 2013).

Organisation for Economic Cooperation and Development (OECD) (2013) *Education at a Glance 2013: OECD indicators.* Paris: OECD.

Plumer, B. (2013) America's Staggering Defense Budget, in Charts. *Washington Post,* January 7. http://www.washingtonpost.com/blogs/wonkblog/wp/2013/01/07/everything-chuck-hagel-needs-to-know-about-the-defense-budget-in-charts/ (accessed December 10, 2013).

Quinto, J.E. (2011) Entitlement Legislation in California: effectiveness of Cal Grant Program SB 1644. PhD thesis, California State University, Fresno.

Rivlin, A. (1969) *Toward a Long-range Plan for Federal Financial Support for Higher Education: a report to the president.* Washington, D.C.: Department of Health, Education, and Welfare.

Rodda, A.S. (1970) Tuition: considerations of interest to democratic legislators, via The Rodda Project: paying for a university education. http://thebackbench.blogspot.co.uk/2007/08/tuition-at-university-of-california.html (accessed January 6, 2014).

Rothblatt, S. (2011) *What is Happening to the California Dream? Revisiting Clark Kerr in 2011*. Oxford: University of Oxford.

Sallie Mae (2011) *Annual Report*. Delaware: SLM Corporation.

Shapiro, R.J. & Pham, N.D. (2010) *Taxpayers' Costs to Support Higher Education: a comparison of public, private not-for-profit, and private for-profit institutions*. Washington, DC: Sonecon.

Shierholz, H., Sabadish, N. & Finio, N. (2013) The Class of 2013: young graduates still face dim job prospects. EPI Briefing Paper #360, April 10, Economic Policy Institute.

Stampen, J.O. & Fenske, R.H. (1988) The Impact of Financial Aid on Ethnic Minorities, *Review of Higher Education*, 11(4), 337-353.

St John, E.P. (2002) *The Access Challenge: rethinking the causes of the new inequality*. Bloomington, IN: Indiana Education Policy Center.

University of California, Berkeley (UC Berkeley) (2012) 2012-13 UC Berkeley Budget Plan. http://cfo.berkeley.edu/sites/default/files/BerkeleyBudgetPlan2012-13.pdf (accessed January 6, 2014).

University of California, Berkeley (UC Berkeley) (2013) *Cost of Attendance*. http://admissions.berkeley.edu/costofattendance (accessed December 20, 2013).

University of California, Berkeley (UC Berkeley) (2014) International Student Expenses. http://internationaloffice.berkeley.edu/students/current/expenses (accessed January 5, 2014).

UC Commission on the Future (2010) First Round of Recommendations from the Working Groups. University of California. March. http://ucfuture.universityofcalifornia.edu/presentations/cotf_wg_first_recs.pdf (accessed December 10, 2013).

University of California Office of the President (2011) UC Mandatory Student Charge Levels. December. Budget and Capital Resources. http://www.ucop.edu/operating- budget/_files/fees/documents/history_fees.pdf (accessed 25 eptember 2014).

University of California (2013a) Paying for UC. http://admission.universityofcalifornia.edu/paying-for-uc/ (accessed January 6, 2014).

University of California (2013b) Student Debt. Accountability Report 2013. http://accountability.universityofcalifornia.edu/index/3.7.1 (accessed January 7, 2014).

University of California History (2014) A Historical View of Today's University. http://sunsite.berkeley.edu/uchistory/general_history/overview/tour1.html (accessed January 5, 2014).

University of New Hampshire (2013) Tuition. http://admissions.unh.edu/tuitionfees (accessed December 20, 2013).

University of Wyoming (2013) Cost of Attendance. http://www.uwyo.edu/admissions/scholarships/cost-of-attendance.html (accessed December 20, 2013).

US Census Bureau (2013) State and County Quick Facts: California. http://quickfacts.census.gov/qfd/states/06000.html (accessed December 20, 2013).

US Department of Education (2009) Institutional Characteristics Component. National Center for Education Statistics, Integrated Postsecondary Education Data System (IPEDS). Fall. http://nces.ed.gov/das/library/tables_listings/showTable2005.asp?popup=true&tableID=7072&rt=p (accessed December 20, 2013).

US Department of Education (2013a) Types of Aid. http://studentaid.ed.gov/types#federal-aid (accessed December 28, 2013).

US Department of Education (2013b) TEACH Grants. http://studentaid.ed.gov/types/grants-scholarships/teach (accessed December 31, 2013).

US House (2003) 108th Congress, 1st Session. *H.R. 3311, Affordability in Higher Education Act of 2003*. Washington: Government Printing Office.

US House (2007) 110th Congress, 1st Session. *H.R. 2669, College Cost Reduction and Access Act*. Washington: Government Printing Office.

US House (2008) 110th Congress, 2nd Session. *H.R. 5715, Ensuring Continued Access to Students Loans Act of 2008*. Washington: Government Printing Office.

US Senate (2000) *SB 1644, Ortiz-Pacheco-Poochigian-Vasconcellos Cal Grant Act*. California: Senate Rules Committee.

White House (2014) Higher Education. http://www.whitehouse.gov/issues/education/higher-education (accessed January 5, 2014).

Wilensky, H.L. (1975) *The Welfare State and Equality: structural and ideological roots of public expenditures*. Berkeley: University of California Press.

Wilkinson, R. (2005) *Aiding Students, Buying Students: fnancial aid in America*. Nashville: Vanderbilt University Press.

CHAPTER 7

Tuition Fees and Participation in Chinese Higher Education: the long march to marketisation and massification

KAI YU & JIN JIN

ABSTRACT The introduction of tuition fees has been one of the most significant reforms in Chinese higher education. This chapter first traces the history of tuition fee policies in China and offers analysis on why China introduced tuition fees. It then looks at the current tuition fee system in Chinese higher education, including the decision-making mechanism, variations between regions and disciplines, as well as the student support system. In the last part, the chapter discusses the impact of tuition fees on Chinese higher education, with a focus on the impact on equality. Although the introduction of tuition fees has driven massification and marketization in Chinese higher education, there is still a long way to go to build a system that can accommodate both the concerns of the market and equality.

Introduction

The introduction of tuition fees has been one of the most significant reforms in Chinese higher education since the founding of the People's Republic of China in 1949. University tuition fees have been a subject of much discussion within and beyond higher education, particularly the determination of a socially-acceptable level of fees and their influence on university participation. The Ministry of Education (MoE) has identified fine-tuning of tuition fees and improving the university student support system as two of the most important objectives for the long-term development of Chinese higher education (MoE, 2010). This chapter discusses the evolution of tuition fee policies in China, the rationales that led to the introduction of tuition fees, the decision-making mechanism for setting fee levels, the disparities in fees within higher education, and the impact of tuition fees on university participation in China.

History of Tuition Fee Policies in China

The policies on tuition fees in Chinese higher education have undergone three significant stages since 1949 – Free education from 1949-1979, dual-track tuition fees from 1980-1996, and one-policy up-front fees from 1997.

Free Education (1949-1979)

Since the founding of the People's Republic of China, the Chinese government has implemented a policy of central planning in every segment of industry. To best utilise limited resources for socialist construction projects, central and provincial governments have strictly planned, monitored and shared production in every industry. The field of higher education has been no exception. In this period, higher education graduates were urgently needed as senior human resources for social construction projects, and the government controlled the recruitment and assignment of university graduates. Only a small number of the most talented students could enter higher education, and they all received tuition fee waivers, in addition to a stipend covering living costs during their years of study (Bao, 2008). At this stage, the tuition fee policy tended to be based on primarily political considerations of socialist construction (Zhang, 2002).

Dual-track Tuition Fees (1980-1996)

In 1978, the Chinese central government transformed its management philosophy with the introduction of market principles. Market-oriented reforms affected the field of higher education, as it did other economic sectors. Expansion in industry demanded more talent, putting pressure on the state quota system in higher education. Higher education institutions (HEIs) gradually began to increase their enrolment by recruiting self-funded or employer-funded students. The National College Enrolment Meeting in 1980 approved this practise resolving that 'from this year onwards, institutions that have satisfied the enrolment plan the government set, can recruit fee-paying students' (Bao, 2008, p. 70). Under this agreement, some universities began to enrol self-funded students in 1980. In 1984, the State Education Commission (SEC) (predecessor of the Ministry of Education [MoE]) allowed universities to admit students recommended and funded by employers (SEC et al, 1984). Normally, self- and employer-funded students were admitted according to standards which usually were less strict than the general admission requirements; the students then were responsible for finding their own employment after graduation (Huang, 2010). Although this reform gave rise to concerns regarding educational equality, it was confirmed in the Decision on Educational System Reform issued by the Central Committee of the Communist Party of China in 1985 (Bao, 2008). University students were divided into two tracks: publicly-funded students who received free education and were assigned jobs after graduation, and self- and employer-funded students who were educated at a university, but had to find their own employment after graduation. Table I shows a decade's change of self- and employer-funded students as a percentage of university enrolment from 1986 onwards.

Year	Employer-funded students	Self-funded students	Total fee-paying students
1986	8.25	0.52	8.77
1987	8.48	1.72	10.30
1988	9.42	6.30	15.72
1989	9.49	4.32	13.81
1990	8.83	2.85	11.68
1991	9.21	1.93	11.14
1992	15.24	11.44	26.68
1993	24.49	14.50	38.99
1994	20.49	14.61	35.10
1995	18.96	13.16	34.12

Table I. Self- and employer-funded students as a percentage of university enrolment, 1986-1995 (%). *Source*: Wang, 2010.

One-policy Up-front Fees (1997 – until present)

Since the late 1980s, the free-tuition track in higher education has gradually been abolished, with the dual-track fee regime representing an interim stage. In 1989, the SEC, State Price Control Bureau and Ministry of Finance published a document stating that the free-education policy no longer aligned with economic and social development and that universities must charge tuition fees (SEC et al, 1989). In 1993, several institutions abandoned the dual-track policy and charged all newly admitted students. In the next year, 39 institutions charged all students. By 1995, that number had increased to 246 (Bao, 2008). In 1996, the SEC, State Price Control Bureau and Ministry of Finance published *Provisional Regulation on College Tuition Fees*, stating that higher education was non-compulsory, and therefore colleges could charge students tuition fees as stated in the Regulation. The government also established the standard for setting the level of tuition fees at 25% of the average per capita annual teaching cost in higher education (SEC et al, 1996). Since 1997, all HEIs in China have charged students tuition fees.

Rationales

The major Chinese higher education policy documents related to tuition fees do not discuss in detail the rationales for moving from free education to charging fees; however, the authors believe that the main cause was the market forces released by the reform and opening up in China starting in 1978. To identify these causes, it is important first to understand why China implemented a policy of free education before the 1980s. First and foremost, against a background of state-planned management, the social benefits of higher education held greater weight than personal benefits. The government assigned university graduates to positions taking into consideration the needs of socialist construction, ignoring graduates' personal desires or ambitions (Zhang, 2002). Moreover, the salaries of university graduates were aligned with non-graduates according to the principle of equal sharing adopted in the era of the planned economy. Personal benefits were of little significance in the framework of planned management. Talented individuals were trained for the state and paid by the socialist state. Second, the free education policy was related to the mission of higher education as explicated by the government of that time. During the first National Education and National Higher Education work meetings in 1949 and 1950, the government described the mission of higher education as 'increasing the access of children of peasants and workers and cultivating them to be intellectuals serving state construction' (p. 34). Waiving tuition fees was an important measure to increase access for students from lower social classes. At that time, regardless of social class, Chinese earnings met only basic living costs, leaving little additional income for extras including higher education (Zhang, 2002). This situation provided another pragmatic reason for implementing the policy of free education.

However, these rationales for free education became less valid amid the economic and social transition in China that began in 1978. First, the introduction of tuition fees reflected the larger market-oriented reform movement in the sector of higher education. The movement had affected all aspects of Chinese society since the government abandoned the philosophy of central planning and initiated market mechanisms. One such market-oriented change, the dual-track policy categorising students as self-funded or employer-funded, broke the tight link between higher education and state needs. After graduation, students could find jobs based on their own interests rather than the needs of the state. Receiving higher education was no longer in preparation for socialist construction, but a kind of personal investment. This reform allowed individuals more personal choices and benefits; consequently, students were required to share part of the higher education cost.

Second, the government chose to implement the dual-track policy instead of increasing the state quota partly due to the limited public funding available to deal with the fast growth in demand for higher education. Fuelled by dramatic economic developments after 1978, university enrolment increased 120% from 1980 to 1985 (Li, 2008), resulting in a sharp rise in costs for HEIs. However, the gross domestic product (GDP) increased by only 98.4% in the same period (National Bureau of Statistics of China, 1996), and the government education budget remained at 2.3% of GDP (Bao, 2008); thus, government funding had limited ability to cover the rapidly increasing tuition fees and teaching costs of the growing student population. A number of studies highlighted the financial tension in Chinese higher education since the 1980s and concluded that it prompted the introduction of the cost-recovery policy (Li & Min, 2001; Zeng & Zhang, 2007; Bao, 2008).

In addition, Chinese families could better afford higher education because of increased income from the rapid economic development. As seen in Table I, only 0.52% of students at university paid tuition fees in 1986, but the figure rose to 14.5% in 1993, a 30-fold increase. This dramatic rise in the proportion of self-funded students provides evidence that Chinese families could afford higher education. This ability to afford higher education is also supported by the percentage of family income spent on tuition fees. When HEIs began to charge students tuition fees in the early 1980s, the government required that the fee level be between 100 to 300 Renminbi (RMB) (Bao, 2008; Zhao & Song, 2008). When some institutions charged all students in 1993, the fee level rose to approximately 600 RMB. Although the tuition fees increased year by year, higher education was affordable for Chinese families when measured by the percentage of income spent on tuition fees. According to Table II, tuition consumed just over 15% of income for a rural family and less than 10% for an urban family. Even when compared to corresponding figures (generally between 10-15%) in other countries (Zhao & Song, 2008), the fee level in China in the early years was perceived as reasonable.

	1993	1994	1995	1996	1997
Average tuition fees	610	889	1,114	1,319	1,620
Average rural family income	3,686.4	4,884.0	6,310.8	7,704.4	8,360.4
Average urban family income	7,732.2	10,488.6	12,849	14,516.7	15,480.9
Tuition fees as a percentage of rural family income	16.5%	18.2%	17.7%	17.1%	19.4%
Tuition fees as a percentage of urban family income	7.9%	8.5%	8.7%	9.1%	10.5%

Note: The exchange rate of pound sterling (GBP) against RMB on 16 December 2013, according to the Bank of China, was 9.9638.

Table II. Tuition fees and family income in China 1993-1997 (RMB).
Source: Zhao & Song, 2008.

If political considerations were paramount in the age of central planning, market forces tended to drive higher education reform in China after 1978. Introducing tuition fees was a cost-sharing strategy to handle the financial burden caused by the expansion of the student population, and simultaneously, growing family income created the conditions necessary to support the strategy.

A Glance at the Current Tuition Fee System in China

Since 1997, when China first implemented the tuition fee policy at all universities, tuition has continuously trended upward. There are no official statistics on the national average fee level in China, but some studies (Zhao & Song, 2008; Wang, 2010; Zhu, 2011) have estimated the levels from 1998 to 2007 (see Table III). Tuition doubled between 1998 and 2001, reaching nearly 4000 RMB. The drastic increase concerned the government, so in 2001 the MoE, State Planning Commission (predecessor of the National Development and Reform Commission) and the Ministry of Finance released a joint circular (MoE et al, 2001) stipulating that tuition and accommodation fees should remain at 2000 levels. After the circular was released, tuition fees grew steadily, but at a much lower rate.

Year					Fee level				
1998	1999	2000	2001	2002	2003	2004	2005	2006	2007
1974	2769	3550	3895	4224	4419	4785	4968	5233	5986

Table III. National average tuition fee level from 1998 to 2007 (RMB).
Sources: Zhao & Song, 2008; Wang, 2010; Zhu, 2011.

To better understand the setting of fee levels in China, this chapter will now discuss the decision-making mechanism and criteria, as well as the variations between regions and across the higher education sector.

Decision-making Mechanism

In China, tuition fee levels of universities are determined jointly by the central government and provincial authorities. This decision-making mechanism was formulated in 1989 when the central government published a tuition fee policy document (SEC et al, 1989) stating that tuition and accommodation fees should be determined by provincial authorities based on local economic and educational conditions. The *Provisional Regulation on College Tuition Fees* document reaffirmed that mechanism, establishing that the central government formulated the general management principles for setting tuition fee levels and set a national threshold to serve as a reference for provinces, who then determined a specific tuition fee level based on local economic circumstances, educational conditions and residents' financial ability (SEC et al, 1996). Although the higher education landscape in China has changed over several stages, this decision mechanism has remained the same in practice and been restated in several important documents related to higher education tuition fees.

Although the policy documents do not assign a role to HEIs in this process, they are in practice positioned as an important stakeholder when setting tuition fee levels. Of 31 provinces, 23 allow universities some flexibility in deciding their own tuition fee levels. Generally, the major universities can raise their fee levels above the provincial standard, and within individual institutions, the tuition fees for some popular subjects may be higher than for others (Xu, 2007). The HEIs in these 23 provinces have some right to determine their fee levels following the basic threshold set by the local authority. Consequently, tuition fees vary among different HEIs, and within a single university, the fee levels might vary among subjects, as discussed in detail later.

Decision-making Criteria

Along with the localised decision mechanism, two standards have a role in determining university tuition fee levels. The core standard is the level of the average per capita teaching cost within Chinese higher education and a subsidiary standard is the affordability of higher education in each province.

The average per capita teaching cost is the basis on which the central government determines the national threshold. The tuition fee level has been set at 25% of the average per capita teaching cost in higher education. This standard was stated in policies from the onset of introducing tuition fees, while the specific value of 25% was first explicated in 1996 (SEC et al, 1996). Notably, the standard of 25% refers to the average teaching cost in the entire higher education sector, not the teaching cost for any individual institution (Wu et al, 2011). To avoid overly steep increases in tuition fees, the MoE has released data on the national average per capita operating cost as a reference for provinces annually since 2001 (MoE et al, 2001).

Although the central government publishes the national standard for higher education tuition fees, provincial governments can adjust local fee levels according to local circumstances. This flexibility was first granted in the 1989 official document which allowed tuition fees to vary from 100 to 300 RMB depending upon local economic and educational conditions (SEC et al, 1989). Since then, each provincial government has set university tuition fee levels based on the published national criterion. This mechanism ensures the localisation of the unified national standard, making the fees suitable for local circumstances.

Variations in Fee Levels

Regional differences. Under this decision-making mechanism, tuition fee levels vary among provinces. Yuan and Cui (2010) compared the tuition fees for sciences and engineering subjects and the fees as a percentage of per capita family income between provinces (the results are shown in Table IV). The data on tuition fees in this study came from the 2010 university enrolment plans at Jiangxi Province, which included 630 HEIs in 30 provinces, while the data on family income was taken from national statistics. The highest tuition is charged in Chongqing, 1.8 times higher than the lowest figure, which is charged in Ningxia. Tuition fee levels were not positively correlated to provincial economic development levels as measured by local per capita GDP, but an obvious relationship was found between the affordability of higher education and provincial per capita GDP. Families in underdeveloped provinces have more difficulty affording higher education.

However, when examining the disparities between regions rather than between provinces, tuition fee levels are seen to reflect regional economic conditions. Tuition fees in eastern China are the highest, followed by the middle and finally western China, which is the most underdeveloped. In 2007, the average tuition in the eastern developed provinces was between 4000 and 5000 RMB, compared to 3000 to 4000 RMB in the middle region, and 2500 to 3500 RMB in the west (Hu, 2011).

Province	Tuition fees in sciences and engineering (RMB)	Tuition fees as a percentage of per capita urban family income in the province (%)	Tuition fees as a percentage of per capita rural family income in the province (%)
Chongqing	5371	34.1	119.9
Shanghai	5097	17.7	40.8
Guangdong	5056	23.4	73.2
Peking	5047	18.9	43.3
Hainan	5039	36.6	106.2
Hubei	5022	35.0	99.7
Sichuan	4817	34.8	108.0
Jiangxi	4816	34.3	94.9
Liaoning	4798	30.4	80.5
Hunan	4766	31.6	97.1
Shaanxi	4658	33.0	135.5
Yunnan	4609	32.0	136.8
Jiangsu	4553	22.2	56.9
Anhui	4495	31.9	99.8
Jilin	4405	31.4	83.7
Fujian	4396	22.5	65.8
Heilongjiang	4344	34.6	83.4
Gansu	4320	36.2	145.0
Zhejiang	4216	17.1	42.1

Shanxi	4129	29.5	97.3
Tianjin	4053	18.9	46.7
Guangxi	4028	26.1	101.2
Shandong	3889	21.8	63.6
Hebei	3851	26.2	74.8
Henan	3737	26.0	77.7
Xinjiang	3517	28.7	90.6
Inner Mongolia	3516	22.2	71.2
Guizhou	3473	27.0	115.5
Qinghai	3238	25.5	96.8
Ningxia	2935	20.9	72.5

Table IV. 2010 tuition fee levels by province.
Source: adapted from Yuan & Cui (2010).

Differences between types of HEIs. Undergraduate education in China can be undertaken at regular HEIs or HEIs for adults. Regular HEIs are open to students who take the National College Entrance Examination, while HEIs for adults admit students who have left high school, but still want to pursue undergraduate education. This chapter discusses only tuition fee levels at regular institutions, which attract an overwhelming majority (87.2%) of all students in higher education (Yu et al, 2010).

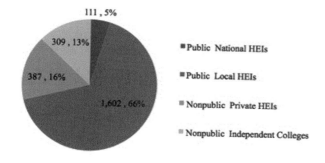

Figure 1. Composition of Chinese HEI by type.
Source: National Bureau of Statistics of China, 2012.

Regular HEIs in China can be divided into public sector and non-public sector institutions. The main difference between them is that public institutions receive funding from the central or provincial governments, while the non-public institutions do not (Yu et al, 2010). Regular public HEIs can be further divided into two categories: national HEIs administered by the MoE or other central ministries in the capital of Beijing, and local HEIs administered by provincial or municipal authorities. Non-public HEIs can also be divided into two types: private institutions which are owned by a private entity, and independent colleges which are funded by a private investor, but connected to a public university. The numbers of each type of institution and their respective share of all HEIs are shown in Figure 1. Public universities account for the majority of Chinese HEIs, with 1602 local HEIs and 111 national institutions. Non-public HEIs make up only 29% of all HEIs, with similar numbers of private HEIs and independent colleges.

To demonstrate the disparity in tuition fees between different types of HEIs, this study noted and examined the different tuition levels in three cases from the east, middle and western regions of China for each of the four types (see Table V).

Public Sector			
Institutions	Province	Benke	Zhuanke
National HEIs			
Shanghai Jiao Tong University	Shanghai	5,000	-
University of Science and Technology of China	Anhui	4,800	-
Xi'an Jiao Tong University	Shaanxi	4,950	-
Local HEIs			
Shanghai University	Shanghai	5,000	7,500
Hefei University	Anhui	3,900	-
Xi'an University	Shaanxi	4,500	5,500

Non-public Sector			
Institutions	Province	Benke	Zhuanke
Private Institutions			
Sanda University	Shanghai	14,000	-
Anhui Xinhua University	Anhui	11,000	7,000
Xi'an Eurasia University	Shaanxi	12,000	8,000
Independent Colleges			
Shanghai Normal University Tianhua College	Shanghai	17,000	-
Anhui University Jianghuai College	Anhui	11,000	-
Xi'an Jiao Tong University City College	Shaanxi	12,000	-

Notes: Given the variations among disciplines, the data used in the this table refers to tuition fees for general natural sciences and engineering subjects, excluding the most popular subjects in this disciplinary area. Shanghai is the economically most developed province in the sample, followed by Anhui and Shaanxi.

Table V. 2013 tuition fee levels at four types of HEIs in China (RMB).
Source: http://www.eol.cn/

Generally, a clear disparity existed between the public and non-public sectors of universities, while, within a single sector, the differences among the various types of institution were marginal. Annual tuition fees for *Benke* education [1] at non-public institutions were between 11,000 and 17,000 RMB, twice as high as the equivalent fees for public institutions, while fees for *Zhuanke* education [2] in both sectors were approximately 7000 RMB. The gap between the public and non-public sectors can be explained by their different funding structures. Income from tuition fees contributed as much as 80% of non-public HEIs' total income, while government funding is the most important source of income of public HEIs (Chu, 2007).

Regarding variation within the public sector, as noted in the policy documents, the national universities, which include almost all of the major universities in every province, charged slightly more than local public universities; however, a similar variation did not seem to exist between different types of non-public HEIs. In addition, only the non-public sector HEIs demonstrated regional disparities. Private institutions and independent colleges in Shanghai charged much more than institutions of the same type in underdeveloped provinces. Differences in fee levels charged by public institutions in different provinces are less pronounced.

Differences between disciplines. Regardless of the type of institution, tuition fees by subjects show a distinct pattern (see Table VI).

Institution	General Subjects	Popular Subjects	Arts and Design	International Programmes
Public HEIs				
Shanghai Jiao Tong University	5,000	6,500	10,000	45,000-50,000
Renmin University of China	5,000	6,000	10,000	60,000
Hefei University	3,900	4,290	7,000	10,000
Liaoning University	4,600	5,200	10,000	23,000
Non-public HEIs				
Sanda University	14,000	-	16,000	20,000
Xi'an Eurasia University	10,000	12,000	15,000	-
Southeast University Chengxian College	14,000	15,000	16,500	-
Xi'an Jiao Tong University City College	10,000	12,000	15,000	-

Table VI. Disparity of annual tuition fees by subjects in Chinese HEIs (RMB).
Source: http://www.eol.cn/

Generally, popular subjects, such as information sciences, business management, foreign languages and medical sciences, charge 20% higher fees than other subjects. Popular subjects usually represent an institution's academic strengths or lead to high-income employment after graduation. Compared to other subjects, the arts or related subjects charge the highest tuition fees at every kind of HEI. International programmes developed in recent years have a similar fee structure, usually exceeding 20,000 RMB annually, five to ten times higher than other subjects.

There should be one point to be clarified. Some readers might be confused why the tuition fees of Shanghai Jiao Tong University in Table V use the figures for its general subjects as shown in Table VI, while Xi'an Jiao Tong City College and Xi'an Eurasia University use the rates for popular subjects as their tuition fees in Table V. This is because Table V shows the tuition fees for general natural sciences and engineering subjects, which happen to be the popular subjects at Xi'an Jiao Tong City College and Xi'an Eurasia University. Tuition fees for general natural sciences and engineering subjects at Shanghai Jiao Tong University, used in Table V, are the same for humanities and social sciences, although certain natural sciences and engineering subjects at Shanghai Jiao Tong University charge higher fees as popular subjects.

Student Support

Since introducing tuition fees, the Chinese government has stressed the importance of student support. The government and HEIs should provide adequate financial support to students with economic difficulties in order to ensure their access to universities (SEC et al, 1996). Student support in China includes student loans, scholarships, studentships, work-study programmes and subsidies (see Table VII for details). The national scholarships and studentships are funded by the central government, and institutional scholarships and studentships by institutions, either on their own or through donations. According to the MoE (2012), student support, including government investment and social investment funds, reached 50.06 billion RMB, distributed among 41.7 million students, in 2011.

Student Support	Amount	Capacity	Criteria
National Level			
National Scholarship	8000	50,000 students	Merit-based
National Aspiration Scholarship	5000	510,000 students	Combination of merit- and needs-based
National Studentship	1000-3000	3,400,000 students	Needs-based, may be combined with the above two scholarships
National Student Loan	No more than 6000	No more than 20% of the enrolment	Needs-based; students at private *Zhuanke* and independent colleges are ineligible.
Local Level			
Local Student	No more	Province-	Needs-based; local residents who are

Loan	than 6000	based	admitted into higher education
Institutional Level			
Scholarships	Institution-based	Institution-based	Merit-based
Studentships	Institution-based	Institution-based	Needs-based
Work-study Programmes	Institution-based	Institution-based	Needs-based
Subsidies	Institution-based	Institution-based	Tuition waiver and stipend subsidies for economically deprived students

Table VII. Student support in Chinese higher education (RMB).
Sources: Wangyi Education, 2011; Ministry of Finance, Ministry of Education & China National Centre for Student Assistance Administration, 2012.

The impact of student support programmes (or lack thereof) on participation in higher education are discussed in the next section.

The Impact of Tuition Fees on Participation in Chinese Higher Education

The introduction of tuition fees in China boosted higher education development by increasing HEIs' income, efficiency, and opportunities for participation. Initially, tuition fees were an important source of funding for expanding higher education. As noted, the increase in government funding lagged behind the pace of development in higher education; due to the emphasis on basic education, only 20% of the government's education budget has been allocated for higher education (Wang, 2010). Amid limited government funding, tuition fees play an important role in increasing income and support for the expansion of Chinese HEIs. As shown in Table VIII, tuition fees contributed just under 30% of university funds in 2007, second only to government funding.

	1978	1990	1992	1995	1997	2003	2007
Government Funds	95.9	87.7	81.8	73.57	67.62	64.24	55.19
Tuition Fees	0.0	1.8	4.6	11.89	15.72	27.92	29.63
Services	4.1	10.3	12.8	8.30	8.73	1.15	7.66
Donations	0.0	0.2	0.8	6.24	7.93	6.69	7.52

Table VIII. Funding sources for Chinese higher education, 1978-2007 (%).
Source: Wang, 2010.

In addition, the introduction of tuition fees spurred competition within higher education and increased institutional responsibility for improving management efficiency. Institutions were forced to enhance their teaching quality and effectively manage their finances to be competitive in the higher education market (Tan & Zhang, 2005). The tuition fee policy also strengthened the link between HEIs and society. In the planned economy, HEIs restricted themselves to the state's interests, but tuition fees drove institutions to focus on the needs of customers, which, in turn, promoted innovation in higher education (Zeng & Zhang, 2007).

Regarding tuition fees' effect on university participation, the first point to note is that increasing tuition fees have occurred alongside rapidly increasing enrolments. According to the data in Table III, average tuition fees in China rose from 1974 RMB at their introduction in 1997 to 5233 RMB in 2006, a 165% increase in a decade. The rise, though, seems to have had little negative influence on higher education enrolment. From 1997 to 2006, the enrolment rate in Chinese higher education rose from 9.1% to 22%, nearly the same rate of increase as that of tuition fees (see Figure 2). This situation can be explained by China's economic development which increased demand for higher education. Tuition fees as a percentage of per capita GDP (shown in Table IX) shows that the pace of tuition fee increases compared to the pace of economic development. This ratio peaked in 2001 and then trended downward, suggesting a relatively steady increase in tuition fees compared to the pace of economic development in China.

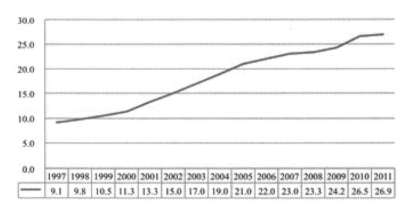

Figure 2. Gross participation rate in higher education, 1997-2011 (%).
Source: MoE, 1997-2011.

However, the increasing participation rate does not ensure equal distribution of economic and educational resources across the social strata. Social inequality exists despite the rising participation in Chinese higher education. After a drastic increase in the late 1990s, tuition fees have exceeded the economic reach of students from disadvantaged social classes, hindering their access (Liu & Zhang, 2004; He, 2007; Wu & Fan, 2007). Affordability is an important influence on access to higher education. Wu and Fan (2007) analysed tuition fees as a percentage of per capita disposable income and concluded that the fees in China are much higher than in other countries. As seen in Table IX, higher education tuition as a percentage of per capita family income has grown since the launch of one-policy tuition fees, peaking at 56.78% for urban families in 2001 and of 170.63% for rural families in 2002.

Year	Tuition Fees (RMB)	Per Capita GDP (RMB)	Tuition Fees as a Percentage of Per Capita GDP (%)	Tuition Fees as a Percentage of Per Capita Urban Family Income	Tuition Fees as a Percentage of Per Capita Rural Family Income
1997	1589	6,420	24.75	30.79	76.03
1998	1974	6,796	29.05	36.39	91.30
1999	2769	7,159	38.68	47.30	125.28
2000	3550	7,858	45.18	56.53	157.54
2001	3895	8,622	45.18	56.78	164.60
2002	4224	9,398	44.95	54.84	170.63
2003	4419	10,542	41.92	52.16	168.52
2004	4785	12,336	38.79	50.79	162.95
2005	4968	14,103	35.23	47.35	152.63
2006	5233	15,973	32.76	44.50	145.89

Table IX. University tuition fees, per capita GDP and per capita family income, 1997-2006.
Source: Wang, 2010.

Liu and Zhang (2004) investigated perceptions of higher education tuition fees amongst Chinese citizens based on 1997-2001 data from the *China Statistics Yearbook*. They found that, after the drastic increase of tuition fees in 2000, 60% of urban citizens and 80% of rural citizens could not afford higher education. He (2007) assessed the ability to pay for higher education among residents of 30 provinces from 2000 to 2005 and found that 40% of urban citizens and 80% of rural citizens could not afford higher education. These studies show that tuition fees became barely affordable for disadvantaged groups in 2000, leading to economic hardship for many low-income poor students at university.

In addition, many studies (Liu & Jiang, 2008; Kuang, 2009; Li & Wu, 2010) demonstrate that current student support in China has a limited effect at meeting students' financial needs. The national student loan programme is the most important financing source for low-income students, but according to Kuang, it has not had the expected effect. Low-income students made up 20% of the higher education cohort and numbered 13.3 million in 2004. Based on the annual standard support of 6000 RMB for one student, low-income students required 16 billion RMB in loans; however, only 6.5 billion RMB was released in loans (Kuang, 2009). According to one study (Wan, 2006), 36.9% of students from an economically deprived family with a per capita annual income of less than 2000 RMB did not receive student loans.

For those who did, the loans were insufficient to cover tuition fees and living expenses during the years of study. According to a national survey (He, 2007), the annual expenses for a university student in 2005, including tuition and living expenses, was 12,153 RMB, while the loan was 6000 RMB annually (Liu & Jiang, 2008). High tuition fees make higher education less affordable for low-income families, and the current student support does not meet the financial needs of disadvantaged students, hindering access to higher education for those from lower social classes.

In addition to unequal access to higher education, enrolment behaviour also demonstrates social inequality. Students from advantaged social classes are more likely to enter more prestigious universities, while disadvantaged students tend to enter low-tier institutions (Li, 2006; Xie & Chen, 2007; Wang, 2011). Based on the data collected from 14,500 questionnaires distributed in a nationwide study, Wang (2011) determined the intergenerational transition rate (the percentage of students from one social class at university compared to the distribution of social classes in the national population) of each social class at different types of HEIs (see Table X).

Table X. Intergenerational transition rate at HEIs by social class. *Source*: Wang, 2011.

HEIs	Classes									
	Government Officials	Senior Managers	Entrepreneurs	Professionals	Clerks	Small Business	Staff in Business	Manual Workers	Peasants	Unemployed
National Major Universities	5.33	2.69	3.71	3.54	0.92	1.46	0.37	0.71	0.69	0.29
Public Benke Institutions	3.52	1.94	3.20	2.70	0.74	2.25	0.46	0.89	0.69	0.54
Public Zhuanke Institutions	2.57	1.81	3.50	2.09	0.63	2.20	0.57	0.88	0.81	0.46
Private Benke Institutions	4.19	3.75	19.2	1.61	0.83	3.90	0.56	0.49	0.22	0.11
Private Zhuanke Institutions	3.38	3.13	10.0	2.09	0.82	3.48	0.62	0.73	0.37	0.40
Independent Colleges	5.57	4.88	12.56	2.96	1.08	2.69	0.51	0.58	0.23	0.29

Here a '1' means that a social class is exactly proportionally represented in a particular type of HEI. Two conclusions can be drawn from Wang's work. First, the intergenerational transition rate in higher education for the highest four social classes is higher than for the lowest four social groupings. This discrepancy supports the claim that students from disadvantaged social classes have less access to higher education. Second, the disadvantaged students who enter higher education choose different types of HEIs. Advantaged students tend to enter major national universities and independent colleges, the best HEIs in the public and non-public sectors. In contrast, disadvantaged students tend to study at low-tier public institutions and private *Zhuanke* institutions. For instance, children of government officials at major universities have the highest intergenerational transition rate at 5.33, seven times higher than peasants and seventeen times higher than the unemployed.

While lower academic achievement influenced by a lack of social, cultural and other capital restricts access to major public universities for disadvantaged students, their exclusion from private education can be largely attributed to the high cost. As noted, if the tuition fees of approximately 5000 RMB have made higher education unaffordable for 40% of urban families and 80% of rural families (He, 2007), disadvantaged families have even more difficulty paying for private *Benke* education whose cost exceeds 10,000 RMB. The disparity in tuition fees at different types of HEIs pushes disadvantaged students into the public sector and lower-tier *Zhuanke* institutions in the private sector.

The unequal representation of students from different social backgrounds in higher education is problematic. Privileged students dominate prestigious universities and underprivileged students enter other public universities (Yu & Ertl, 2010). However, the prestigious universities provide more scholarships due to higher social donations (Li & Wu, 2010). A national survey conducted by Li (2006) in 2004 also demonstrated that students at major universities (key universities which are selected by the government to receive more funds in order to build world-class universities) receive more subsidies on tuition fees. Given the representation of social backgrounds in HEIs, this trend means that rich students pay less for potentially better education at prestigious universities and have more access to financial support, while poor students pay higher fees at less well-recognised HEIs and receive less financial support.

Social stratification exists not only among types of institutions, but also within institutions. Wang (2011) extended his study to investigate students' social backgrounds in different majors and found that privileged students were over-represented in popular subjects, while underprivileged students were dominant in majors that promise lower labour market returns. This discrepancy can be attributed to variation in costs across disciplines. Tuition fees in popular subjects are higher than for other majors, potentially discouraging price-sensitive students from lower social classes from choosing these subjects. Popular subjects usually lead to more promising employment with higher salaries, so the unbalanced distribution of social backgrounds among subjects will lead to unequal labour market returns, extending educational inequality into social inequality. Low-income students are similarly under-represented in international programmes. Although they offer many advantages through connections with premier international universities, the cost of 20,000 to 50,000 RMB is out of the reach of students from underprivileged families.

Conclusion and Discussion

Two principles have operated in the implementation and evolution of tuition fee policies in China: the market and equal access to higher education across the nation and social hierarchy. Although these principles have to some degree played complementary roles in the reform of Chinese higher education, both can be better brought into play with more support.

The market principle has been manifested in the evolution of Chinese tuition fee policies. Since the categories of self- and employer-funded students were introduced in the 1980s, Chinese higher education has sought to meet and accommodate the demands of customers. Although tuition fee levels are still determined through a government-controlled mechanism, market demand is reflected in the pricing of higher education, such as higher fees for popular subjects. The openness to the market generates more income and efficiency in Chinese higher education, but the current decision-making mechanism limits the effects. The largest problem posed by this system is that the price of a university's education services does not reflect its quality. Non-public institutions always charge the most because of their different funding structure, but their quality of education is not in line with their high price, giving them a constantly weakened position in the higher education market. Prestigious universities with premier education services, on the other hand, charge prices similar to other public universities, although government policies allow them to charge more. While the market mechanism has been introduced into Chinese higher education, the government retains significant powers to determine higher education prices.

One likely reason that the government insists on using the central-planning decision mechanism to set tuition fees is to protect under-privileged students. The localisation of tuition fee levels by provinces ensures that different educational and economic conditions can be taken into account and gives students in underdeveloped regions more opportunities with fewer economic burdens. Student support in the form of scholarships, studentships and loans has been offered since the introduction of tuition fees. However, for a considerable number of Chinese citizens, especially from deprived rural areas, tuition fees still exceed their ability to pay for higher education, and student support is far from sufficient to cover university costs. Policy makers and higher education institutions should devote more attention to building a more efficient student support system. Special schemes could be devised to give disadvantaged students access to premier education resources, such as international programmes. Business and other societal groups could be encouraged to become more involved in strengthening student support in China.

The market mechanism increases the efficiency of the development of Chinese higher education, while the government-controlled management plays an important role in ensuring equal access across the nation. However, how to balance these two principles and construct an efficient, socially fairer fees system in the field of higher education is a long-term issue that deserves further attention.

Notes

[1] *Benke* education leads to a bachelor's degree, normally following the academic track.

[2] *Zhuanke* education is a vocational track which leads to an undergraduate diploma, but not a degree.

References

Bao, H.Q. (2008) Changes in Higher Education Tuition Policies in China, *Tsinghua Journal of Education*, 29(2), 70-76.

Chu, Z.W. (2007) The Objectives and Reality of Multi-channel Financing at Chinese Universities, *Education & Economy*, 1, 50-55.

He, Z.Y. (2007) Analysis on the Affordability to Advanced Education for Rural Family in China, *Issue in Agricultural Economy*, 6, 40-43.

Hu, Y. Z. (2011) A Comparative Study of Financing between the National Universities and the Provincial Universities, *China Higher Education Research*, 11, 17-20.

Huang, L. (2010) The Evolvement of Higher Education Tuition Fee Policies in China Since 1949, *Higher Education Exploration*, 6, 54-58.

Kuang, Q. (2009) The Role of Education Bank in the Cost Sharing within Higher Education, *Heilongjiang Research on Higher Education*, 3, 25-28.

Li, L.S. & Wu, L.B. (2010) *A Study on the System Design to Achieve Equality within Higher education.* Beijing: Science Press.

Li, W.L. (2006) The Role of Higher Education Financing Policy in Providing Equal Enrolment Opportunity and Resource Distribution, *Peking University Education Review*, 4(2), 34-45.

Li, W.L. & Min, W.F. (2001) Tuition, Private Demand and Higher Education in China. http://www.tc.columbia.edu/centers/coce/pdf_files/v4.pdf

Li, W.S. (2008) *A Study on Equal Access to Higher Education in China.* Beijing: Beijing University Press.

Liu, J.M. & Jiang, Z.F. (2008) Empirical Analysis on Adjusting the Credit of the National Student Loan, *Zhejiang Finance*, 5, 62.

Liu, Y. & Zhang, F. (2004) Empirical Analysis on Citizens' Ability to Afford Higher Education and the Tuition Fee Policies, *China Soft Science*, 2, 14-20.

179

Ministry of Education (MoE) (1997-2011) Statistical Report on the National Educational Development. http://www.moe.edu.cn/publicfiles/business/htmlfiles/moe/moe_633/201308/155798.html

Ministry of Education (MoE) (2010) The Outline of the National Plan for Medium and Long-term Education Reform. http://www.gov.cn/jrzg/2010-07/29/content_1667143.htm

Ministry of Education (MoE) (2012) Economic Concerns Should Not Be The Reason for Students Declining Education. http://edu.163.com/12/0809/08/88F0LHQ700294JD5.html

Ministry of Education, State Planning Commission & Ministry of Finance (2001) Circular on Higher Education Institutions Charging Fees to 2001's Enrolment. http://www.gov.cn/gongbao/content/2001/content_60735.htm

Ministry of Finance, Ministry of Education & China National Centre for Student Assistance Administration (2012) A Brief Introduction on the Undergraduate Student Support. http://www.gov.cn/banshi/2012-11/20/content_2270886.htm

National Bureau of Statistics of China (1996) *China Statistics Yearbook*. Beijing: China Statistics Press.

National Bureau of Statistics of China (2012). *China Statistics Yearbook*. Beijing: China Statistics Press.

State Education Commission, State Planning Commission & Ministry of Finance (1984) *Tentative Scheme on Higher Education Institution Acceptance of Employer-funded Students*. http://fagui.eol.cn/html/201008/4064.shtml

State Education Commission, State Planning Commission & Ministry of Finance (1996) *Provisional Regulation on College Tuition Fees*. http://cwc.fudan.edu.cn/s/41/t/76/0b/c1/info3009.htm

State Education Commission, State Price Control Bureau & Ministry of Finance (1989) *Regulation on Charging the Tuition Fees and the Living Fees at Regular Higher Education Institutions*. http://www.chinaacc.com/new/63/64/80/2006/3/zh64035429236002740-0.htm

Tan, Z.L. & Zhang, X.P. (2005) Analysis on Higher Education Pricing in China, *Heilongjiang Research on Higher Education*, 12, 1-3.

Wan, X.L. (2006) *Protection of the Rights and Interests of Disadvantaged Groups within Higher Education: a comparative study between the United States and China*. Changchun: Jilin People's Press.

Wang, T.X. (2010) *A Study of the Tuition Fees at Chinese Universities*. Beijing: Peking University Press.

Wang, W.L. (2011) *A Study on Chinese Higher Education Participation Based on Social Strata*. Guangzhou: Guangdong Higher Education Press.

Wangyi Education (2011) An Introduction on the Student Support in China. http://edu.163.com/special/gaokao/pkszz.html

Wu, H.Q., Zhong, F.F. & Chen, Y. (2011) Two Kinds of Forms for the Tuition Pricing of Higher Education, *Education & Economy*, 2, 58-61.

Wu, K.J. & Fan, X.Z. (2007) The Dilemma of the Tuition Criterion According to the Cost of Education, *Journal of Higher Education*, 28(1), 26-30.

Xie, Z.X. & Chen, X.W. (2007) Analysis on the Impact of Tuition Fees on the Higher Education Participation of Students from Different Social Strata in the Mainland China, *Education & Economy*, 2, 12-15.

Xu, G.X. (2007) The Third Party in the Tuition Fee Decision Making: an analysis of the relationship between the government and the university in China, *Jiangsu Higher Education*, 3, 34-36.

Yu, K., Andrea, S., Liu, L. & Chen, H.Z. (2010) *Tertiary Education at a Glance: China*. Shanghai: Shanghai Jiao Tong University Press.

Yu, K. & Ertl, H. (2010) Equity in Access to Higher Education in China: the role of public and non-public institutions, *Chinese Education and Society*, 43(6), 36-58.

Yuan, L.S. & Cui, S.Q. (2010) An Empirical Study on the Undergraduate Tuition Disparity in China, *Exploring Education Development*, 23, 1-6.

Zeng, D.R. & Zhang, D. (2007) Higher Education Cost Sharing in China and the Tuition Fee Policy, *Finance and Economics*, 11, 70-76.

Zhang, J.Q. (2002) The Policy of Free Education: its formation and influence, *Tsinghua Journal of Education*, 4, 33-38.

Zhao, J.H. & Song, S.L. (2008) An Analysis of the Relationship between Tuition Fees in Higher Education and the Income of Residents or the Increase of GDP per Person in China, *Journal of Liaoning Normal University*, 31(3), 59-61.

Zhu, J. (2011) Why the Higher Education Expansion Achieved in China: based on the Resource Dilution Model, *China Higher Education Research*, 4, 19-22.

CHAPTER 8

University Financing Policy in Québec: the test of the 'printemps érable'[1]

CHRISTIAN MAROY, PIERRE DORAY & MAMOUNA KABORE

ABSTRACT This chapter focuses on the higher education (HE) funding policy in Québec. Recently, the Québec Liberal Party government (2008-2012) put forward policy aimed at increasing university revenues with a very substantial tuition fees hike, i.e. 75% over five years. During the so-called '*Printemps Erable*' of 2012, students mobilized against this policy and went on strike until it became a major conflict that led to general elections and a government change in Québec. The first part of the chapter focuses on funding in the history of HE policies in Québec. The second section presents the various public arguments that were mobilized by the key protagonists of the *printemps érable*. The strong controversies between the narratives reveal a path dependancy of the debate and of the policy to some of the ideals of the so-called Quiet Revolution (in particular the necessity to deal with the problem of democratic access to HE). The chapter concludes that a pure neoliberal policy of marketization has been made difficult, due to this path dependancy and the relative balance of power enacted by the mobilization of the student movement. The third section focuses on the impact of the student movement on recent trends in Québec policies with respect to university funding.

Our chapter focuses on the recent post-secondary education policy in Québec, which includes the Collèges d'enseignement général et professionnel (CEGEPs) [2] and universities. For several years, the Liberal government tried to increase the income of universities through a substantial tuition increase of 75% over five years. Students rallied against this decision in the spring of 2012. A strike movement developed and grew into a major conflict, known as the 'printemps érable'.[3] This became a significant political and social event as the strike lasted six months. It mobilized up to 400,000 individuals (students and beyond, citizens of all generations) and led to new elections and a change of government. The new government proposed less onerous terms for tuition increases (with annual indexation), accompanied by new tools to adjust these fees, a restructuring of the student loan and scholarship system, and the monitoring of university governance.

The first section of this chapter provides a historical analysis of the policy debates and instruments that gave rise to the 2012 Liberal reform proposal. The second section presents the various public arguments of the key protagonists of the printemps érable: the Liberal government, universities, student associations, opposition parties, and trade unions. We highlight the different policy narratives (Radaelli, 2000) employed to support or oppose the increase during the printemps érable. The third section focuses on the impact of the student movement on recent trends in Québec universities' funding policies.

This chapter argue that, since the Quiet Revolution, Québec's policies on funding higher education (HE) have been characterized by the ideal of free education, considered as a means to increase accessibility to post-secondary education and to develop Québec society as a whole. However, since the 1980s, neoliberal discourse and a context of enhanced international competition among universities has led to a growing perception by governmental and university elites of an 'underfunding problem' in HE. This has challenged the influence of the Quiet Revolution philosophy with respect to financing education, and has also led to successive policies to raise tuition fees, most recently in 2011-12 by the Liberal government. The heated controversies stemming from the narratives emerging during the printemps érable reveal a path dependency of the debate and the policy on some of the ideals of the Quiet Revolution, and in particular the necessity of dealing with the problem of democratic access to HE. We conclude that a purely neoliberal policy of marketization has been made difficult due to this path dependency and the relative balance of power as a result of student mobilization. Thus, the printemps érable is a major event clearly depicting various and contradictory trends in Québec HE policy, in attempting to balance social justice principles and emerging marketization trends.

Policies on Financing University Education in Québec: 1960-2010

In this section, we will show how the trajectory of HE policy since the Quiet Revolution has shaped the recent political debate on tuition fees. We present: (1) the inception of contemporary HE policy in Québec, with its emphasis on a social justice rationale; (2) the debates on HE funding and ensuing attempts at policy change from the late 1990s and early 2000s, along with emerging new policy rationales; and (3) the impacts on access to HE of this policy trajectory.

The Quiet Revolution and the Ideal of Free Education

Like many other societies, Québec witnessed a major shift in educational policy in the 1960s. (The Coleman Report in the USA is another example of this [Coleman et al, 1966].) The seminal document behind Québec's educational system overhaul was the report of the Royal Commission on Education in the Province of Québec, also known as the Parent Report (Parent, 1964-66). While education had been largely provided by religious organizations (Catholic or Protestant school boards and religious universities), the reform favoured by the Parent Report first ensured a state-run education system. Moreover, there was a major reform of school organization, curriculum and educational pathways for students, from kindergarten to university. The goal of this reform was to upgrade the province's education sector. Access to education needed to be increased, particularly as regards post-secondary education. Measures were implemented to facilitate geographical accessibility (the creation of CEGEPs), social accessibility [4], and affordability (free compulsory education and free junior college education, the creation of a system of loans and bursaries, etc.). Other measures proposed included: greater investment by the state in universities; development of postgraduate studies programs; and increased research, especially in French-language universities. This major educational reform was part of a modernization movement and assertion of the Québec state within the Canadian confederation. This period of the 1960s was called the 'Quiet Revolution' because it combined significant reforms and a process of gradual and peaceful change. The educational reform, the introduction of a public health insurance plan and the nationalization of private electricity companies were its three political highlights. The development of education for all and the promotion of a public education project (including HE) have since been important symbolic referents in Québec's educational policies. The Parent Report is still frequently quoted and celebrated today (Corbo, 2002; Rocher, 2004).

The last volume of the Parent Report had not yet been written when the reform package was launched. The university sector experienced a major transformation with the creation of the Université du Québec in Montreal (UQAM) and in the main town of each region (the Université du Québec in Trois-Rivières [UQTR], the UQAC in Chicoutimi [UQAC], and the Université du Québec in Rimouski [UQAR]). Québec increased its investment in universities, old and new, and created a system of loans and bursaries [5] to meet the economic needs of less fortunate students.

The authors of the Parent Report favoured free university tuition, but they thought:

> That, during this period of educational reorganization, increasing enrolment, and expansion of educational services, the government cannot afford to give priority to free education at the university level, nor thus deprive itself of moneys that it could use to enable

poor students to study. We believe that free education is a desirable long-term goal, but it would not be wise to apply it immediately. And of course, it does not address the case of needy students and those who could not go to school if they were not financially supported during this period of their lives. (Parent, 1966, para. 621) [6]

Instead, the government decreed a tuition freeze [7] that lasted until the early 1990s, as outlined in Figure 1. We find that, between 1970 and 1975, the average tuition of Québec universities (in constant dollars) was slightly lower than that of Ontario.[8] The difference between the two provinces increased between 1976 and 1990.

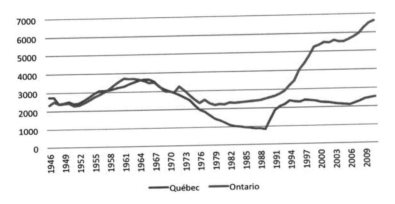

Figure 1. Tuition fees in constant dollars (2011 = 100) in Québec and in Ontario, 1946-2011.

The Québec Liberal Party was re-elected in 1985 with the stated objectives of supporting economic growth and establishing 'good management' in public spending. As elsewhere, this resulted in a deficit-reduction campaign coupled with budget cuts (absolute or relative) in all spheres of public activity. The government program was widely influenced by neoliberal policies to reduce public spending and transform the management of public administration under the impetus of 'new public management' principles. In 1989-90, the government announced an increase in tuition fees. Students were opposed to it, but failed to force the government to alter this decision. Between 1989 and 1994, tuition increased by $567 [9] to $1668.[10]

The growing gap between tuition fees in Québec and Ontario narrowed during this period, as can be seen in Figure 1. Subsequently, it widened again as a result of a new freeze on tuition fees in Québec, enacted in 1994 by the freshly-elected Parti Québécois government, and as a result of the increase in such fees in Ontario. Tuition represents a smaller share of university budgets in Québec than in Ontario.[11] Starting in 1984, the growth of federal-provincial transfer payments was progressively reduced. In 1995, federal transfers for HE were cut significantly, thus decreasing the money available for funding universities. Therefore, provincial governments were forced to find alternative means of funding or reduce their spending.

A Growing Debate: the 'underfunding' of Québec universities

With the policy of deficit-reduction in public sector budgets and a freeze on tuition, the stage was set for a debate on university funding. It took place amongst the various organizations involved in the development of HE, as well as in the media. In some ways, the debate was technical, insofar as it was necessary to estimate the budgetary shortfall as accurately as possible (Conference of Québec University Rectors and Principals [CREPUQ], 2002, 2010, 2013). In other respects, the debate was political since the period was marked by governmental decisions and subsequent student opposition.

In 2002, the CREPUQ and the Ministry of Education of Québec (MEQ) published a study on Québec universities' financial resources, compared to those of other Canadian universities (CREPUQ, 2002). The report established the 'shortfall in general operating resources of Québec universities compared to other Canadian universities, including $114 million related to the trust fund and $261 million related to the general operating fund' at $375.3 million for 2002-03 (p. 19). Following this, the position taken by university management revolved around these figures and concluded that Québec universities were no longer 'competitive' and must therefore increase their funding. This study was updated in 2010 and 2013. In 2010, the CREPUQ estimated the shortfall at $620 million for the period 2007-08. This update highlighted another element: 'the fact that the Québec government's contribution to universities is higher than the national average while the contributions from students and those from other sources are inferior' (2010, p. 7).[12]

These findings triggered the CREPUQ's repeated proposals to rectify the perceived so-called 'underfunding' of Québec universities (CREPUQ, 2004, 2011a, 2011b). However, a ministerial study published in 2011 (Demers, 2011) showed that, on a per capita basis, the Québec government finances education more than other provinces.

The last decade has seen vigorous political debate between various experts on the issue of university funding. On one hand, it was a matter of establishing the actual extent of the 'underfunding' of universities compared to other provinces. On the other, it was a question of how to address this issue. The idea of students assuming a larger share of the funding was gaining ground, firstly, because HE would bring them benefits in the future, and, secondly, because the state of public finances would make it impossible to sufficiently increase governmental subsidies.[13] One could say that this period marked the end of the uncontested influence of the Quiet Revolution philosophy on financing education, that is, of the promotion of publicly-funded education and potentially free education.

The issue of the allocation of subsidies between universities is also on the agenda. In the spirit of the 'Québec University Funding Policy' (Ministère de l'Éducation du Québec, 2000), the government was committed to increasing funding for universities ($300 million from 2000-01 to 2002-03), while at the same time obliging them to sign a 'performance contract', whereby they pledged to achieve operational targets, such as specific graduation rates.[14]

The new university policy also introduces a change in the funding formula. Until 2000, funding for each university's operation was provided by a formula that added to a 'lump sum' amount determined on the basis of annual variations in student enrolment weighted by the levels and fields of study. In 2000, the Ministry did away with the 'lump sum'. Henceforth, only the number of students enrolled in full-time equivalence in each university, weighted according to the fields of study and graduate levels, was to be considered in allocating the public sector's university 'teaching' budget. The consequence was the increasing weight of the number of enrolled students as part of each university's funding. In a context of a declining population, this contributed to increased competition.

The Liberal Party was returned to power in 2003. Two years later, the government made an important decision with respect to financial assistance for students: the share of aid disbursed in the form of loans was increased by reducing the share of bursaries. This transfer is valued at $100 million. The students went on strike and expressed their disagreement with this policy, which they perceived as infringing on students' rights. A compromise was reached after the intervention of the Canada Millennium Scholarship Foundation, an organization created by the federal government at the dawn of the twenty-first century, to distribute scholarships under agreements signed with each province. It was agreed to fund Québec scholarships and to even increase them in exchange for the partial withdrawal of the provincial government's proposed policy shift.

Two years later, in April 2007, the government announced an increase in tuition fees (i.e. it 'lifted the freeze'). Tuition was to be increased by $50 per semester over the next five years. Student associations protested, but no movement was organized to counteract this decision. Parallel to this increase, universities can also impose service charges. In early 2008, because of the significant increase in service charges in some universities, the Minister of Education set new rules for increasing such fees, adjusted according to their previous level. The objective was to reduce the variations in the effective cost of education depending on the university.

Access to HE: Québec vs Ontario

What was the impact of these policies on enrolment in HE? Québec's university student population grew by recruiting from social strata that had been less likely to attend university. This will be demonstrated in a comparison of Québec and Ontario (see Figure 2).[15]

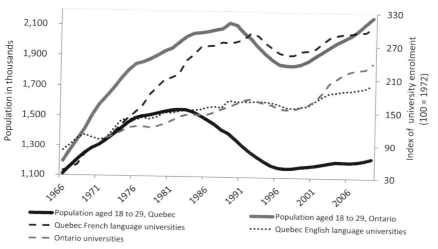

Note: Annual estimates from 1966 to 1970 have been adjusted using a derived estimate of 1971 compensation.

Figure 2. Population aged 18 to 29 by province in thousands, 1966 to 2009. Index of University Enrolment, 100 in 1972, Québec (1966 to 2009) and Ontario (1972 to 2009).
Sources for population 18-29: Statistics Canada.
Sources for university enrollment in Québec: Ministry of Education, Recreation and Sports (online); Lahaye (1989).
Sources for university enrolment in Ontario: Association of Universities and Colleges of Canada (special request).

In Québec, the educational reform of the 1960s resulted in the growth of access to university education. The number of students increased continuously from 1966 to 1990, especially in French-speaking universities. Between 1991 and 2001, enrolment stagnated and even declined. Higher tuition fees in the early 1990s were followed by a decrease in the student population of francophone universities.[16] Since then, growth has resumed, but at a lower rate.

The proportion of 18-29 year olds declined between 1980 and 1995 in Québec, and stabilized thereafter, while university enrolment continued to grow. In contrast, in Ontario, the university enrolment curve follows the same trend as the demographic curve, the ratio of young people aged 18-29 in the province's population. Following Bastien et al (2013, 2014), we suggest that the freezing of fees favoured increased access to university in Québec, while in Ontario, rising fees did not favour a higher rate of post-secondary education..

After this presentation of the context of the funding policy for Québec universities until 2010, and its impact on student enrolment, let us turn toward the main arguments for and against tuition increases put forward by the principal actors mobilized during the printemps érable.

Policy Narratives at the Heart of the Student Movement (2011-2013)

Student protests developed and expanded following the presentation of budget options (December 6, 2010) related to university funding and the subsequent tabling of the 2011-12 provincial budget by the Liberal government's Minister of Finance. The budget intended to provide a 'structured and predictable financial framework over six years' for Québec universities (Doc 57, GVT, March 2011).[17] Among other measures, it proposed increasing tuition by $325 per year, starting in the financial year (FY) 2012-13 (i.e. a total increase of $1625 over five years). Other measures included: (1) an increase of $320 million for state-funded university budgets; (2) creation of a fund for excellence and academic performance ($530 million) to finance 'partnership agreements' with universities (associated with performance targets in terms of research and graduation rates); (3) creation of a fund (*Placements Universités*) to motivate universities to seek private donations from individuals and companies (with a public premium proportional to the increase in donations, the size and the performance of the university); and (4) endowments and complementary amendments to the student loans and bursaries program so that 'less affluent students receive full compensation for increases in tuition by awarding complementary scholarships' (Doc 57, GVT, March 2011).

Following several awareness-raising activities with their constituents (starting in March 2011), the different student associations triggered a 'student strike' on February 7, 2012, which escalated dramatically. Student mobilization fluctuated [18], and there were several attempts 'to find a way out of the crisis'. Nevertheless, the strike lasted until August 2012, when the Liberal leader called for new elections.

Our analysis aims to identify the different policy narratives [19] developed by the main collective actors (and coalitions of actors) to justify or condemn the policy on Québec university funding.[20] These narratives are integral to the ideological and political controversies to determine the priority issues to be addressed and the 'best solutions', which are often in conflict, both in action and theory.[2]

Three policy narratives emerge: a dominant narrative in favour of the 'tuition increase' called 'Québec universities in the knowledge economy'; a narrative favouring 'university education as a public asset'; and finally, a narrative focussing on 'the maintenance of financial access to university education for the middle-class'.

Narrative 1: the Québec university in the knowledge economy

This policy narrative was mainly advanced by the government, but also, subsequently, by university spokespersons and in the CREPUQ reports (Docs 23, 24, 25).[22] In addition, it had the support of the private sector and business associations (Docs 28, 29) and a group of public figures (personalities) who exercised high-level responsibilities (ministers, university rectors, representatives of employers, economists and directors of research centres or renowned think tanks), all of whom claimed to be concerned about Québec's collective future (Doc 58). Several think tanks, including an academic think tank, the Center for Interuniversity Research and Analysis of Organizations (CIRANO) (Docs 48, 49), and a think tank that openly advocates liberal ideas, the Montréal Economic Institute (MEI) (Docs 51, 52), also developed arguments or policy proposals to operationalize this policy line.

This first narrative links the problem of university funding to the future and prosperity of Québec's society and its economy. Québec's competitive position in the world is changing due to two factors: greater global competition and wealth creation increasingly linked to 'knowledge' (the knowledge economy). In addition, Québec society is aging, which calls for increasing its productivity and ensuring its growth in order to maintain the level of wealth and social benefits it currently offers (Doc 59 and 24; CREPUQ, 2010, 2011a, b).

However, apart from its natural resources, Québec has no other wealth than its population's 'knowledge' or 'human capital'. This means that Québec needs to invest sufficiently in the quality of its HE and research and attract the best students and researchers. Failure to do so may result in economic and social decline. Thus, Québec must have the means to compete with other societies, and especially with other Canadian provinces. Yet, Québec universities are 'underfunded', particularly when compared to their Canadian counterparts (Doc 58 *Personnalités*, February 2010; Doc 59 and 24; CREPUQ, 2010, 2011a, b). It is, thus, essential to 'catch up' and ensure Québec universities' competitiveness in the context of an increasingly internationalized tertiary education. It is necessary to invest in the 'quality' and 'excellence' of universities (Doc 58 *Personnalités*, February 2010, and Doc 20, GVT, March 2011).

This level of quality means investing more in education and university research, but the investment must be shared equally between the government, the private sector and students. Public investment in education and university research must be maintained or increased; donations (by companies or individuals) must be encouraged; and the proportion financed by students, the users and future beneficiaries, must be increased. Hence, tuition fees must be raised. In fact, tuition fees are much lower in Québec than in other provinces. Students must, therefore, pay their 'fair share' (Doc 20, GVT, March 2011) of the funding for their studies, inasmuch as they will benefit in terms of wages and access to employment.

This narrative also emphasizes that it is crucial to maintain accessibility and equity in HE. Accessibility and enrolment would not be jeopardized by the proposed measures because, when comparing enrolment rates in Canadian provinces, we see no link between those and the levels of tuition fees. In addition, these measures would restore a form of intergenerational equity as the 'freezing of tuition' in the past has tended to reduce the actual financial burden of tuition for today's students compared to those of previous generations. There is potential for an increase without compromising accessibility, and this increase would be fairer from an intergenerational perspective.

Equity in individual access to HE based on the level of family income would be maintained through several measures (whose formulation changed with the evolution of the debate and the printemps érable): (1) the need to develop scholarships for 'deserving' and less affluent students to avoid an increase in their indebtedness and not discourage them from continuing their studies [23] (Docs 20 and 24); and (2) the need to adjust the repayment of loans based on future employment income [24] (Docs 20 and 24) or the need to adjust tuition fees based on the level and type of education (more or less expensive, or more or less [economically] profitable) [25] (Doc 58).

Ultimately, this investment would benefit the whole of Québec society. It would ensure accessibility and opportunities for social advancement for everyone, and maintain 'equity' because all pay their 'fair share' (depending on their ability to pay, before or after schooling). The current situation is not 'fair' or 'good' for the future of Québec. It is, therefore, 'urgent' to act (Docs 58 and 24) and deal with 'university underfunding'.

It is striking that this narrative offers a justice-related argument that refers to accessibility and social justice objectives promoted in Québec since the Parent Report. This discourse is not limited to calling for investment in human capital. It also invokes principles of equity, since the government and the rectors want to emphasize that their proposals will not reduce accessibility. They wish to show that they care about preserving fairness and equality of opportunity for the 'less fortunate and deserving' through enhanced loan arrangements and scholarships. This illustrates that the framing of HE issues in Québec is partly path-dependent, and that the publication of the Parent Report constituted a critical juncture in Québec's education policy. The result is a policy which proponents claim is balanced, in sharing the cost of HE 'equitably' between government, business and students. As could be expected, these claims of justice were vigorously contested by policy narratives 2 and 3.

Narrative 2: university education as a public asset

This policy narrative was initially propounded by the Coalition Large de l'Association pour une Solidarité Syndicale Etudiante (CLASSE) faction of the student movement. It was also developed (with variations and less systematically) by other actors who participated in the debate and the student crisis, particularly labour unions (Docs 34, 35), a leftist opposition party (Québec Solidaire, Doc 40), the 'professors against the increase' collective, and a number of intellectuals. It should also be mentioned that IRIS, a progressive think tank (Docs 43-45), and the institutional research offices of CLASSE, played a role in shaping the ideas and action theories of this narrative.

In this second narrative, the challenge for students, citizens and Québec society as a whole is to maintain a conception of education and knowledge as a 'common asset' (Doc 4 CLASSE, 2011) and a public service, rather than as a private asset or commodity. 'Contrary to what the government says, education is not a personal investment; it is a fundamental right. Everyone should have access to it, regardless of the thickness of his or her wallet' (Doc 3, CLASSE, March 17, 2011). It is therefore a matter of promoting 'free education' (university) through 100% tax-based public funding.

Trends towards 'privatization of education' and 'pricing these services' (Doc 4 CLASSE, 2011) impact access to HE and affect the content of university education and research (which is increasingly utilitarian and oriented to the needs of economic development). In short, knowledge becomes a 'commodity' and the university a 'business' (Doc 5, CLASSE, March 18, 11). The integration of universities as 'links to a broad financial system: the knowledge economy' is the main problem facing society and students.

For CLASSE, the problem is not 'underfunding', but the 'solutions' proposed by the government to resolve this 'fake' problem. They maintained that the policy of the Liberal government would have a negative impact on several levels. First, it would increase student debt and strain their families' budgets, likely discouraging them from entering university or compelling them to work more to pay for their studies and therefore jeopardize their success. Second, it would constitute a frontal 'attack' on 'the benefits from the past', as it was the policy of 'freezing tuition' (a benefit and extension of the Quiet Revolution) which enabled Québec to offer the 'most accessible post-secondary education system' in Canada. This freeze was a positive step towards consolidation, improvement and evolution into an ideal free education system (Doc 4 CLASSE, 2011). In addition, by encouraging their donations to universities, governmental policy reinforces the stranglehold of private business interests on universities' strategic orientations. Finally, it would encourage ineffective university management and waste (such as excessive real estate investments, extra remuneration for rectors, the multiplication of branch campuses, etc.) by promoting management principles (competition, performance contracts, etc.) that are 'the source of the recurring waste of resources in the province's universities' (Doc 61, CLASSE, March 31, 11). In other words, the Liberals 'are pushing universities towards the global economy, to which they shackle them' (Doc 5, CLASSE, March 18, 11). Faced with this situation, the proposed response was a call to action, a strike to 'stop the tuition increase' and a militant struggle for 'free education'.

This second narrative argues for a continuation of the social democratic discourse in education that marked the Quiet Revolution: it is a matter of ensuring access to a humanistic and emancipatory HE, protected by public funding and strong support from the state. The concern about accessibility and empowerment, however, confronts new situations and issues related to the emergence of the knowledge economy, the internationalization of universities, and economic globalization. Hence this narrative makes frequent links to the 'anti-globalization' movement and other student and social struggles in the world.

Narrative 3: the maintenance of financial access to university education for the middle class

This narrative was advanced by two student associations, Fédération étudiante collégiale du Québec (FECQ) (grouping associations at the CEGEP level) and Fédération étudiante universitaire du Québec (FEUQ) (university students). Their views were often expressed together, including through joint press releases. The narrative was partially shared by other collective actors on the political and media scene. This was particularly the case with the opposition Parti Québécois.[26]

This narrative does not respond to the government arguments on the 'challenges' faced by the university system in Québec and by the province in general (the need to invest in education and research as the key to future wealth, the need to face international competition, etc.). In fact, these issues are scarcely addressed in their position statements [27]; on these, there appears to be a relative consensus. However, the government's solutions are regarded as problematic in terms of a double challenge: increased indebtedness and access to education.

According to narrative 3, government policy leads to several major problems. First, it would increase the financial pressure on the budgets of middle class families and add to student debt levels while the measures supposed to 'reduce this indebtedness' are ineffective (so-called improvements to the student loans and grants program). As a consequence, university access for 'less affluent' or poorer students will be reduced. These 'solutions' are therefore doubly unfair. On one level, they tend to shift the brunt of the burden of funding adjustments to the 'younger generations' who will be penalized in the future by the weight of the debts contracted for their studies. On another level, they are supposed to make the students pay their 'fair share' but, in fact, they fail to require university authorities to 'do their part' and better manage their budgets. Actually, the government is unable to 'better manage' and do some 'house cleaning' in universities, whose mismanagement is flagrant (rectors' high salaries, real estate scandals, multiplication of branch campuses, etc.), as is wasteful spending of Québec taxpayers' money (Doc 53, FEUQ and FECQ, December 2, 11).

Therefore, several alternatives are proposed in this narrative. The proposed solution is to 'freeze tuition fees' in order to avoid exacerbating students' indebtedness and that of their families. In addition, student loans and scholarship programs need to be improved. Finally, these solutions are financially feasible if universities are better supervised by the government and ordered to be more 'accountable without being judge and jury', as this will force them to avoid waste and manage their budgets more effectively without penalizing students. Consequently, a commission to evaluate Québec universities (Commission d'évaluation des universités du Québec [CÉUQ]), an 'independent watchdog', is proposed, as is a moratorium on the establishment of branch campuses (FEUQ proposals).

This narrative does not question governmental assumptions about the issues and challenges facing universities and HE and their value for Québec. It does, however, raise doubts about the government's policy instruments (raising tuition) and their impact (on youth, the poor and Québec in general).

It strongly promotes another policy instrument (greater control and accountability of universities), which implies a strong critique of a secondary opponent, that is, the CREPUQ and university management. In other words, those who presented this narrative share the government's perspective on universities (the paradigm of the knowledge economy and construing education as an investment in human capital). This narrative questions the range of public policy instruments proposed which it considers adverse to its constituencies, and it focuses attention on another set of actors (university managers), largely ignored by governmental policy.

To conclude the presentation of these three arguments, we will highlight some shared features. There is considerable reference to the collective figure of 'Québec society', of a Québec whose (economic, social, and – especially for narrative 2 – cultural) future we care about.

The recipient of university education (or of investments in education) is obviously, at least partially, collective. Yet the recipient is also individual, even if the generic individual of each narrative is different. The second narrative emphasizes the student as citizen, while the first highlights the student as a private investor in human capital. The third narrative depicts the student as one who uses and pays for services.

It is striking that all three narratives present an argument regarding fairness which refers to accessibility and social justice, as promoted in Québec since the Parent Report. These references to collective figures and to values such as accessibility and equity must be understood in relation to the history of education in Québec, particularly since the Quiet Revolution.

Thus, beyond the clear opposition between the action theories advocated by the protagonists in their narratives, some societal conventions were commonplace, and necessary symbolic resources in the argumentation: for example, the impact of education on Québec's collective destiny; the question of access to education; and the right to education.

The Impact of Students' Narratives on Recent Policy Orientations

To what extent did the student movement influence university funding policy? Did the movement affect the policy paradigm of Québec governments? Or has it just resulted in a change in public policy instruments and their mix (Hall, 1986)? Can we identify players who have 'lost' in relation to the theses they defended and which, in one way or another, reflect their interests? We can link the narratives and the latest policy guidelines for funding and governance of universities since the advent of a new government (Parti Québécois, September 2012), although many guidelines are still not yet established.

Let us first suggest that the new minority Parti Québécois government has already taken several successive decisions since coming to power: (1) cancellation of the tuition fee increase voted on by the previous government; (2) holding of a 'summit' on post-secondary education; (3) decision (February 2013) to increase tuition by 3% based on the consumer price index and to maintain the policy of improving the student loans and grants system decided on by the previous government; (4) following the summit, the establishment of five working committees (to develop a framework law for universities; a national university council; a financing policy; financial assistance to students; and the supply, or offer, of college education) to be steered by various key public figures [28]; and (5) with respect to the 'plan for university funding' of the Liberal government, which increased universities' budget allocations as of FY 2012-13, the postponement of increased funding for universities and the imposition of temporary fiscal austerity as part of the fight against a fiscal deficit.

As regards winning or losing protagonists, it is clear that the student movement has 'won' at least with respect to one issue – the cancellation of the Liberal government's planned tuition increase.[29] It can also be said that several criticisms and proposals raised by narrative 3 have been taken into account. Thus, 'improvements' in the system of student loans and grants, already proposed by the Parti libéral du Québec (PLQ) [30] during the conflict, were adopted by the Parti Québécois government.

In addition, one of the 'working committees' that the new government established is based on a student proposal for an 'independent watchdog' for university management (a 'national university council', distinct from the CREPUQ). Thus, university rectors have 'lost', both because of this new regulatory body that seems likely to become a reality, and especially because their increased public funding has been deferred, and the authorized increases in tuition were severely reduced compared to what was in the PLQ plan.

Yet, other than that, the student movement has not secured substantial changes (at least in the short term) in Québec's funding policy paradigm (which was what narrative 2 was mostly targeting, as it clearly denounced the ideology and problem definition developed by narrative 1).

The new government continues to insist on the need to invest in quality university education and seeks to preserve accessibility, but changes the instruments to achieve this and their intensity, as requested in narrative 3. The government adjusts the instruments for limiting increases in tuition and in budgetary allocations to universities. It also adds a new public action instrument with the likely creation of a mechanism for monitoring, evaluating and controlling universities' governance and effectiveness (the national council of universities).[31]

Conclusion

From the outset, Québec's policies for funding HE have been characterized by a concern about increased accessibility to post-secondary education as a means of contributing to the economic, cultural and social development of Québec society as a whole. Indeed, free education – including at the university level – is an ideal which has been defended since the Quiet Revolution. From the 1960s to the 1980s, a 'tuition freeze' reduced the actual cost paid by the students (in constant dollars), but it did not lead to free education for two reasons: the North American tradition of using various funding sources for universities (including philanthropy), and the Québec government's budgetary limitations.

These limits were accentuated in the 1980s and 1990s, due to a triple trend: neoliberal denunciation of public sector deficits; the drying up of federal transfers; and the development of a diagnosis of the 'increased funding needs' of Québec universities, in a context of comparison and competition with their Canadian and US counterparts.

As a result, the early 1990s witnessed periods of 'lifting the freeze' on tuition and, in the 2000s, an extensive expert debate about the extent of university 'underfunding' and how to reduce it. We have also shown that this funding policy has had some success with respect to accessibility: there was a clear increase in enrolment that is not wholly attributable to population growth. Recruitment by universities has expanded to social strata which did not, previously, have access to HE. This tendency was somewhat mitigated due to higher student fees in the 1990s.

This contextualization helps us put the various policy narratives of the main organized protagonists during the printemps érable into perspective. We have demonstrated the clear opposition between different policy narratives. Defenders of a partial privatization of university funding (rectors, government, and some think tanks), including an increase in students' financial contribution, have done so on the basis of arguments that were both economic (public budget management, necessary investment in human capital, and the knowledge economy) and social (equity in contributions and payments to beneficiaries).

The advocates of narrative 1 were opposed to the student associations' position that the collective destiny of Québec society requires maintaining key societal conventions that Québec has defended since the Quiet Revolution: ensuring the public nature of university education and its accessibility through free education. A third narrative carried by other student organizations was especially opposed to the instruments chosen by the government to increase university funding: rising tuition burdening students, while the internal management of universities was clearly deficient in their eyes.

Ultimately, updating a markedly neoliberal policy of university funding has been difficult in Québec for two reasons. On one hand, part of the student movement has revived the legitimacy of certain societal conventions derived from the Quiet Revolution (the ideal of free education, and the importance of access to education for individuals and society), which had diminished in recent decades. On the other hand, the fluctuating balance of power during the strike succeeded in weakening the Liberal government in power and led to political change. The new government has been able to pave the way out of the 'student' crisis by adjusting the instruments of public action employed by the previous government to secure funding for universities. These include a reduced increase in tuition fees, further modifications in financing for students based on their ability to pay, and increased supervision of university governance. This new configuration of public policy mechanisms allowed for pragmatic compromises in the absence of agreement on ideological discourses and the theories underpinning the various funding policies advocated.

Notes

[1] The publication of this chapter was made possible by a grant from the Fonds Recherche Québec Société et culture (programme Équipe) and from the Canada Research Chair in Education Policy. The authors thank Guy Girard (CREPUQ) for his contribution to the understanding of the different ways of funding universities in Québec. The authors take full responsibility for the opinions expressed in this text.

[2] Junior colleges providing general and vocational education.

[3] Refers to the name used by francophone media. In English it means 'maple spring', but in French it is a play on 'Printemps arabe' or 'Arab Spring'.

[4] For stakeholders, social accessibility involved ensuring equality of opportunity for individuals from different social classes. For example, the elimination of

programs and curricula reserved for women and giving women access to the same programs as men was considered a measure of social accessibility.

[5] The Loans and Bursaries Program is the main source of educational financial assistance offered by the Ministère de l'Éducation, du Loisir et du Sport du Québec. It allows approximately 140,000 students, whose financial resources are insufficient, to pursue HE or vocational training. Financial assistance is determined on the basis of the student's income (or that of the parents' or the spouse's). The assistance first takes the form of a loan that the student must repay after graduation. If this loan is insufficient to cover the needs, the student can then receive a bursary that does not need to be repaid. There is a revenue cap inversely proportional to income. During the entire study period, the government ensures financial institutions receive interest on the loan contracted. After graduation, students begin repayment of the debt (principal and interest) to the financial institution if they draw an employment income.

[6] All quotations in this chapter are unofficial translations by its authors.

[7] Funding sources for universities are diverse. Tuition fees are only one element. Sources also include: service charges (that is to say, mandatory administrative or institutional fees, such as those for access to sports facilities, computer equipment, etc.), government grants for operating costs, research grants, indirect costs of research, endowments from donations, income from auxiliary enterprises (such as continuing professional training), and trust funds (financial investments).

[8] In Canada, education falls under provincial jurisdiction. There are 13 education systems, one for each province or territory. Each system has its particular political and organizational features. In this context, we chose to compare the situation in Québec with that prevailing in Ontario, Canada's most powerful province economically and politically. It is also in Ontario that post-secondary education is the most developed; thus, it tends to be the standard of comparison.

[9] In November 2013, one Canadian dollar was worth €0.711.

[10] The increase in direct education expenses incurred by students must take into account the increase in tuition fees, as well as what are called 'service charges' in university jargon. The rules concerning tuition fees fall under provincial jurisdiction and those for service charges are set by the universities. We have to remember that tuition fees must be paid at the beginning of each semester.

[11] Moussaly-Sergieh and Vaillancourt (2007) determined that, in 2001, the Québec government's share of university funding was 53.9%, compared to 39.3% in Ontario. Tuition provided 10.7% and 26.3% respectively.

[12] At the beginning of 2013, after the student crisis and the provincial election in September 2012, the underfunding for 2009-10 was estimated at $850 million.

[13] For example, researchers at the Center for Interuniversity Research and Analysis of Organizations (CIRANO), a centre for the transfer of knowledge in the field of economics, have produced reports on these issues (Montmarquette, 2006; Lacroix & Trahan, 2007; Castro & Poitevin, 2013).

They are based on human capital theory, emphasizing that HE is both a private and public investment. Therefore, the government may legitimately ask for a greater contribution from individuals, and thus increase tuition. The Institut de recherche d'informations socio-économiques (IRIS), a left-leaning private research center, has also intervened through research notes or reports (Hurteau & Martin, 2008; Gagné, 2012) and criticized previous works. In addition, student associations have produced reports on university funding and on students' living and financial conditions.

[14] These performance contracts were later abandoned by the Liberal government in 2003.

[15] We chose to compare university student enrolment with the population aged 18-29 because of a peculiarity of universities in Québec and in the rest of Canada, i.e. a high proportion of adult students. As an indication of the latter's importance, students aged 25 years and over comprised more than half of university enrolments. Currently, the figure is 45%. In such a context, it is best to use the population aged 18-29, rather than that of 18-24, for the purposes of our comparison.

[16] For a more detailed analysis of the correlation between rising tuition fees and participation in university education, please see, Bastien et al (2013, 2014).

[17] Full details of each document are presented in Appendix 2. It shows the list of the documents analysed, with the number, name of the document, publication date, the generic type of actor (for example, government or students' organisation) promoting the document and the name of the author of the document, and finally the type of document (for example, press release or tribune, report, etc). Doc 57, GVT, March 2011, means the document no. 57, published by the government, in March 2011.

[18] On February 20, 132,500 students were reported on strike, 305,000 out of 400,000 students on March 22, and 199,000 on April 4. Furthermore, mass demonstrations (from 100,000 to 300,000 people) were held, in addition to daily demonstrations in Montréal.

[19] The notion of policy narratives (Radaelli, 2000) is part of a so-called 'cognitive approach' to public policy, which focuses on the 'ideas' on which these are constructed. We do not analyze the various sources of these ideas (at the provincial, national or international level), but rather their shaping by a range of key players in the printemps érable. For Radaelli, narratives incorporate various ideas and causal theories that constitute the content of the policy to be implemented with respect to the challenges and issues facing the HE system. This problematization, therefore, encourages the proposal and development of a range of actions and solutions with a set of expected consequences stemming from the effective implementation of these solutions and/or inaction.

[20] Our goal here is not to analyze the 'student movement', its strategies against the government's actions, nor the support or opposition it encountered among Québec's population. Nor shall we address the management of the strike and protests by the government and security forces. We will not, therefore, analyze the 'crisis' and the 'student movement'. For this kind of analysis, see the articles in Bédard (2013).

[21] The reader will find in Appendix 1 the means used for selecting the corpus of texts and the guidelines for the subsequent content analysis.

[22] The latter has also produced a number of arguments and proposed several measures that were subsequently adopted by the government.

[23] This measure was presented when the 2011-12 budget was tabled, but it was 'enhanced' with the proposals made by the government to the student movement as part of the negotiations during the conflict. The Marois government (PQ) adopted these proposals afterward.

[24] Measure proposed by the government during the conflict.

[25] Measure proposed by the Conseil du patronat and the authors of the 'For a Clear Sighted Vision of Québec' manifesto, but which was not adopted by the Liberal government.

[26] However, starting in June 2012, Pauline Marois, the leader of this party, would defend the proposal of 'indexing tuition on the basis of the consumer price index' rather than 'freezing tuition fees'.

[27] Please refer to FECQ, Note d'information économique sur la hausse des frais de scolarité. Impact de la hausse des frais de scolarité sur la diplômation et les finances publiques, November 8, 2011. http://fecq.org/Centre-de-documentation (accessed October 16, 2013).

[28] The recommendations of these committees are not yet fully known (as of September 2013), but we can recognize in their statements several of the issues that were raised during the student crisis.

[29] In a press release dated September 8, 2012, FECQ and FEUQ stated that 'the cancellation of rising tuition' promised on September 7 by Pauline Marois, winner of the elections of September 4, is a 'victory' and terminates the student conflict.

[30] During the conflict, the Liberal government proposed raising the threshold for access to loans and grants from $28,000 to $45,000. This proposal was taken up by the Parti Québécois government.

[31] This diagnosis of the effects of the strike should be interpreted with caution for two reasons. First, the government policy is still in development. Second, the effects of the symbolic questioning of narrative 1 ('the university in the knowledge economy') by narrative 2 probably should not be underestimated since they may be more subtle and occur over a longer time frame.

References

Association of Universities and Colleges of Canada, *Special request – University Enrolment in Ontario by Registration Status, Program Level, 1972-2009*.

Bastien, N., Chenard, P., Doray, P. & Laplante B. (2013) Society, Economy and Access to Postsecondary Studies in Québec, in N. Murray & C.M. Klinger (Eds) *Aspirations, Access and Attainment in Widening Participation: international perspectives and an agenda for change*, pp. 67-81. London: Routledge.

Bastien, N., Chenard, P., Doray, P. & Laplante, B. (2014) L'effet de l'augmentation des frais de scolarité sur l'accès aux études, note de recherche CIRST, Montréal, CIRST, Université du Québec à Montréal.

Bédard, Eric (2013) Dossier Le peuple selon la CLASSE, *Argument Politique Société Histoire*, 15(2).

Castro, R. & Poitevin, M. (2013) *Éducation et frais de scolarité*. Montréal: Centre interuniversitaire de recherche en analyse des organisations (CIRANO).

Coleman, J.S.., Campbell, EQ., Hobson, C.J., et al (1966) *Equality of Educational Opportunity*. Washington, DC: National Center for Educational Statistics, US Government Printing Office.

Corbo, C. (2002) *L'éducation pour tous: une anthologie du Rapport Parent*. Montréal: Presses de l'Université de Montréal.

Conference of Québec University Rectors and Principals (CREPUQ) (2002) *Le niveau des ressources de fonctionnement des universités québécoises: comparaison aux autres universités canadiennes, 1995-1996 à 2002-2003*. Montréal: CREPUQ.

Conference of Québec University Rectors and Principals (CREPUQ) (2004) *Le financement des universités québécoises: un enjeu déterminant pour l'avenir du Québec*. Montréal: CREPUQ.

Conference of Québec University Rectors and Principals (CREPUQ) (2010) *Le financement des universités québécoises en comparé à celui des universités des autres provinces canadiennes de 2000-2001 à 2007-2008*. Montréal: CREPUQ.

Conference of Québec University Rectors and Principals (CREPUQ) (2011a) Recommandations présentées par la conférence des recteurs et des principaux des universités au ministre des Finances dans le cadre des consultations prébudgétaires 2012-2013. Montréal: CREPUQ.

Conference of Québec University Rectors and Principals (CREPUQ) (2011b) *Un appel à agir pour permettre aux universités de contribuer pleinement au développement économique, culturel et social du Québec*. Montréal: CREPUQ.

Conference of Québec University Rectors and Principals (CREPUQ) (2013) *Le niveau des ressources de fonctionnement des universités québécoises: comparaison aux autres universités canadiennes, 2003-2004 à 2009-2010*. Montréal: CREPUQ.

Demers, M. (2011) L'effort financier pour les universités en 2008-2009: comparaison entre le Québec et les autres provinces canadiennes, Bulletin Statistique de l'Éducation, Québec, Gouvernement du Québec, ministère de l'Éducation, du Loisir et du Sport.

Gagné, G. (2012) *Les revenus des universités selon la conférence des recteurs*. Montréal: Institut de recherche et d'informations socio-économique.

Hall, P.A. (1986) *Governing the Economy: the politics of state intervention in Britain and France*. Cambridge, MA: Polity Press.

Hurteau, P. & Martin, E. (2008) *Financement des universités: vers une américanisation du modèle québécois*. Montréal: Institut de recherche et d'informations socio-économique.

Lacroix, R. & Trahan, M. (2007) *Le Québec et les droits de scolarité universitaire*. Montréal: Centre interuniversitaire de recherche en analyse des organisations (CIRANO).

Lahaye, J. (1989) *Données statistiques sur la population étudiante*. Québec: Ministère de l'Enseignement supérieur et de la Science, Direction générale de l'enseignement et de la recherche universitaire.

Ministère de l'éducation, du Loisir et du Sport, (1995-2011) *Statistiques de l'éducation Enseignement primaire, secondaire, collégial et universitaire.* Québec: Government of Québec.

Ministère de l'Éducation du Québec (2000) *Politique québécoise de financement des universités.* Québec: Government of Québec.

Ministère de l'Enseignement supérieur, de la recherche, de la science et de la technologie (n.d.) *Système de gestion des effectifs étudiants (GDEU).* Québec: Government of Québec.

Montmarquette, C. (2006) *Le remboursement Proportionnel au Revenu (RPR): un système pour les prêts d'études alliant efficacité et accessibilité.* Montréal: Centre interuniversitaire de recherche en analyse des organisations (CIRANO).

Moussaly-Sergieh, K. & Vaillancourt, F. (2007) Le financement des institutions d'enseignement post-secondaire au Québec, 1961-2005, *McGill Journal of Education,* 42(3), 427-442.

Parent, A.-M. (1964-6) *Rapport de la Commission royale d'enquête sur l'enseignement dans la province de Québec,* 5 vols. Québec: Gouvernement du Québec.

Radaelli, C. (2000) Logiques de pouvoir et récits dans les politiques publiques de l'Union européenne, *Revue française de Sciences politiques,* 50(2), 255-276.

Rocher, G. (2004) Un bilan du Rapport Parent: vers la démocratisation, *Bulletin d'Histoire politique,* 12(2), 117-128.

Statistics Canada. Estimates of population, by age group and sex, Canada, provinces and territories, annual (Persons), 1921 to 1971, CANSIM table 051-0026; Estimates of population, by age group and sex for July 1, Canada, provinces and territories, annual (Persons), 1971 to 2009, CANSIM table 051-0001.

APPENDIX 1
Methodology

The policy narrative analysis started with an examination of the discourse of the main protagonists in the conflict. The discourse corpus was constituted in two phases. For document retrieval, we first identified the different protagonists involved in the debate (principally government, university management, student associations, trade unions, opposition parties, think tanks, and representatives of the business world), and determined the period during which the debate took place (November 2010 to July 2012).

Then we targeted the websites of these organizations to select all the documents that addressed the issue of tuition fees. In addition, we collected newspaper articles from the *Le Devoir* and *La Presse*, using the ProQuest database and keywords such as 'student crisis', 'printemps québécois' or 'student conflict'.

The second phase consisted of selecting in this first corpus of 172 texts those that were relevant to our objective of analyzing policy narratives. It was a matter of retaining those documents that provided information on how the protagonists were thematizing the issues and problems faced by Québec universities, as well as the solutions to the latter.

A corpus of 61 texts was, thus, subjected to qualitative content analysis, guided by a simple grid (issues identified by the actor, problems to resolve and, related to universities, solutions discussed, and positive or negative consequences of political action or inaction) derived from Radaelli's policy narrative concept. The originators of these discourses were then compared according to the type of narrative carried. The references for these 61 texts are listed in Appendix 2.

APPENDIX 2
List of documents submitted to content analysis

Number	Name of document	Publication date	Type of actor	Author's name (organisation or indivdual)	Type of document
1/ CLASSE/4 nov 10	*Rencontre des partenaires sur l'avenir des universités: l'ASSÉ refuse de participer à cette consultation bidon!*	Nov 2010	Students' organisation	CLASSE	Press release
2/ CLASSE/6 déc 10	*Manifestation*	Dec 2010	Students' organisation	CLASSE	Press release
3/ CLASSE/17 mars 11	*Budget du Québec: 'Une véritable déclaration de guerre!' soutient l'ASSÉ, qui annonce la tenue d'une manifestation*	Mar 2011	Students' organisation	CLASSE	Press release
4/ CLASSE/1 nov 11	*Argumentaire, Ensemble, bloquons la hausse*	Nov 2011	Students' organisation	CLASSE	leaflet
5/ CLASSE/18 mars 11	*Budget Bachand 2011-2012: des mesures illégitimes, une lutte inévitable*	Mar 2011	Students' organisation	CLASSE/A. Theurillat et al	Tribune in *Le Devoir*
6/FEUQ/14 nov 11	*Hausse des frais de scolarité – Legault et Charest, même combat: endetter les générations à venir du Québec*	14 Nov2011	Students' organisation	FEUQ	Press release
7/FEUQ/8 déc 2011	*Trois années depuis la dernière élection des libéraux: les étudiants ne se laisseront pas passer un sapin*	8 Dec 2011	Students' organisation	FEUQ	Press release
8/FEUQ/27 jan 12	*Réaction de la FEUQ sur l'endettement des ménages canadiens: Les*	27 Jan 2012	Students' organisation	FEUQ	Press release

	étudiants ont aussi atteint leur limite				
9/FEUQ/23 fév 12	*Comme la FEUQ, le Conseil supérieur de l'Éducation constate que la gestion des universités québécoises manque de rigueur et de transparence*	23 Feb 2012	Students' organisation	FEUQ	Press release
10/FEUQ/8 mars 12	*Hausse de 1625 $ des frais de scolarité: les femmes seront particulièrement frappées par la hausse du gouvernement Charest*	8 Mar 2012	Students' organisation	FEUQ	Press release
11/FEUQ/2 9 mars 12	*Réaction de la FEUQ au budget fédéral: Des dizaines de millions de dollars toujours détournés par Québec*	29 Mar 2012	Students' organisation	FEUQ	Press release
12/FEUQ/1 0 avril 12	*La FEUQ rappelle que l'entêtement du gouvernement coûte 104 000 $ de l'heure*	10 Apr 2012	Students' organisation	FEUQ	Press release
13/FEUQ/1 4 avril 12	*Une commission d'évaluation des universités indépendante pour améliorer la gestion universitaire*	14 Apr 2012	Students' organisation	FEUQ	Press release
14/FEUQ/1 1 mai 12	*La FEUQ rejette à l'unanimité l'offre gouvernementale*	11 May 2012	Students' organisation	FEUQ	Press release
15/FECQ/17 juin 11	*Campement étudiant contre la hausse des frais de scolarité: 'Jean Charest écrase notre génération' – disent les campeurs*	17 Ju 2011	Students' organisation	FECQ	Press release
16/FECQ/8 nov11	*Hausse des frais de scolarité: 1,1 à 2,4 milliards de dollars en moins pour les finances publiques*	8 Nov 2011	Students' organisation	FECQ	Press release
17/FECQ/6 déc11	*Hausse des frais de scolarité: plus de 1 000 000 de familles ne sont pas pleinement admissibles aux prêts et bourses*	6 Dec 2011	Students' organisation	FECQ	Press release

18/FECQ/13 mars 12	*Grève étudiante: À une semaine du dépôt du Budget, la FECQ rappelle au gouvernement que des solutions existent*	13 Mar 2012	Students' organisation	FECQ	Press release
19/FECQ/18 juin 12	*Conflit étudiant: La FECQ lance un ultime appel à la médiation*	18 Jun 2012	Students' organisation	FECQ	Press release
20/ GOUV/17 mars 11	*BUDGET 2011-2012*	17 Mar 2011	Government	Government	Press release
21/ GOUV/31 mai 12	*Négociations sur les droits de scolarité - Des discussions basées sur l'ouverture, mais l'impasse continue*	31 May 2012	Government	Government	Press release
22/ CREPUQ/1 7 nov 10	*Le financement des universités québécoises comparé à celui des universités des autres provinces canadiennes de 2000-2001 à 2007-2008*	Nov 2010	University	CREPUQ	Institutional report
23/ CREPUQ/0 1 nov 10	*Urgence d'agir pour les universités: le Québec à la croisée des chemins*	Nov 2010	University	CREPUQ	Institutional report
24/ CREPUQ/1 janv 11	*UN APPEL À AGIR POUR PERMETTRE AUX UNIVERSITÉS DE CONTRIBUER PLEINEMENT AU DÉVELOPPEMENT ÉCONOMIQUE, CULTUREL ET SOCIAL DU QUÉBEC*	Jan 2011	University	CREPUQ	Institutional report
25/ CREPUQ/0 1 déc 11	*Recommandations présentées dans le cadre des consultations prébudgétaires 2012-2013*	1 Dec 2011	University	CREPUQ	Recom-mendation
26/ Collège/20 mars 12	*LA FÉDÉRATION DES CÉGEPS REÇOIT FAVORABLEMENT LE BUDGET DU QUÉBEC 2012-2013*	20 Mar 2012	Colleges	Fédération des collèges	Press release
27/ Collège/13	*ALLOCUTION DE M. JEAN*	13 Apr 2012	Colleges	Fédération des collèges	Press conference

avril 12	BEAUCHESNE, PRÉSIDENT-DIRECTEUR GÉNÉRAL, FÉDÉRATION DES CÉGEPS				
28/ Patronat/5 avril 12	Accessibilité financière aux études – Des mesures bénéfiques qui pavent la voie à un retour en classe	5 Apr 2012	Employers	Conseil du Patronat du Québec	Press release
29/ Patronat/2 mai 12	Au tour des étudiants	2 May 2012	Employers	Conseil du Patronat du Québec	Tribune in La Presse & Le Devoir
30/CSN/23 janv 12	Hausse des droits de scolarité - Le gouvernement Charest doit refaire ses devoirs selon la CSN	23 Jan 2012	Trade Unions	CSN	Press release
31/CSN/1 mai 12	Conflit étudiant – Le 1er mai, la CSN appuie les étudiants	1 May 2012	Trade Unions	CSN	Press release
32/FTQ/18 juin 12	Conflit étudiant 'La médiation, c'est faire le choix de la responsabilité'	18 Jun 2012	Trade Unions	Michel Arsenault, président de la FTQ	Tribune in the newspapers
33/CSQ/23 jan 12	Priorité de la FEC-CSQ en 2012, Poursuivre la lutte en faveur de l'accessibilité à l'enseignement supérieur	23 Jan 2012	Trade Unions	CSQ	Press release
34/CSQ/4 avril 12	L'AREQ se prononce contre la hausse des droits de scolarité et réclame un débat social sur le financement de l'éducation	4 Apr 2012	Trade Unions	AREQ	Press release
35/CSQ/3 mai 12	Le Réseau des femmes de la CSQ appuie la grève étudiante	3 May 2012	Trade Unions	Le Réseau des femmes de la CSQ	Press release
36/ON/1 mai 12	Jean-Martin Aussant souhaite une commission parlementaire d'urgence	1 May 2012	Opposition Party	Option nationale	Press release
37/ON/ 28 mai 12	'L'éducation doit être au cœur des priorités du Québec de demain', Patrick Sabourin	28 May 2012	Opposition Party	Option nationale	Press release
38/PQ/21 mars 12	Hausse des droits de scolarité: Pauline Marois	21 Mar 2012	Opposition Party	Parti québécois	Press release

	exhorte le premier ministre à ouvrir le dialogue avec les étudiants				
39/PQ/2 mai 12	*Conflit étudiant: 'Seules des élections générales peuvent dénouer l'impasse' - Pauline Marois*	2 May 2012	Opposition Party	Parti québécois	Press release
40/QS/22 mars 12	*L'éducation gratuite de la maternelle à l'université: le projet d'un Québec solidaire*	22 Mar 2012	Opposition Party	QUÉBEC SOLIDAIRE	Press release
41/ CCAFE/22 sept 11	*AVIS DU COMITÉ CONSULTATIF SUR L'ACCESSIBILITÉ FINANCIÈRE AUX ÉTUDES SUR LES HAUSSES DES DROITS DE SCOLARITÉ ET LES MESURES D'AIDE FINANCIÈRE AUX ÉTUDES PRÉVUES POUR LA PÉRIODE DE 2012-2013 À 2016-2017*	22 Sep 2011	Think tank	CCAFE	Press release
42/ CCAFE/17 juillet 12	*AVIS DU COMITÉ CONSULTATIF SUR L'ACCESSIBILITÉ FINANCIÈRE AUX ÉTUDES SUR L'ÉTALEMENT DES HAUSSES DES DROITS DE SCOLARITÉ DE 2012-2013 À 2018-2019 ET SUR LES MODIFICATIONS PROPOSÉES À L'AIDE FINANCIÈRE AUX ÉTUDES*	17 Jul 2012	Think tank	CCAFE	Press release
43/IRIS/1 oct 08	*Financement des universités: Vers une américanisation du modèle québécois?*	Oct 2008	Think tank	IRIS	Research Report
44/IRIS/1 mars 12	*L'endettement étudiant: un 'investissement'*	Mar 2012	Think tank	IRIS	Research Report

45/IRIS/	*rentable?* *Faut-il vraiment augmenter les frais de scolarité? Huit arguments trompeurs sur la hausse*		Think tank	IRIS	Research Report
46/IREC/2009	*Universités ou foires marchandes? le partenariat public-privé et les errances du monde universitaire, un cas et son clone*	2009	Think tank	IREC	Research Report
47/IREC/1 janv 12	*La hausse des droits de scolarité et ses impacts sur le coût de programme de l'Aide financière aux études*	Jan 2012	Think tank	IREC	Research Report
48/ CIRANO/1 fév 07	*Le Québec et les droits de scolarité universitaire*	Feb 2007	Think tank	CIRANO	Research Report 'Rapport Bourgogne'
49/ CIRANO/1 déc 10	*Le rendement privé et social de l'éducation universitaire au Québec*	Dec 2010	Think tank	CIRANO	Research Report
50/IEDM/16 juin 10	*Accessibilité ne rime pas avec faibles droits de scolarité*	16 Jun 2010	Think tank	IEDM/ Germain Belzile directeur	Tribune in *Le Devoir*
51/IEDM/4 déc 10	*Pour l'équité, il faut moduler les droits de scolarité*	4 Dec 2010	Think tank	IEDM	Tribune
52/IEDM/11 nov 11	*Pancartes et slogans pour une éducation de second rang*	11 Nov 2011	Think tank	IEDM/Youri Chassin, Germain Belzile	Tribune
53/FECQ, FEUQ/ 2 déc 11	*La Fecq et la Feucq lancent une note d'information sur la gouvernance universitaire: mettre de l'ordre dans le chaos de la gestion universitaire*	2 Dec 2011	Students' organisation	FECQ et FEUCQ	Press release
54/FECQ, FEUQ/11 avr 12	*Couper dans le gras: près de 300 millions de $ pourraient être mieux dépenser dans les universités*	11 Apr 2012	Students' organisation	FECQ et FEUCQ	Press release
55/FECQ, FEUQ/ 1	*Contre propositions de la FECQ et de la Feucq:*	1 May 2012	Students' organisation	FECQ et FEUCQ	Press release

mai 12	*une alternative globale à la hausse des frais*			
56/FECQ/10 nov 11	*30 000 étudiants manifestent pour le gel des frais de scolarité*	10 Nov 2011	Students' organisation	FECQ	Press release
57/Gouv/17 mars 11	*Discours sur le budget prononcé à l'assemblée nationale par M. Bachand, ministre des finances*	17 Mar 2011	Government	Government	Minister speech
58/Person-nalités/ fev 2010	*Pacte pour le financement concurrentiel de nos universités*	Feb 2010	Various	Various	Tribune
59/ CREPUQ/2 7 janv 10	*Propositions présentées par la CREPUQ au ministre des finances dans le cadre des consultations budgétaires*	27 janv 2010	University	CREPUQ	Proposition
60/FECQ & FEUQ/20 mars 12	*Réaction dela FECQ et de la FEUQ au budget 2012-13: 'La lutte contre la hausse des frais de scolarité se règlera dans la rue.'*	20 Mar 2012	Students' organisation	FECQ et FEUCQ	Press release
61/ CLASSE/31 mars 11	*Les étudiants et les étudiantes dans la rue contre la hausse des frais de scolarité*	31 Mar 2011	Students' organisation	CLASSE	Press release

Notes on Contributors

Ricardo Biscaia is Assistant Professor in Economics at the University Portucalense Infante D. Henrique, Portugal and is a researcher at the Centre for Research in Higher Education Policies (CIPES). His main research interests are regional and urban economics, the economics of education, and industrial organisation.

Helen Carasso researches and teaches higher education policy at the University of Oxford, and has a particular interest in questions relating to student fees and funding in England. Her career in the sector began when she headed up public relations and then admissions functions, first in a post-92 institution, then at a collegiate university. This gives Helen a practice-based insight into the issues that she studies; she keeps this current, undertaking consultancy projects for a range of institutions.

Margarida Fonseca Cardoso is Assistant Professor in the Biomedical School of the University of Porto, Portugal: ICBAS – Instituto de Ciências Biomédicas Abel Salazar, in the scientific areas of biostatistics and epidemiology. her research interests include epidemiology, public health and education. She is co-author of several publications in the area of higher education as a result of her collaboration with the Centre for Research in Higher Education Policies (CIPES), and has also publications in the biomedical area.

Nicolas Charles is a lecturer at the Centre Emile Durkheim, University of Bordeaux, France. His main research interest is social justice within higher education, covering various subjects including student financing, selection, transition-to-work, with both quantitative and qualitative international comparative analyses.

Pierre Doray is the former director of the Interuniversity Research Centre on Science and Technology and professor of sociology at the University of Quebec, Montreal. His current research focuses on the school careers of students in post-secondary education and on adult participation in education. He is the leader of a research team on school transitions and educational pathways in Canada. He has also worked on the social construction of relations between economics and education. He has conducted extensive research on participation in adult education in Quebec and elsewhere. In addition to research and teaching, he is a member of various advisory bodies including Quebec's Conseil supérieur de l'éducation, where he also chairs the committee on adult and continuing education.

Claire Dupuy is Assistant Professor in political science at University of Grenoble Alpes (Sciences Po Grenoble – Pacte). She works on multilevel governance and is interested in territorial state transformations and regionalisation processes in Western Europe. She studies education policy and social policy in France, Germany and Belgium.

Hubert Ertl is Associate Professor of Higher Education and Fellow of Linacre College, University of Oxford. He is the course director of the MSc. in Higher Education at the Department of Education, Oxford. He is also Senior Research Fellow at the ESRC Centre on Skills, Knowledge and Organisational Performance (SKOPE). His research interests include international aspects of higher education, the transitions of graduates into the labour market, access to higher education, vocational education and training, and European Union educational policies.

Otto Hüther is Assistant Professor for Sociology at the Department for Social Sciences at the University of Kassel, Germany. He is also a member at INCHER-Kassel, the International Centre for Higher Education Research at the University of Kassel. His main research interests include higher education research, governance studies and organisational studies.

Jin Jin is a doctoral student at the Institute of Education, University of London. Her main research interest is social justice within higher education.

Mamouna Kabore is a doctoral student in sociology at the University of Quebec, Montreal, and a research assistant at the Interuniversity Research Centre on Science and Technology.

Georg Krücken is Professor of Higher Education Research and Director of INCHER-Kassel, the International Centre for Higher Education Research, both at the University of Kassel, Germany. He received his PhD in sociology from Bielefeld University in 1996. From 2006 to 2011 he was a full professor at the German University of Administrative Sciences. From 1999 to 2001 and in 2011 he was a visiting scholar at Stanford University (Department of Sociology and School of Education). He taught as a guest professor at the Institute for Science Studies, University of Vienna, and at the Centre de Sociologie des Organisations, Sciences Po, Paris. He is president of the Gesellschaft für Hochschulforschung (Society for Higher Education Research) and spokesman of the research network 'New Institutionalism'. His research interests include higher education research, science studies, organisational studies and neo-institutional theory.

Christian Maroy is full professor at the University of Montreal and chairholder of the Canada Research Chair on education policies since October 2010. Previously, he was professor of sociology at the University of Louvain and director of the GIRSEF research centre between 1998 and 2010. His main research interests are education policies, governance and regulation within education systems, the school market, and social inequalities in education. He has recently published *L'école à l'épreuve de la performance scolaire* (De Boeck, 2013) and *Les marchés scolaires. Sociologie d'une politique publique d'éducation* (Presses universitaires de France, 2013) with Georges Felouzis and Agnès van Zanten.

R.N. Nahai is a doctoral student at the Department of Education, University of Oxford. Her research is focused on student funding in higher education, with an emphasis on student loans. Broadly, her research interests centre on social equality, and humane and ethics-based policy frameworks that support human flourishing.

Vera Rocha is a researcher at the Center for Research in Higher Education Policies (CIPES) and a PostDoc at Copenhagen Business School. Her main research interests are related to higher education (HE funding, competition and diversification), industrial organisation (entrepreneurship, firm and industry dynamics) and labour economics (wage differentials, human capital and occupational choice).

Pedro N. Teixeira is Associate Professor at the Faculty of Economics and Vice Rector of the University of Porto, Portugal and Director of the Center for Research in Higher Education Policies (CIPES). His main research interests are on the economics of education and the history of economics. He has published several journal articles in higher education and economics journals and has edited several collective volumes.

Hans Vossensteyn is the Director of the Center for Higher Education Policy Studies (CHEPS) at the University of Twente, where he is also a senior researcher and lecturer. Hans has been a Professor and Programme Leader of the MBA Hochschul- und Wissenschaftsmanagement at the Osnabrück University of Applied Sciences in Germany since 2007. He completed his Master's degree in Public Administration and Public Policy at the University of Twente in 1991 and completed his PhD (*cum laude*) on student price-responsiveness in 2005. Since 1991, Hans has participated in and managed a multitude of research projects covering a wide array of subjects including: funding of higher education; student financing and access to higher education internationalisation; higher education indicators; selection and study success; quality of higher education; often leading to quantitative and qualitative international comparative analyses. Between

2000 and 2011, he was a member of the International Advisory Board of the International Comparative Higher Education Finance and Accessibility Project, coordinated by Professor Bruce D. Johnstone at the State University of New York at Buffalo, sponsored by the Ford Foundation. Between 2005 and 2010, he was a member of the Adjudication Committee supervising the five-year Measuring the Effectiveness of Student Aid (MESA) project funded by the Canada Millennium Scholarships Foundation. Between 2009 and 2010, Hans served as an external expert and secretary for the Committee on the Future Sustainability of Dutch Higher Education, which set out a new strategic vision for higher education in the Netherlands. He also contributed to a project on widening access for the Higher Education Funding Council for England (HEFCE) between 2012 and 2013.

Kai Yu is Associate Professor and Assistant Dean at the Graduate School of Education, Shanghai Jiao Tong University. His main research interest is management in higher education.

Oxford Studies in Comparative Education

Series Editor: David Phillips

Other volumes in this series....

The Globalisation of School Choice? eds, Martin Forsey, Scott Davies & Geoffrey Walford, 2008

The Changing Landscape of Education in Africa, ed. David Johnson, 2007

Aspects of Education in the Middle East and North Africa, eds. Colin Brock & Lila Zia Levers, 2007

Exploring Cross-national Attraction in Education: some historical comparisons of American and Chinese attraction to Japanese education, ed. Jeremy Rappleye, 2007

Education's Abiding Moral Dilemma, Sheldon Rothblatt, 2007

Partnerships in Educational Development, eds. Iffat Farah & Barbara Jaworski, 2006

Political and Citizenship Education, Stephanie Wilde, 2005

The Challenges of Education in Brazil, eds. Colin Brock & Simon Schwartzman, 2004

Educational Policy Borrowing: historical perspectives, eds. David Phillips & Kimberly Ochs, 2004

New Approaches to Vocational Education in Europe, eds. Regina H. Mulder & Peter F.E. Sloane, 2004

Further details of the over 40 volumes in this series can be found at
www.symposium-books.co.uk
and can be ordered there, or from
Symposium Books, PO Box 204, Didcot,
Oxford OX11 9ZQ, United Kingdom
orders@symposium-books.co.uk